Rowling Revisited

Return Trips to Harry, Fantastic Beasts, Quidditch, & Beedle the Bard

James W. Thomas, PhD

Rowling Revisited

published by Zossima Press
Hamden, CT

10-9-8-7-6-5-4-3-2-1

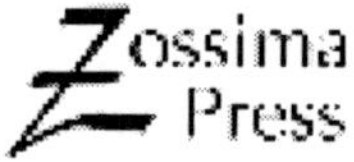

ISBN 13 978-09822385-5-4

This book is dedicated to my grandchildren —

Georgia Claire

Kaiden

Makena

Reese

and Lincoln

— in hopes that some day they will read
Harry's story to grandchildren of their own

Table of Contents

Introduction

I'm the author of *Repotting Harry Potter: A Professor's Book-by-Book Guide for the Serious Re-Reader.* Now I'm back, and this time I invite you to join me for another look at a few more things you might have missed in J. K. Rowling's seven Harry Potter books—though only a fraction of those we looked at in *Repotting Harry Potter.* In that book you'll find my first thoughts on Harry; here you can read my afterthoughts. Moreover, I hope you'll accompany me through *Rowling Revisited* as we look at a few curiosities, some droll humorous elements, a number of foreshadows, and many other matters in Rowling's three ancillary works, *Fantastic Beasts and Where to Find Them*, *Quidditch Through the Ages*, and *The Tales of Beedle the Bard.* I believe these brief books are especially interesting when compared to and contrasted with the now completed Potter series.

As in *Repotting Harry Potter*, here too we will revisit Rowling in an informal, conversational way (*sans* footnotes and academic formalities), and once again I'll be writing in the first person, speaking directly to you, and using lots of contractions (you'll see what I mean as we go along). This is a book for re-readers of Rowling, yet maybe some of you are serious Potter aficionados but haven't read the three short books. No problem. Get your copies and read along with my chapters or, better yet, enjoy these wonderful gems before you start *Rowling Revisited.*

Let me give you a little background to this book. In the summer of 2007 at a Potter conference in Toronto, I presented a paper and participated in a panel discussion of the then just-published *Deathly Hallows.* In preparation for these presentations, I came up with two "Top Ten" lists: "The Top Ten Reasons Harry Haters Hate the Potter Books" and "The Top Ten Reasons Harry Lovers Love the Potter Books." My daughter Alexi, who attended the conference with me, talked me into omitting one of the lists. "Dad," she said, "You don't want to be known as the 'Top Ten Guy.'" (And I believe David Letterman has an edge on me there anyway.)

Well, similarly, I'm not sure I want to be known as the "*Re-* Guy," but I may run that risk after Re*potting Harry Potter* and now *Rowling* Re*visited.* But in my title defense, I'd like to point out that I *am* kind of a "*Re-* Guy." As a literature professor, I both practice and preach rereading rich texts which continue to delight and inform thoughtful and curious readers. Among other time-honored indications of and tests for great and enduring literature, perhaps chief is simply how well a work rereads. Does the work still please us with what we remember and surprise us with what we didn't notice the first time(s) through the text? For me and for many millions of other readers, Rowling's works certainly do.

In *Repotting Harry Potter*, I intended the prefix *Re-* in a number of ways. I tried to argue, implicitly or explicitly, that Rowling's novels needed to be repotted from books for children to books for everyone, from popular literature to enduring literature, and from plot-driven, one-dimensional works to richly encoded, complex books that readers will be enjoying and discussing for decades to come. All that is a lot for my favorite prefix to do; that's a lot of repotting (I think I wore out two trowels and three pairs of gloves in the process). In *Rowling Revisited*, less ambitiously, I intend my *Re-* to mean, first, returning to the already repotted Potter books—our hands are clean now; we've washed up and put away the gloves (and, I know, I need to lose that metaphor). In addition, in this book we will revisit the three related Rowling books, two of which—*Fantastic Beasts and Where to Find Them* and *Quidditch Through the Ages*—were written before Books 5, 6, and 7 in the Potter series, and one of which—*The Tales of Beedle the Bard*—was written after the series was complete. In going through Rowling's brief works, we will see that many elements are linked to the books in the Potter series and add still more to our enjoyment of them. And, by the way, you may already be fearful of an overdose of *re-* words, and well you should be. I ask you to forgive my use of every *re-* word I could think of in some of the section titles (along with some I made up—neologisms, anyone?).

In *Rowling Revisited* we'll begin with a quick trip back through the Potter novels. I'll be sharing a few things about each book that I have noticed since my last reading, along with some things I've rethought; I'll focus on foreshadows, puns, humorous passages, and various other literary elements—much as I did far more extensively in *Repotting Harry*

Potter. Then we'll discuss the author's fantastic beasts. Many of these creatures Rowling had already introduced in the first four Potter books before she wrote her book of beasts. Some were soon to be seen in Books 5-7, and still others never saw later treatment and remain exclusively on Newt Scamander's pages forever. By the way, don't you think "fantastic beasts" is a redundancy? After all, aren't virtually all beasts fantastic indeed? And even if magizoology does have the extra prefix, studying plain old Muggle zoology reveals magic aplenty, it seems to me. *Love* those beasties—Muggle or magic, real or imaginary.

Next I'll ask you to join me on a journey back to that queer ditch, the magical spot where that most popular of wizard games originated. Quidditch, which is now played by Muggles (after a fashion), has a number of elements that parallel aspects of established Muggle games as well; we will discuss Rowling's brief history of the game she invented for her magical characters, as well as her Muggle readers, to enjoy. *Fantastic Beasts* and *Quidditch Through the Ages* are, for the most part, absurd and eccentric, so my afterthoughts about them tend to be as well. So, I hope you'll find some fun in these chapters because I wanted to treat these two books with the seriousness they deserve and in the spirit in which I believe they were written. I mean, how seriously do you expect me to discuss a Fwooper or a Sloth Grip Roll?

Finally in this book I invite you to join me for a focus on *The Tales of Beedle the Bard*—Rowling's wonderful fables that we got to read for ourselves in December of 2008, after all those months of peering over Hermione's shoulder in the tent or on the road, puzzled by the runes and unable to read the lines. At last, Rowling gave us all our own copies, complete with outstanding commentary and annotation by the inimitable Albus Dumbledore, and edited, essentially, by the woman between magical and Muggle worlds, J. K. Rowling herself. In *all* of my discussions in *Rowling Revisited*, I will note literary parallels to and possible influences on Rowling's works, along with a few recommendations of literary works you may not know and which I think you would enjoy.

Once again, if you don't own copies of any or all of these three wonderful ancillary Potter books, please consider purchasing them. In doing so, you'll be contributing to excellent causes that you'll feel very good about supporting. So, whether you've joined me for *Repotting Harry Potter* or are joining me here for the first time, I welcome you to these pages. Remember when Dumbledore tells Harry near the beginning of *Half-Blood Prince*, "And now . . . let us step out into the night and pursue that flighty temptress, adventure"? Well, let us now turn a few pages and pursue whatever that flighty temptress *rereading* has in store for us. I know— "rereading" doesn't sound quite as exciting as Dumby's flighty temptress "adventure," but it's what we do. After all, I'm the "*Re*- Guy."

Abbreviations and Notations

SS	*Harry Potter and the Sorcerer's Stone* (1998)
CS	*Harry Potter and the Chamber of Secrets* (1999)
PA	*Harry Potter and the Prisoner of Azkaban* (1999)
GF	*Harry Potter and the Goblet of Fire* (2000)
FB	*Fantastic Beasts and Where to Find Them* (2001)
QA	*Quidditch Through the Ages* (2001)
OP	*Harry Potter and the Order of the Phoenix* (2003)
HP	*Harry Potter and the Half-Blood Prince* (2005)
DH	*Harry Potter and the Deathly Hallows* (2007)
BB	*The Tales of Beedle the Bard* (2008)

Note: Rowling's works are listed above in chronological order. The publication dates refer to the initial hardback publication of Rowling's books in the United States by Scholastic Press. All of my page references are to these editions and are cited parenthetically in the text.

Chapter 1: A Return to Harry

Re-Stoned: Afterthoughts on *Harry Potter and the Sorcerer's Stone*

How, "in the name of heaven," as Professor McGonagall says, would an incurable Potter reader like me find even *more* matters to talk about by going back through *Harry Potter and the Sorcerer's Stone* yet again? Yet, recently as I began to reread Book 1 in preparation for my upcoming class at Pepperdine University, I was surprised that the simplest and shortest of the Potter books yielded still more unexpected rewards upon still another rereading. Focusing on the categories I employ in *Repotting Harry Potter*—punning, foreshadowing, miscellaneous matters, and problematic elements—led me to the discovery of a number of elements I had overlooked in all my previous readings.

How, for example, did I miss Vernon Dursley's selection of a tie to wear to work at good old Grunnings? He hummingly picks out "his most boring tie" (2). Drills *are* boring, aren't they? In fact, you might say it's *boring* to work with a drill (even if you find it exciting), so why not wear a tie that ties in with the nature of the job? In addition to Rowling's appropriate word choice here, notice that in the same sentence she links the words "snakes" and "slithering" and "snake" and "slithering" twice in Chapter 2 (26, 28) with only three and four words between these two. We are thus prepared for the most notorious house at Hogwarts before Harry even knows he's a wizard and well before the Sorting Hat gives us our profile of the serpentine witches and wizards of the silver and green. One more example of word play is found, I believe, in Ron's comment about Scabbers: "I tried to turn him yellow yesterday to make him more interesting . . ." (104). Ironically, we all discover hundreds of pages later in Book 3 that Scabbers/Peter is far *too* "interesting," that he turned "yellow" years ago, and that, in future actions, he will show his true color yet again.

Notice too that Ron, annoyed by how lethargic his snoozing pet rat is, says, "He might have died and you wouldn't know the difference" (104). A turn of that phrase is tempting: Peter might *not* have died and we wouldn't know the difference (until we get to the truth in the Shrieking Shack).

In the general category of problematic elements, we can't help but notice some oddities about Mary GrandPré's cover art: not only are Harry's glasses wider than they are elsewhere; his scar doesn't really resemble the artist's later drawings of them a great deal either. I much prefer the GrandPré cover on the tenth anniversary edition of *Sorcerer's Stone*, which came out in 2008, depicting Harry looking into the Mirror of Erised. Also in Book 1, Rowling does not match her dates and days of the week with those of 1991-92, the time setting of the book. Vernon's going to work on the morning after Harry has survived and the Dark Lord has been thwarted is a Tuesday (2), but that would be November 1, 1981, which was a Sunday. Harry's eleventh birthday, which is July 31, 1991, is also on a Tuesday (43), but that date actually fell on a Wednesday. This is reminiscent of Gertie Keddle's diary entries in *Quidditch Through the Ages*; they're all "Tuesday" entries because "she only knew the name of one of the days of the week" (8). In later books, Rowling (or a copy editor) surely consulted a perpetual calendar for those days and dates matching reality. As for the first few pages of the first book, "who knew" re-readers like us would be guilty of this kind of *carpe diem* (or carping about *diem*)?

There are a few other things I find myself wondering about on rereading *Sorcerer's Stone*. It's a bit odd that after so many days, months, or even years, Dumbledore feels the need to send Hagrid to move the stone from Gringotts to another safe hiding place, Hogwarts. It is extraordinarily propitious that the stone is taken from the vault just before the break in and attempted theft; and it is even more propitious (or, arguably, a plot contrivance) that the stone is moved *closer* to the potential danger of Quirrell/Voldemort snatching it. I wonder too why the Dursleys have waited a month to have Dudley de-tailed. Was London's most renowned pigtailectomy surgeon on holiday during August? Again, plot-wise this is convenient since the Dursleys are "going up to London . . . anyway" on the day Harry needs to get to King's Cross (90). Come to think of it, how did Vernon and Petunia and newly be-tailed Dudley get off that rock island and back to civilization? In later books, Rowling will not leave such details up in the air. For example, take the case of Aunt Marge: although *she's* left in the air, the explanation of how this matter was resolved is not.

There are a few more minor matters about which I wonder. Why would Molly Weasley ask what platform number she and the kids need to find to get to the Hogwarts Express (92)? Ginny, strangely enough since she hasn't begun school at Hogwarts yet, informs her mother; but what about Molly's seeing off Bill, Charlie, Percy, and the twins in previous years? Or, for that matter, what about her own (we assume) seven years of going off to school? Does the access point (or the station) change from time to time—like portraits' passwords? For the next five years it won't, and the kids in the Epilogue of Book 7 (in 2017) still depart from the same place. Moreover, with regard to Harry's hairy giant friend, how did Hagrid get to the rock where Vernon hoped to escape the Hogwarts letters? "Flew," he says simply without elaborating (64). Yet very few magical persons can fly without a broom, as indicated by the Order members' amazement at Voldemort's broomless flight in Book 7. Hagrid, in fact, seems to have no broom (even one hidden in a pink umbrella), and he tells us in *Deathly Hallows* that neither brooms nor thestrals can take his weight (53). Kennilworthy Whisp tells us in *Quidditch Through the Ages* that no wizard can fly unaided (1); so maybe Rowling should be called in on the *carpet* on this one.

Finally, with regard to these little "blips" on the radar (which Hagrid would surely have been), notice how Hagrid uses *ter* for *to* quite often in his speech. Many of these usages are before words beginning with consonants while *teh* is often used before vowels. A couple of examples (italics mine) are "they were too close *ter* Dumbledore *ter* want anythin' *ter* do with the Dark Side" (55) and "I wouldn' say no *teh* a bit o' yer birthday cake" (63). Yet at times throughout *Sorcerer's Stone*, Hagrid uses *to* before either a consonant or a vowel: "Now listen *to* me" (193). Talking about all of Hagrid's little *t* words might seem *te*dious, but he does seem somewhat inconsistent in his dialect *to*'s, pronouncing that preposition different ways at different times (sometimes while serving tea for two). I doubt that you would want to make a formal study or count of Hagrid's *to*'s in *Sorcerer's Stone* since most of us have better things to/ter/teh do with our time. I mention this and all of the curiosities discussed above in part to underscore how much more detailed, thorough, and accurate the later books are compared to Book 1. I find that as I return to "the stone," there *are* a few stones left unturned.

When you reread *Harry Potter and the Sorcerer's Stone*, here are several miscellaneous matters—footnotes to the text, metaphorically speaking—that might add to your appreciation of the book:

§ The television weatherman reports shooting stars and adds that maybe some folks are "celebrating Bonfire Night early" (6). Bonfire Night is November 5, ending the various observances of Guy Fawkes Day with fireworks and bonfires—all this commemorating the Gunpowder Plot on November 5, 1605, led by Fawkes (the man not the phoenix) and other English Catholics against King James. Since the television report the Dursleys are watching is on November 1, 1981, weatherman McGuffin makes a timely and understandable reference as he introduces his happy report on this surely happy news program.

§ When Dumbledore assures McGonagall that Hagrid is trustworthy to bring baby Harry to Privet Drive, she reminds the headmaster that Hagrid is careless and that he "does tend to . . ." (14). Though McGonagall doesn't finish her sentence, we re-readers surely can since we know that Hagrid, when well into his cups, can talk too much on matters on which he's supposed to be mum.

§ I wonder why Rowling spends half a page on the number of spoiled Dudley's birthday presents—eventually totaling thirty-nine (21). Is that seemingly random number of gifts linked to the thirty-nine lashes St. Paul received from his persecutors (see 2 Corinthians 11:24)? Thirty-nine was the traditional number of lashes inflicted on a prisoner or a slave because if forty or more were inflicted and the beaten person died, the punisher could be subject to murder charges (see Deuteronomy 25:3). All this is interesting in light of Dumbledore's biting comment to the Dursleys in *Half-Blood Prince* regarding "the appalling damage you have inflicted" upon Dudley (55). Harry's gifts of Vernon's old socks, the coat hanger, or the fifty pence piece are, perhaps in the end, less cruel than the thirty-nine lashes which Dudley's lavish gifts really are—gifts which further spoil and damage this favored, but, as Dumby says, "unfortunate" boy.

§ Speaking of numbers, when twenty-four more letters for Harry are unwittingly delivered by the Dursleys' milkman in the eggs, the Muggle deliverer is "very confused" (40). I wonder if he has been hit with a Confundus Charm, though Rowling hasn't told us what they are yet and won't for a few hundred more pages.

§ And now let's consider some numbers with regard to dollars, pounds, and Galleons. If we apply a simple ratio to Dumbledore's translation of about 34 million Galleons being equal to 174 million pounds or to 250 million dollars in *Quidditch Through the Ages* (vii) and *Fantastic Beasts and Where to Find Them* (vii-viii), a Galleon would be about $7.35. Thus Harry's wand would cost just over $50 (85), and the candy he buys would total about $5.00 (101). Both prices work for me; these numbers seem to "add up" (more so than the classic Rowling numbers puzzler of how many students are at Hogwarts, for sure).

§ Hagrid's first comparison to explain Quidditch to Harry is that it's "like soccer in the Muggle world" (79). Later when Oliver Wood gives Harry (and us) the basics of this kind of air soccer, notice how many parallels there are to other Muggle sports. In Quidditch, as in baseball and cricket, there is no clock, and the lengths of the games can vary significantly until the last out is made (or until the Snitch is caught). As in hockey and soccer, there are Quidditch fouls and penalty shots; as in American football and basketball, points are scored when balls pass between or within goalposts and goals. The whole Bludger business reminds me of Dodgeball (along with another baseball link with the Beaters' bats). I'll elaborate on these and other similarities to Muggle sports later in my discussion of *Quidditch Through the Ages*. Among Harry readers, there are surely Quidditch lovers and Quidditch haters, with probably most of us somewhere in between. Nevertheless, what an ingenious hybrid of an imaginary sport Rowling gives us—along with ample explanations of its rules.

§ I love the way Rowling puts our proud Muggle founding dates in perspective—like "Brooks Brothers, Established 1815," or "Harvard University, founded 1636," or "Heidelberg University, founded 1386"—with what's written over Ollivander's door: "Makers of Fine Wands since 382 B.C." (82). Now *that's* an old establishment, and hopefully the sign was painted *Anno Domini*. (Do you recall the old joke about someone finding a rare Roman coin dated "48 B.C."; could *that* have been a fake—what do you think?)

§ George Weasley, Hagrid, and Ron yell "Oy" to Fred, Neville, and the mountain troll respectively (94, 112, 175), but Rowling doesn't use this British "hey" much in all the later books. I have no idea why *Oy*'s wane and *Hiya*'s and *Hey*'s take their place.

§ In the rich tradition of initiation stories ("coming of age" fiction), *Sorcerer's Stone* contains a wonderful line as Harry, aboard the Hogwarts Express, is heading for his first year at school: "He didn't know what he was going to—but it had to be better than what he was leaving behind" (98). This line reminds me of the last line of William Faulkner's beautiful initiation story "Barn Burning" ("He did not look back") and, even more so, of the ending of Thomas Wolfe's sprawling, often-incoherent, but overall magnificent *Look Homeward, Angel*: "he was like a man who stands upon a hill above the town he has left, yet does not say 'The town is near,' but turns his eyes upon the distant soaring ranges." Rowling's Harry, like these other literary initiates, is focused on the future rather than the past; and, among other things, *Sorcerer's Stone* is an excellent "first chapter" of a multi-volume coming-of-age story *for* the ages.

§ I find it interesting that the Dumbledore Chocolate Frog card contains mostly information that will be important later (from Flamel's name to the Grindelwald duel to Dumbledore's love of music) with the exception of the last detail: his enjoyment of "tenpin bowling" (102-03). Rowling never makes anything of this, never takes us bowling with Dumby; maybe this little tidbit was included as a clue to the pronunciation of the author's last name. If so, it didn't help with those who rimed her with *howling*—and, in some cases, still do.

§ Isn't it ironic that one Rubeus Hagrid, Keeper of Keys and Grounds at Hogwarts, has to knock on the castle door to get in (112)? The Keeper of Keys doesn't have one to the front door.

§ Many attempts have been made to find some significance or hidden meaning in those "few words" Dumbledore speaks, "Nitwit, Blubber, Oddment, Tweak" (123), including my own futile efforts in *Repotting Harry Potter* (19). Is it possible to apply the four words to the speech Dumbledore makes after all have been "fed and watered" (126)? In his first announcement, the headmaster *tweaks* his warning about the Forbidden Forest by adding a special reminder to a few older students, his eyes "twinkling" as he looks at Fred and George (127). Later, he issues the dire warning about the third-floor corridor, but does not explain why the area is dangerous. Notice that Percy tells Harry that it's "odd" that Dumbledore gave no reason for this prohibition; it's odd that there's no *oddment* about the reason. The reaction of the other teachers (with their "fixed" smiles) when Dumby leads all in the school song might indicate that they may think having hundreds of people singing all different tunes at once is the kind of thing a *nitwit* might do. The song is surely beautiful to Dumbledore, though, and in fact it moves him to tears, as he *blubbers* "Ah, music . . . A magic beyond all we do here!" (128). To say that all this is a stretch on my part is to state the obvious, and I admit I have now said far too *many* words about Dumby's famous *few*.

§ The title of Chapter 9, "The Midnight Duel," promises what it doesn't deliver—another example of Rowling's characteristic misdirection. You might recall similarly the misleading Chapter 5 title, "Fallen Warrior," in *Deathly Hallows* when we think that surely Hagrid is a goner. The midnight duel in *Sorcerer's Stone* is not a potentially deadly duel between Draco and Harry, but, in actuality, is Ron and Harry versus the obstreperous Hermione, who fears being expelled from school—a fate, to her, "worse" than death (162).

§ How about the significance of the number of the Gringotts vault from which Hagrid removes the stone (and which is broken into shortly thereafter): vault seven hundred and thirteen? Once Harry figures Fluffy is guarding the package that he saw in the vault and tells Ron all about it, Ron concludes that what was in seven hundred and thirteen is "either really valuable or really dangerous" (162-63). Seven is a "really valuable" number in a sense—a number with special significance and positive associations from antiquity to contemporary authors who write seven-part epics; and thirteen for centuries (as well as in the Potter books) is traditionally unlucky, ominous, or "really dangerous." Before *Sorcerer's Stone* is over, this really valuable stone will lead to some really dangerous situations. Additionally, in *Harry Potter and the Prisoner of Azkaban*, Rowling will have Sirius Black imprisoned at Hogwarts and awaiting his Dementor's Kiss in the thirteenth window from the right, unlucky for him, but on the seventh floor, lucky for him (393).

§ Moreover, Rowling will, in *Prisoner of Azkaban*, indulge in a bit of droll troll humor with regard to their clubs, but I find it of interest here that she features the foul stench of the mountain troll at Hogwarts (as she will later as well). Yet Newt Scamander makes no reference to this smelly characteristic of trolls in *Fantastic Beasts and Where to Find Them*. Maybe Newt had been fortunate enough in his long career not to be within whiffing distance or not to experience troll boogers first hand. If so, all the better for Newt and all the worse for Harry and Ron and us.

§ Many people in the crowd at Harry's first Quidditch match are watching with binoculars (184), and Hagrid later brings out his pair (187). Omnioculars, anyone? I know, maybe they'd only be available for important World Cup matches, maybe they're too expensive for a lot of students (or Hagrid) to own, or maybe Rowling just hadn't invented them yet. At any rate, these fans have to look up in the sky with the same Muggle magnifiers you and I might use to look down at the field.

§ As I look back at Harry's first adventure while he's wearing his father's cloak, I would revise what I say in *Repotting Harry Potter*—that Harry heads for the library without a clear purpose (28-29). Book 1 indicates that he headed for the library first, and to the Restricted Section in particular, to continue the search for information about Flamel (205). It does strike me, though, that something that has nothing to do with Flamel (or any other facts within those books) drew Harry there. Unwittingly, he's drawn to a place where just a few letters—twenty-six in our language—form groups called words which are arranged in ways that can excite, enrage, enlighten, convince, persuade, perplex, and provoke thought or action. To a bibliophile, like Rowling and, I assume, all of us Potterites, cloaked Harry is on almost sacred ground that first night he is embraced by his father's cloak.

The last area I'd like to consider with regard to *Sorcerer's Stone* is Rowling's deftness with foreshadowing, another of her characteristic literary devices. For example, the author foreshadows later events, great and small, that will be a part of life at Hogwarts soon and in the years to come for Harry and the others. Hagrid mentions Cornelius Fudge (65), though the bowlered minister will not appear until *Chamber of Secrets*. When Hagrid is looking for the key to Harry's vault at Gringotts, some "moldy dog biscuits" are emptied out of his pockets (73); thus we have a little Fang foreshadowing. Ron's complaints about his hand-me-downs succinctly foreshadow later events as well (100). He bemoans his old robes (already too short for him), Charlie's old wand (soon to be broken), and Percy's old rat (soon to be a rat of another sort). Moreover, Ron doesn't have to fight a troll to be sorted into a house at school, as Fred (who else?) has told him; nevertheless, Ron and Harry will be fighting one by their first Halloween. Speaking of sorting, notice that the hat "took a long time to decide" that Neville is a Gryffindor (120)—just as it takes a long time for him to demonstrate his bravery and for readers to admire him. Forgetting to remove the hat, Neville returns it "amid gales of laughter." Eventually for readers of the Potter books, Neville will be no laughing matter. In fact, just as Harry earlier tells Neville regarding the ever-lost Trevor, "He'll turn up" (104), so will the toad's owner turn up—big time in the end. While still at the opening feast also, Seamus Finnigan asks Nearly Headless Nick why the Bloody Baron is bloody (124). Nick can't answer, and Rowling won't either for a few thousand pages yet.

As the days and weeks go by during Harry's first year, we see several more examples of events and devices of Hogwarts life foreshadowed. In the description of the oddities of the place, we find a reference to "doors that weren't really doors at all, but solid walls just pretending" (132). Is the Room of Requirement referenced here in rudimentary form? We read further that Filch knows the secret passageways of Hogwarts better than anyone, with the possible exception of the Weasley twins (133)—a nice anticipation of our later finding out Fred and George are in possession of the Marauder's Map. The twins too later steal some goodies from the Hogwarts kitchens for the post-Quidditch celebration (227). Eventually, we learn how they get there and do that, with the house-elves never letting them leave empty-handed.

Several other foreshadows anticipate scenes, events, and people yet to come in the Potter series. We learn in *Sorcerer's Stone* that the Prewetts fell victim to Lord Voldemort (55-56) long before we know this is Molly's maiden name and that these slain wizards were her brothers. Just after hearing Hagrid talk about the Prewetts and the others, Harry "for the first time in his life" recalls hearing a "high, cold, cruel laugh" (56). It surely won't be the last time he remembers or hears in person that awful laughter. Also early in *Sorcerer's Stone* as Harry attempts to find *his* wand at Ollivanders, the old wand maker tells him "you will never get such good results with another wizard's wand" (84). Rowling will *show* us in *Deathly Hallows* what Ollivander *tells* us here a few thousand pages earlier. Notice too the economy of Rowling's foreshadowing as Ron tells Harry that his brother Charlie is "studying dragons" and that Bill does "something for Gringotts" (107). This sets us up nicely for Charlie's friends' aid in the de-Norberting caper and for his role in *Goblet of Fire* in preparation for the dragon trial in the Triwizard Tournament. Bill's work at and familiarity with Gringotts and goblins will be a significant factor in *Deathly Hallows*. Rowling definitely has plans for Ron's yet unseen older brothers. And she has plans for a couple of yet-to-be-written ancillary books as well. In the first Potter book, we have references to *Fantastic Beasts and Where to Find Them* (67) and to *Quidditch Through the Ages* (144, 181, 182). Rowling is a few years away from bringing Newt's and Kennilworthy's works to us Muggles, but their titles await them.

To me, the most emotionally satisfying foreshadowed element in *Sorcerer's Stone* is the composite picture of soon-to-be-first-year Harry on the train to Hogwarts. What's anticipated here are three aspects of Harry's "goodness" (for lack of a better term). Sainthood he deserves not; brilliant he isn't; and to make Harry an allegorical Christ figure is problematic as well. But he is good, a very good-hearted young lad indeed. Consider how Harry responds to Ron when asked what Muggles are like: "Horrible—well, not all of them" (99). As a decade-long, spider-infested-cupboard dweller in the house of Dursley, this boy can still say "not all of them." Give Harry high marks in tolerance. When Ron clearly indicates his family's financial difficulties, Harry "didn't think there was anything wrong with not being able to afford an owl" and reveals how Spartan-like he has lived (100). Harry immediately understands Ron's circumstances and shows empathy. And, best of all perhaps, when newly rich Harry can treat his new friend-for-life to all the junk food he has bought, it's a good feeling indeed, since Harry "had never had anything to share before or, indeed, anyone to share it with" (102). He is instinctively generous. We see how his tolerance, empathy, and generosity, first demonstrated here on the Hogwarts Express, make up a major part of who he is. It is his very nature to be this way. His rashness, daredevil nature, boldness, and quickness to act may come from the parent he so resembles, but he does indeed have his mother's eyes and, I assume, her kind heart. I'm not sure I can imagine James Potter reacting to a Ron Weasley of his generation in these ways, but I can surely see Lily doing so. After all, she befriended as long as she could the social outcast "Snivellus"; she yelled across the lake "LEAVE HIM ALONE!"; she treated *her* childhood friend with tolerance, empathy, and generosity; and, whether she realized it or not, she gave Severus Snape something to love "always."

I would like to look finally at a foreshadowed scene involving Snape and Harry. Notice the moment when Harry and the teacher with "greasy black hair" and a "hooked nose" first make eye contact (126). Rowling, masterful at misdirection, writes: "The hook-nosed teacher looked past Quirrell's turban straight into Harry's eyes—and a sharp, hot pain shot across the scar on Harry's forehead" (126). *Post hoc ergo propter hoc* ("after this, therefore because of this") is what Rowling is "up to" here. Surely, first-time readers conclude that the black eyes of evil Snape bring the pain to poor Harry's forehead. Why, as Harry often thinks, *does* Snape "hate him so much" (139), a question Rowling leaves us pondering for almost four thousand pages. Rowling contrasts the warmth of Hagrid's beetle-black eyes with those of Snape, whose eyes "were cold and empty and made you think of dark tunnels" (136). Many hundreds of pages later, in *Deathly Hallows*, Harry will see Snape's living eyes for one last time as he has traversed a long dark tunnel and witnesses Voldemort's virtual murder of Snape. Here, in *Sorcerer's Stone*, Snape's eyes strike Harry as "cold and empty"; in death Harry sees Snape's eyes as "fixed, blank, and empty" (*DH* 658). In the former case, perhaps Rowling intends us, looking back and only retrospectively, to realize that Severus's eyes are cold because his life is without Lily's presence, esteem, and love. In the latter description, his fixed and blank eyes are empty of life itself. If all this seems a stretch or a lot to make of that first look between Harry and Snape, I apologize. But Rowling, who plans so much so masterfully, in my view, could well have had the moving last words of Snape, "Look . . . at . . . me," clearly in mind the first time the eleven-year-old innocent child of his life-long love casually looked his way.

Re-Chambered: Afterthoughts on *Harry Potter and the Chamber of Secrets*

Harry Potter and the Chamber of Secrets has never been my favorite in the series; in fact, it's probably my least favorite, even though I still think it's wonderful, and I enjoy going back through the book just as much as I do rereading any of the others. As many richly humorous elements as I've appreciated in my previous readings of *Chamber*, I found still a few more my last time through. For example, the first time Harry enters a wizard house, the wonderfully eccentric "Burrow" of the Weasleys, he hears a radio announcement that Celestina Warbeck is about to sing (34). Most of the Celestina references (and all of her awful lyrics) Rowling will save for later; but encountering the singer as early as Book 2 as a re-reader makes me smile, knowing that to Molly Celestina Warbeck's singing is so much celestial warbling, while to Fleur it's more like hellish howling (or maybe *'ellish 'owling* since Fleur calls the singing "'orrible"). There's more good wordplay to come soon in Book 2. It's appropriate that Fred and George, our two future joke shop entrepreneurs, are shopping at Gambol and Japes Wizarding Joke Shop (58). To *gambol* is to frolic or skip playfully, and a *jape* is a joke or a gibe. Hamlet asks of Yorick's skull, "Where be your gibes now? your gambols?" (V.i.175).

With regard to more word-related humor, I wonder if Rowling wants us to make a connection when Harry passes McGonagall's classroom where someone has "turned his friend into a badger" just three lines before he comes upon some Hufflepuffs (198). The victim of the classroom badgering, who "still had black-and-white-striped hair" (203), is present just as Hufflepuff Ernie Macmillan accuses Harry of the attack, again just three lines from the badgered student reference. I believe such juxtapositions as these are little winks to the reader and are not accidental or coincidental, like Rowling's uses of *grim*, *grimly*, *serious*, and *seriously* in the Sirius-dominated Book 3. If you're skeptical about these *badger-Hufflepuff* matters, it gets worse. In Professor Binns's grudging discussion of the location of the Chamber of Secrets, Parvati "piped up" with a comment (152). Many pages later Professor Flitwick "piped up" to confront Lockhart about his alleged knowledge of the Chamber (294). I mention the latter, the Professor's piping up, in *Repotting Harry Potter* (80-81), but I've only recently noticed Parvati Patil's piping. In both cases, I think Rowling is enjoying the word humor associated with a verb, *piped*, linked to the noun, the *pipes*, the bathroom plumbing, which is linked, which literally leads, to the Chamber of the title of the book.

Now let's consider a few curiosities in Book 2 (cracks in the Chamber, maybe). Early on when Harry's foul-weather friends rescue him, they're revving the flying car's engine, pulling bars off Harry's window, and pushing his trunk through the window. Yet, they are not making enough noise to awaken the Dursleys—until, of course, they pull off the getaway (25-27). Secondly, we wonder that gnomes can talk—albeit somewhat inarticulately (37). When Harry and the Weasleys are de-gnoming the garden, one of the pests squeals, "Gerroff me!" (37). Newt Scamander makes no reference to gnomes talking in *Fantastic Beasts and Where to Find Them*; maybe Newt never de-gnomed a garden and thus never got a gnome-tongue-lashing "gerroff." You might recall that when we first meet Ron in *Sorcerer's Stone* and Molly is trying to wipe his nose before he boards the Hogwarts Express, Ron says, "*Mom*—geroff" (95). I suppose we could conclude that Ron speaks Gnome, which would seem to be as impressive as speaking Troll. Thirdly, I wonder why Rowling describes the Whomping Willow as an "ancient tree" (76). In a few hundred pages, we're about to learn when the Whomper was planted and why, and it was not so long ago as to warrant "ancient," was it? Then again, maybe it was a new planting of an already old tree back in Lupin's student days.

The next curious matter I notice in *Chamber* is that Ron complains about his detention, saying that he is "no good at Muggle cleaning"(119). Wouldn't his chores at the Burrow, as an under-aged wizard, probably have involved a good deal of non-magical cleaning? Recall too that in *Half-Blood Prince* Ron and Harry are ridiculed by Fred and George (who now *can* use magic at home) as they are peeling sprouts as Muggles would do (*HP* 326-27). Admittedly, though, Ron might have done a lot of elbow-grease work and just be no good at it; after all, Molly's still trying to get him to clean up his room in Book 7. Speaking of cleaning, wouldn't hundreds of Hogwarts students have wondered over the years why Filch has to clean Muggle-fashion? It seems that his Squibness would be widely known and, by some, ridiculed throughout the school. Then again, like a few hundred other matters, maybe *we* just don't know something until Harry knows it.

As I go back through Book 2 this time, I have to question the Quidditch strategy the team decides on during the time out in "The Rogue Bludger" chapter. The plan is for Fred and George to *protect* the Chasers as they try for ten-point goals and leave the beleaguered (or bebludgeoned) Seeker *unprotected* while he goes for one-hundred-and-fifty points and the game-ending, potentially game-winning, Snitch snitch. Besides, during the somewhat lengthy time out, where's that rogue of a Bludger? Why not just bludgeon Harry's arm as he stands there talking bad strategy; now *that* would be a roguish thing to do indeed. We need to ask Dobby about all this. Speaking of whom, when Dobby disappears with a crack (Rowling hasn't given us the word *Apparate* yet), Harry, who has been clutching the house-elf's wrist, finds that his fist is then "clenched on thin air" (179). In later books we'll see Side-Along Apparition (*HP* 58), as well as a Death Eater holding on to the Apparating Hermione and going where she is going (*DH* 267). So it would seem from these later examples that touching the disappearing one takes the toucher along, unlike the case in Book 2 with Harry's *not* having the vanished house-elf in his clutches. Maybe elf Apparition is different in this respect too, like *where* they can Apparate to and from is different.

Here's one more oddity to think about, this one regarding Crabbe and Goyle. When the sleeping giant friends of Draco awaken following the mildly successful Polyjuice caper in *Chamber of Secrets*, wouldn't they have said something to their gang leader about that experience? Or wouldn't Draco have said at some point, "I've already *shown* you two the *Daily Prophet* article about Arthur Weasley"? Come to think of it, though, since it's Crabbe and Goyle that we're talking about figuring out Draco was talking to imposters, probably *not*. Here's one more really little matter. It has to do with how Harry-as-Goyle sounds compared to the real thing, who finally talks in Book 7. Polyjuiced Harry/Goyle speaks in a "low rasp of a voice" (*CS* 217), yet the real Goyle "grunted" his line (complete with two subject-verb agreement errors) in *Deathly Hallows* (629). Harry/Goyle speaks grammatically correctly in his dialogue with Draco. Similarly, Ron's Polyjuiced voice of Crabbe in Book 2 is described as a "deep grunt" (*CS* 217), yet the real Crabbe's voice is "surprisingly soft for such an enormous person" (*DH* 628). That's probably more than enough for most of you regarding the real and Polyjuiced henchmen of dreaded Draco. You might be thinking: Crabbe, Goyle, fake Crabbe, fake Goyle, grammatical or not, grunting, soft, let's call the whole thing off.

And now a final matter that might make you go "hmmm." Tom Riddle makes such a convincing point to Harry as to why young Hagrid was assumed to be the one who opened the Chamber that we too are almost persuaded (311-12). No wonder the beastie-loving, eccentric, uncultured giant lad who was constantly in trouble (the trouble almost always involving forbidden and/or dangerous creatures) would be Suspect Number One when the Chamber was opened. Yet, as Riddle says, "I thought *someone* must realize that Hagrid couldn't possibly be the Heir of Slytherin" (312). No kidding! We're supposed to believe that no one but Dumbledore figured Hagrid was WRONG for the Heir of Sytherin. With apologies to Hagrid, I'd say that the man who could be a dragon's Mommy and who produced Blast-Ended Skrewts *could* surely, as a boy, have loosed a basilisk on Hogwarts . . . but as for *this loveable oaf* being the heir of Salazar Slytherin? No way. What were they all (except Dumby) thinking fifty years ago?

As we continue back through Book 2, as we are *re-Chambered* once again, I invite you to consider with me now a number of miscellaneous matters that I think you will find of more interest now that we re-readers know Harry's whole story. Rowling defines Muggles as humans who have "not a drop of magical blood in their veins" (3). She seems not only to be readying us for Squibs, but this line also brings to mind the comparisons that John Granger and others have made over the years that a person's being magic or not is linked to a recessive gene. Thus our favorite Muggle dentists, Hermione's parents, must have both had a recessive magic gene—producing, therefore, the wonderful Hermione—and, alas, poor Filch (and poor Figg) must have had magical parents who both had recessive non-magical genes. While we're on the subject of Muggles and magic folk, I find it interesting that young Harry has a good grip on what Muggles think of as magic. Recall that he frightens Dudley with some "*Hocus pocus*" and other lame phrases (9) and that Harry's first reaction upon seeing the Sorting Hat is that the first years will have to pull a rabbit out of it (SS117). Well worth noticing too is that Dobby's green eyes stare at Harry through the hedge (8) and that his large green eyes are almost the first features mentioned when he appears in Harry's bedroom (12). I appreciate Rowling's vision (sorry) with regard to the house-elf's green eyes: after all, green-eyed Lily and Dobby both die for the green-eyed boy.

Going now from the sublime to the ridiculous, I can't help but wonder if Mr. Mason's "very funny story about those American plumbers" would have included a guy named Joe from Ohio (sorry, but I couldn't resist that reference—though by the time you read this, Joe the plumber's fifteen minutes of fame may have been up so long ago that he may not even be Googleable). Still on the silly side of things (and focusing on the first letter of *plumber*), think of how often Rowling shows her love of letters that alliterate—how she seems particularly pleased with patterns of specifically the same starting letters (OK, I'll stop)—how she loves alliterations. In characters' names alone—take *P* characters for example—she gives us Piers Polkiss, Peter Pettigrew, Pansy Parkinson, Padma Patil, Parvati

Patil, and Poppy Pomfrey. The *P*'s go on and on beyond persons with things like the Pepperup Potion, Lockhart's *Peskipiksi Pesternomi* charm, Polyjuice Potion, the Porskoff Ploy (a sophisticated Quidditch move), *The Practical Potioneer* (an academic journal in the wizarding world), the Pride of Portree (a professional Quidditch team), Probity Probes, Puking Pastilles, Pumpkin Pasty, and (remember Arnold?) pygmy puffs.

So it's no surprise that the most famous fraud in the Potterverse is apparently *wild* about alliteration. Look back at Gilderoy Lockhart's book titles (43-44) and add his recently published *Magical Me* to the Hogwarts list. I figure he had at least thirteen more books to write to finish off the alliterative consonants left in the English alphabet. Isn't it sad that the gilded one lost his own memory before he could erase others' and write *Bonding With Bundimuns*, *Journeys With Jarveys*, or *Roaming With Re'ems.* Before we leave Gilderoy, notice that he is "definitely" sure that a curse, "probably the Transmogrifian Torture" (141), has killed Mrs. Norris. The only problems here for the gilded one are that the cat is not dead, and she's still a cat (transmogrifying involves a change in form—as from a frog to a prince). Yet the name of the curse *sounds* good, as does the charm *Peskipiksi Pesternomi* (102), which Lockhart apparently makes up on the spot—at least the pesky pixies pay it no heed.

While we're on the subject of fantastic beasts, I find it interesting that some which Rowling mentions in *Chamber of Secrets* are not later described by Newt Scamander. The bicorn and boomslang (186) we can't read about in *Fantastic Beasts and Where to Find Them*; the latter is a real snake in the Muggle world, thus not fantastic; the bicorn would have been well described by Newt, though, yet it somehow isn't. Hagrid later mentions the "Blood-Suckin' Bugbear" (201) which likewise doesn't make Newt's list. On the other hand, Scamander's description of the basilisk matches what is said about and what is done by the beast in *Chamber of Secrets* (though Newt's Basilisk rates a capital *B* and Book 2's doesn't). The inclusion of the basilisk and exclusion of the above-mentioned minor beasts (though "minor beasts" may be an oxymoron) may grow out of the on-the-page presence of the snake, as opposed to mere references to the others.

I noticed four further miscellaneous matters as I was *re-Chambered.* First, Madam Hooch is called a "Quidditch teacher" (167), but is she? She seems to be a flying teacher—one, we assume, who both teaches flying and flies while teaching—and a Quidditch referee; but we don't really see anyone teaching Quidditch besides the various team captains, do we? Secondly, notice that when Harry enters Tom's diary and his past, it's June

13 (242), and that can't be lucky. Third, McGonagall uses a megaphone to address the students (256) rather than touching her wand to her neck and saying a magic word, as others will do later. Maybe like the Omnioculars, the magical method of addressing a crowd is still on the drawing board. Fourth, it's very much in keeping with later books that Harry's chamber adventure takes place on a very long day. The action in the novel that begins on May 29, 1993, takes place over fifty-five pages, beginning on page 284 and concluding only slightly over two pages from the book's end. We can know this precise date in *Chamber of Secrets*, incidentally, since the events take place three days before exams were to begin (283-84). The long June day in Book 3 and the long day's journey into the dawn when the Dark Lord will die (also a May day) are nicely prepared for here.

Understandably, Book 2 contains a significant number of foreshadows of things to come later in the series—as do all of the early books in the Potter series. Here are some for you to think about as you reread *Chamber of Secrets* and beyond:

§ All the early furor over "the 'M' word," "magic," on Privet Drive (2) foreshadows the pronounced reactions to another "'M' word," "Mudblood," at Hogwarts (112).

§ Fred Weasley points out that house-elves "have got powerful magic of their own" (28). From Dobby's disappearance from Harry's bedside in *Chamber of Secrets* to his appearance in the Malfoys' cellar in Book 7, we will see the truth of Fred's words.

§ Hagrid claims he's in Knockturn Alley to buy some "Flesh-Eatin' Slug Repellent" (55). Ron could use some slug repellent later, though maybe he's not plagued by the flesh-eating kind. Newt missed a chance to describe *these* magical mollusks too.

§ After Ron, Hermione, and Harry come upon Percy Weasley reading a book about Hogwarts prefects who went on to the proverbial bigger and better things, Ron tells his friends that Percy is "very ambitious," has things "all planned out," and "wants to be Minister of Magic" some day (58). I'll bet that few first-time readers took Percy's character or his brother's characterization as seriously as we must later on. Pompous, perfect prefect Percy evolves all too soon into a power-hungry Ministry minion who breaks his mother's heart one cold Christmas day four years later and doesn't come "home" again until the Battle of Hogwarts.

§ Hedwig's screeching at Ron and Harry at King's Cross (69)

anticipates McGonagall's question as to why the stranded boys didn't send an owl rather than fly a car. To assume that Hedwig was asking that same question in owl talk is not too far-fetched, I would say, especially since Rowling continues to humanize Harry's owl throughout the later books.

§ When Ron "patted the dash board" of the struggling Anglia (73), Rowling sets up the later comparisons of faithful car to faithful cur. Note that she compares the car to a "large turquoise dog" (274), and later Harry gives the car "a grateful pat" (280) as it has whisked them away from the giant spiders, about to disappear forever. Good dog/car.

§ Ron's broken wand and the important role this plays in Book 2 remind me of Harry's broken wand and of the subsequent wand-watching we have to do in Book 7.

§ Already within *Chamber of Secrets*, we learn that a malfunctioning wand (or using another's malfunctioning wand) is a serious thing. Such a wand doesn't just *slug* its owner, but can put someone in St. Mungo's for good.

§ Harry had a feeling that Snape can read minds in Book 1 (221), and he has the same feeling in *Chamber of Secrets* (79). Rowling is hundreds of pages away from introducing us to Legilimency and Occlumency, but I'll bet by Book 2 she'd already imagined some future scenes (it's almost as if we can read her mind).

§ Dumbledore's calmness over the Anglia incident, along with the "disappointment in his voice" (81), is more painful to Harry than if the headmaster were shouting and enraged. This foreshadows Dumbledore's calm demeanor in dealing with Harry following the death of Sirius Black, as well as his reaction to Harry's failure to procure Slughorn's memory in Book 6. In all cases, wise old Dumby is calm, and it's the quiet treatment that significantly affects the boy.

§ During Lockhart's first class, the new D.A.D.A. teacher tells the students, "You may find yourselves facing your worst fears in this room" (101). They certainly won't *that* day or any other during Lockhart's time at Hogwarts. But the line does nicely foreshadow what these students will experience the next year when Professor Lupin brings out the boggarts.

§ Long before we know the *when* of James and Lily Potter's deaths, not to mention not knowing the *why*, we find that someone else died on Halloween night as well—five hundred years before the present time of *Chamber of Secrets* Nearly Headless Nick's demise came. Incidentally, the hardbound editions of Books 1 and 2 contain minor errors that were corrected for the paperbacks. One involves Nick, since he tells Harry he hasn't eaten in four hundred years (*SS* 123), yet he died on October 31, 1492, *five* hundred years ago (*CS* 133)—a mistake, assuming that ghosts don't get a free century of still being able to taste food after death. It seems hard for Potterites to believe *any* kind of error sneaked past copy editors and proof readers of the early books after the immense success later and the world-wide readership and attention. Yet the first printed hardbacks have a few little surprises, like "Perry" instead of "Percy" (*CS* 157) and "Fawke's head" instead of "Fawkes's head" (*CS* 321).

§ Hermione's prowess with conjured, waterproof little warming fires (183) foreshadows a few of her fires to come, such as during the wilderness wanderings of Book 7.

§ Though the Polyjuice caper doesn't accomplish that much in *Chamber of Secrets*, the venture will turn out to be quite helpful to Harry as he claims to be Slytherin student Vernon Dudley in Book 7. His knowledge of the Slytherin common room adds to the credibility of the lie he tells the Snatchers.

§ The Expelliarmus spell is first used in *Chamber of Secrets*, and it will be used by Harry all through the series, becoming his signature spell. I mention in *Repotting Harry Potter* (81) that Harry's first use of the spell is to disarm Lockhart, but I missed his earlier, actual first attempt of the spell when Harry de-diaries Draco (239).

§ Just before Harry hears the voice for the first time, Hermione is reading a book about runes (254). She will spend a lot of time ruminating about runes in Book 7, and, later in her life, Hermione will "translate" the stories of Beedle from runes into English for us Muggles.

§ Reread the near-death experiences of Ron and Harry among the giant spiders with "The Forest Again" chapter of Book 7 in mind. I'd say the forest "death" scene in *Deathly Hallows* is here in *Chamber of Secrets* in embryonic form (279). Here Harry knows that reaching for his wand is "no good," and he is "ready to die." I know I have omitted words to serve my purpose and strengthen my point of foreshadowing, but I did say "embryonic form."

§ Ron's concern for Hermione and his now clearly implied fondness for her shows up in *Chamber of Secrets* when he looks at the empty seat the now petrified Hermione formerly occupied in class (270) and when he is "happier than he'd looked in days" (285) when the Mandrakes are ready to reanimate the petrified.

§ What a deft foreshadowing we have too when Harry asks Dobby to promise *not* to try to save his life again (339)—followed by a smile from Dobby, but no such promise. This seems a very appropriate response from our favorite house-elf, who will save Harry and the others five years later at the cost of his life.

As we conclude this reexamination of *Chamber of Secrets*, I'd like to consider Rowling's treatment of Gilderoy Lockhart in Book 2, especially in light of her later dispensation of this character. After Harry's explanation of what happened in the Chamber and after Dumbledore's decision not to expel but to reward the rule breaker, Harry "had completely forgotten about Lockhart" (331). This is appropriate since Lockhart has completely forgotten about himself. Yet what follows seems to foreshadow a cured, though not necessarily improved, Lockhart. Ron "explained quietly" to Dumbledore that the professor's Memory Charm had backfired without mentioning what exactly Lockhart was trying to do with that charm (331). Dumby then makes the impaled sword joke, which is followed by more sword silliness and, finally, the headmaster's request of Ron to take Lockhart to the infirmary. Rowling could have chosen to have Gilderoy healed by Madam Pomfrey so that, as with Ginny and all other matters in *Chamber of Secrets*, we could say (along with Dumby), "There has been no lasting harm done . . ." (330). By book's end, Dumbledore has announced that Professor Lockhart will not be returning to teach the next year since he "needed to go away and get his memory back" (340). This hasn't happened by Book 5, has it? And it seems unlikely ever to have occurred. So, I wonder if, after Book 2, Rowling had second thoughts about giving Lockhart his thoughts back because even if Ron and Harry don't talk about it afterwards, we readers know exactly what Lockhart was willing to do to them and to Ginny in the Chamber. He was within a working wand of doing them lasting harm, so no wonder Rowling allows Lockhart's self-inflicted harm to last. Many readers have seen Gilderoy as

Rowling's most effective comic character in the entire series. As effectively comedic as this mindless character/caricature is, though, he's also still in St. Mungo's—perhaps to remind us of this lightweight's very dark side.

Re-Prisonered: Afterthoughts on *Harry Potter and the Prisoner of Azkaban*

As I returned to *Harry Potter and the Prisoner of Azkaban* one more time, I found a "little something" in almost every chapter that I hadn't noticed before. So, I invite you to go back through this third book in the series with me in the proverbial "orderly fashion" beginning with Chapter 1. There I find it ironic that Uncle Vernon, following his abortive phone conservation with Ron, puts the receiver back as if it were a "poisonous spider" (4). Ron would like that simile even less than he enjoyed his phone chat with Vernon Dursley, I suspect. By the way, Rowling gives us such good reasons that Hermione *would* have called Harry and averted a Ron-like tele-catastrophe with Vernon (5), that we wonder why she *didn't* call. It's too bad these events take place way back in the summer of 1993; after all, these days Harry would have just given his mates his cell number, and they'd have been calling, texting, or twittering him all summer long. Notice too in the opening chapter of Book 3 the reference to what Ron thinks is his sub-par Pocket Sneakoscope that lights up too often (10). Here, I assume—and later when the Sneakoscope falls out of the sock (226), I *know*—that Scabbers is surely near. Maybe the device isn't unworthy and a bit of "rubbish," as Bill has said, after all; and maybe it wasn't lighting up because the twins put beetles in Bill's soup that night in Egypt, but because a certain rat was nearby. I figure Scabbers set it off, not scarabs, as Scabbers/Peter seems to do many times later in Book 3 (see 70, 76, 78, and 226). Here's one more matter I find of interest from early on in *Prisoner of Azkaban*: Hogsmeade is finally named for the first time in the Potter books (14) instead of just being "the village." As is the case with so many names of people, places, and things, we readers don't know something until Harry knows it or until it's about to affect his life in some relevant way.

As we progress through the next three chapters of *Prisoner of Azkaban*, let me invite you to consider some miscellaneous matters you might not have thought much of before. For example, Aunt Marge inflating and floating (29) is one of the last purely sight-gag moments in the Potter books—enjoyable not exclusively, but primarily, by the youngest of readers and comparable to such scenes in *Mary Poppins*, *Willy Wonka and the Chocolate Factory*, or some of the Pippi Longstocking tales. Next, Harry's charge for riding the Knight Bus is in Sickles (which are silver), but he pays in gold (35). The number of people Sirius (actually Peter) killed is thirteen (38), a consistently (and traditionally) unlucky number in Rowling's Potter books. Did you notice how toothless Tom of the Leaky Cauldron starts a nice roaring fire (43) with a click of his fingers (we Americans might say that's a *snap*)—something McGonagall does with her wand in *Chamber of Secrets* (80)? We Muggles deserve a little credit here, I'd say, for developing remote controls that fire up gas logs in the old grate with a *whoosh*. We also learn early in Book 3 that the matter of floating Aunt Marge has been taken care of by a nameless dynamic duo from the Ministry's Accidental Magic Reversal Department (44), which is, to me, much better than Rowling's leaving us in the dark about Ron's healing from his dragon bite or the return of the Dursleys from the rock in *Sorcerer's Stone*. I find myself wishing the Accidental Magic Reversal Department were the Accidental Reversal of Magic Department, so they could be nicely acronymed as ARMD. Here's another question: when Fudge conversed with the guards at Azkaban about Sirius (66), was he talking to dementors? Can they talk? And now one last little thing to think about: Hermione is taken with the ginger colored Crookshanks, whose color is referred to in Book 3 on occasion (see 60, 213, and 251); but later in the Potter books Ron will be referred to as "ginger" from time to time. Does the cat attraction parallel the boy attraction later?

Going through these first few chapters of *Prisoner of Azkaban*, I confess that I smiled again at the account of the *Invisible Book of Invisibility* (53), the copies of which were never found since they were apparently invisible (or, technically, not apparently visible). I wonder if Flourish and Blotts bookstore's trying to stock *that* book means that invisibility is taught at Hogwarts. Heretofore, I had assumed that only great wizards like Dumbledore don't need a cloak to become invisible, like those magic folk who are adept at the Disillusionment Charm. Maybe invisibility classes are conducted at Hogwarts and we just don't see them; or maybe they never got started after the trouble at Flourish and Blotts since the potential students have no visible textbooks or a visible teacher to teach them invisibility. Speaking of classes and changing the subject matter (*thankfully*, I know you're thinking), why *is* Hermione taking Muggle Studies, as Ron wants to know (57)? Hermione's answer, that "it'll be fascinating to study them from the wizarding point of view," reminds me of, say, an American taking an American literature class at the Sorbonne. Furthermore, isn't what Hermione says a major part of what Rowling is doing in the Potter books? Isn't she "studying" Muggles from a wizarding perspective—ranging from those who hate us, like Lucius Malfoy and You-Know-Who, to those, like Arthur Weasley, who find us fascinating with all our escapators, plugs, and post offices? Practically speaking, I might remind you that Hermione's other reason to take Muggle Studies could be the "easy A" or, in wizarding terms, the "easy O" she hopes to get. Even though she drops the course later, she made 320% on the exam (430), which might imply that this Muggle-born young witch knows about three-and-a-quarter times more about us than we know about ourselves—which may be about what gifted, insightful Muggle-born authors seem to know about the human race.

Over the next few pages we re-readers come across a number of foreshadowing elements. Harry notices that the stagecoaches take the returning students to Hogwarts castle by an invisible (to Harry) means. Recall that, as a first year, Harry was taken to his first night and the opening feast in Hagrid-supervised boats; his second year, he and Ron arrived (sort of) by air; and so now he experiences for the first time the traditional way second years and older kids go back to Hogwarts for a new school year. Also foreshadowed in the first chapters set at school are Hermione's Time-Turner deal with McGonagall (90) and the fact that Dumbledore is a young-acting old man—"though very old . . ." giving the "impression of great energy" (91)—which is still descriptive of him throughout Book 3, but which will not be so true of the headmaster from Book 4 on. Rowling tries to give us a hint about Hermione's upcoming third year at Hogwarts, incidentally, by italicizing *time* in Ron's comment (98). *Harry Potter and the Prisoner of Azkaban* is, indeed, all about time in the end, isn't it?

As we progress through a rereading of Book 3, let's go now in some different (and random) directions. How about looking back at the futures that Harry and Ron "read" for each other in the tea leaves (105) in Trelawney's class? Ron's "crooked sort of cross" means that he'll suffer but eventually be very happy (think about Ron in Book 7). Harry's "blob a bit like a bowler hat" means, so Ron thinks, that Harry might work at the Ministry of Magic. I wonder if the bowler hat led Ron to think of Fudge and, thus, the Ministry. Harry working for the Ministry in the long run makes sense since he, according to Rowling in interviews, becomes an Auror; but in Book 6 the new Minister tries unsuccessfully to get Harry to "work" at the Ministry or, as Harry says, to serve as a mascot there. Throughout *Repotting Harry Potter*, I trace through a number of "rights" and "lefts"—directions, wand-hand maneuvers, etc.—and suggest that there seem to be links between right and good and between left and evil (I remind readers that, after all, *sinister* is Latin for *left*). So, in Book 3, when Snape makes Neville's toad the Potions class guinea pig, he picks up Trevor "in his left hand" (128). Similarly, Harry sees those scary eyes "to his left" as he and Ron walk the castle grounds (256); Hermione speaks into Harry's right ear when she tells him to do the right thing and not sneak into Hogsmeade (275); and when Hermione and Harry are seeking Ron in the Shrieking Shack, they take "a door to their right" (337), which will eventually lead to the truth and the right course of action (but only after a *lot* of shack talk).

We've probably all heard the expression "smoking gun," and we'd probably all not want to be caught holding one. I like what I believe is Rowling's subtle allusion to this cliché as she has Snape bring in Lupin's monthly wolfsbane and writes, "Snape set down the smoking goblet . . ." (156). The Hogwarts professor Harry is continually convinced is guilty of something here actually *holds the smoking goblet*—how appropriate, or so Harry thinks anyway. Furthermore, at this point in *Prisoner of Azkaban*, we find still another violent act happening on Halloween night (recall Harry's parents' murder and Nick's almost-beheading) as Sirius Black slashes the Fat Lady's portrait (160-61). All this further prepares us to hear later in detail about the Halloween attack in Godric's Hollow by You-Know-Who on you know whom.

In my discussion of Book 3 in *Repotting Harry Potter*, I point out a number of Rowling's usages of *serious* and *seriously*, most of which are parts of discussions about or involving Sirius Black. I noticed a couple of other *seriously* usages, however, that are not directly related to Sirius and actually are part of discussions about Quidditch. Fred assures a worried Oliver Wood that the Gryffindor team is "taking Hufflepuff very seriously. *Seriously*" (169). Now let's fact it: such a dialogue as this could take place in any book wherein Quidditch is played, and under Captain Wood for *sure*; so I wonder if it's accidental that Rowling takes advantage of just imbedding two more uses of the ubiquitous adverb in her story of Sirius Black. Now, it gets worse. Is it too farfetched to suggest that Rowling orchestrates still another *serious* passage? Check out the fact that Ron, currently famous at Hogwarts for surviving the serious Sirius Black attack, figures that when Hagrid summons him and Harry to have tea, he wants to hear all about serious/Sirius matters (272). What Hagrid wants to discuss, however, is the boys' treatment of Hermione. Hagrid is, quite appropriately, "looking uncharacteristically serious" (273), which is fitting for the un-Sirius discussion that follows. That all may be way over the top, and, if it strikes you so, I'm sorry; but, I vow, I'm now *done* with all further Sirius/serious matters in Book 3 (or maybe way *overdone*).

Here are a few more minor matters you may want to notice in going back through the middle chapters of *Harry Potter and the Prisoner of Azkaban*:

§ In Book 3, Cedric Diggory is a fifth-year student (174), which means he's probably fifteen years old at the beginning of the school year since Hogwarts students begin their first year at age eleven, and it's still pre-Christmas at this point in Cedric's school year. So it seems odd that he's seventeen the next September in *Goblet of Fire*, fully able and eligible to place his name in the fire.

§ When Hermione aids Harry's Quidditch vision on that windy, rainy day with her "*Impervious*" wand touch of his glasses, Oliver Wood "looked as though he could have kissed her" (177). This is a nice little touch with regard to a rather wooden minor character, Oliver Wood. This is the first and only time he has shown any interest in the opposite sex (remember when he addresses his mixed-gender Quidditch team in *Sorcerer's Stone* as "men"?). And, don't forget that a few pages later, Wood, the classic fanatic, insanely competitive athlete (and isn't that guy always the captain?) is trying to drown his sorrows and probably himself in the showers after poor Harry has fallen off his broom (180).

§ It's important to note that just as Fred and George bestow the Marauder's Map on Harry, Rowling makes sure that Fred brings up the matter of the Whomping Willow (193). Thus she reminds us readers, and, more importantly, us re-readers, of the tree involved in the Anglia car caper of *Chamber of Secrets*, and she foreshadows the trip through the tunnel and to the Shrieking Shack coming up soon in *Prisoner of Azkaban*.

§ As an old, as well as former, teacher of English Composition, I happened to notice the difference in prepositions in the words that appear on the Marauder's Map. "Aids *to* Magical Mischief-Makers" (192, italics mine) becomes "Aids *for* Magical Mischief-Makers" (194, italics mine). Sure, Harry may just be remembering the words on the map imprecisely, but at no point in the other books in the series does Harry recall a speech or a passage in a book incorrectly.

§ As Alanis Morissette said so long ago (long ago in Rowling years, that is), isn't it ironic? Isn't it ironic that Rosmerta finds it hard to believe that the Sirius she remembers as a boy would go over to the Dark Side (203)? Similarly, McGonagall regrets that she wasn't nicer to Peter Pettigrew when he was at Hogwarts (207).

Re-readers want to assure Rosmerta that her instincts were correct and to assure McGonagall she shouldn't feel bad for not finding a rat endearing.

§ Here's a bit more irony. Recall that Hermione is convinced that Sirius Black gave Harry the Firebolt, and bear in mind that Fudge is worried that once Voldemort has "his most devoted servant" back, he will quickly rise to power again (209). In both cases the observation is correct, yet the all-important particulars are different from what the speaker thinks. Sirius does give Harry the Firebolt, but not to harm him; and the Dark Lord's "most devoted servant" is not a dog, but a rat.

§ Even before Luna Lovegood enters the Potter books reading her *Quibbler* on the train bound for Hogwarts, we come across a girl reading a book upside down in *Prisoner of Azkaban*. In this case, it's Hermione acting like she's not hearing McGonagall confiscate Harry's Firebolt (231)—another nadir for the Hermione-Ron-and-Harry relationship.

§ In Mary GrandPré's drawing at the beginning of Chapter 12, why is right-handed Harry handling a boggart/dementor left handed (or left wanded)? And since he wipes sweat and tears "off on his robes" (240-41) as he struggles in his Patronus practice, why is he wearing Muggle clothes in the drawing?

§ I wonder if Rowling is foreshadowing Fred's death by having him console Ron on his loss of Scabbers, saying, "It was probably better for him to snuff it quickly . . . he probably didn't feel a thing" (253). The comment is thoroughly within character, reminiscent of the things Fred says and does and, perhaps, of the way he dies.

§ Upon first hearing of Cho Chang, we learn from Oliver Wood that "she's had some problems with injuries" (254). And so Cho in the near future will have "problems with injuries" that follow the loss of Cedric.

§ It seems odd that when Harry casts his Patronus at the "dementors" (Draco and friends), he "didn't stop to think" (262). Likewise, when he later casts the Patronus at the dementors closing in on Sirius, there is no reference to his achieving a sufficiently happy thought beforehand (411).

§ Draco's mimicry of Hagrid's grieving over Buckbeak contains the line, "There's no 'arm in 'im, 'onest" (279). The very person who supposedly came to *harm* when Buckbeak injured his *arm* now brings harm to Hagrid's hippogriff. Come to think of it, I probably am imagining this Draco's *'arm* as an intentional pun (if so, here's hoping no permanent harm was done).

§ As with Cho, we get our first view of the Slytherin Chaser Montague in a Quidditch scene (307-08). This seemingly throw-away name will come up later, as Montague offends the Weasley twins, gets himself locked in a cabinet, and later gives Draco an evil idea based on his experiences.

In the last few pages of *Prisoner of Azkaban*, I find three somewhat problematic passages. When Ron, Hermione, and Harry are quickly leaving Hagrid's cabin as Fudge and company have arrived to execute Buckbeak and Harry wants to turn back, Ron says, "We can't . . . He'll be in worse trouble if they know we've been to see him . . ." (332). What trouble is Hagrid in exactly, and how could things be worse? Would Macnair kill Fang next? I tend to think Rowling just needs to get the kids out of there quickly for reasons we'll all know in due *time*. Secondly, I wonder why the name "Peter Pettigrew" wouldn't have shown up on the Marauder's Map at some point when the rat was at Hogwarts or hiding in Hagrid's cabin. The map shows "every detail of the Hogwarts castle and grounds" (193); Lupin seems to have seen the kids on the map when they're at Hagrid's (347); and he sees Sirius's name there even though he's in dog form (348). Thirdly, I wonder how Sirius, the escaped mass murderer sought by magical and Muggle authorities alike, pulled off getting the gold from his Gringotts vault, sending the Firebolt order to the owl office and having Harry's wonder broom birthday gift delivered (433). Even with Crookshanks's help, all this seems like a tall order indeed.

I have found several matters of interest related to the final exams ending Harry's third year at Hogwarts. Hagrid's exam is of the classic "piece of cake" easy test variety—just keep your flobberworm alive and you're done (317). I assume this couldn't be too difficult since Newt Scamander tells us the Ministry of Magic Classification of the "perceived dangerousness" of flobberworms is "X"—meaning that they are "Boring" (*FB* xxii, 17). (The easy exam made even easier for a stereotypical "dumb jock" type provides good humor, incidentally, in James Thurber's story "University Days"—it's an oldie but a goodie.) Speaking of *Fantastic Beasts*, Newt describes two of the three creatures Lupin challenges the D.A.D.A. students with—grindylows (XX creatures) and Red Caps (danger rating

XXX)—but neither Newt nor Lupin gives us much information on the hinkypunk (318), though I have to think that with a name like *that* a hinkypunk couldn't rate too many X's. The final day of exams is a Thursday (318), and this turns out to be the longest day, June 6, in the book page-wise. In *Repotting Harry Potter* I discuss that famous date with regard to D-Day and Rowling's "T-Day," as I call it (126-27). But suffice it to say here that Rowling, unlike certain days in *Sorcerer's Stone* and *Chamber of Secrets*, matches the day and date in Harry's world with the day and date in the Muggle world. June 6, 1994, was indeed a Thursday (but it didn't have an extra three hours in it). Notice that Harry's last final exam that day was Divination, and Trelawney seems to summon her students for the one-on-one exams in random order (it's surely not in alphabetical order). So, imagine this, Harry comes last (322). Of course, the truth of the matter is that Rowling needs for Professor Inner Eye to examine Harry last, then prophesy, then attribute it all to being sleepy on a long, warm afternoon.

The final three chapters of Book 3 contain three passages I'd like you to notice especially in rereading. I am quite impressed with Rowling's pronoun shift as Lupin is transforming into the werewolf (381). She uses "his" and "he" until the kind man fully becomes the fearsome beast; then she employs "it," "its," and "itself" to describe the werewolf's appearance and actions. All this is deftly done and is quite appropriate because the *he* who cares deeply for the kids has become an *it* that would now devour them—and all by the light of the full moon. Secondly, Harry says the proverbial mouthful when, bidding farewell to Lupin, he says, "You're the best Defense Against the Dark Arts teacher we've ever had!" (424). Right, Harry; if you only *knew*, you could add ". . . or ever *will* have"—with Fake Moody, Dreaded Dolores, and Slimy Snape next in line to teach the Dark Arts.

Finally, Rowling masterfully and movingly gives us one of those scenes where Harry comes so close to being able to touch some essence related to his lost loved ones. As the Patronus that Harry first thinks his father has cast is later cast by Harry himself, it comes back to him. The stag "stared at Harry with its large, silver eyes. Slowly, it bowed its antlered head" (411). Harry then whispers his father's boyhood nickname, "*Prongs*"; yet, "as his trembling fingertips stretched toward the creature, it vanished" (412). As with the images in the Mirror of Erised, the voices just beyond the veil, the essences of his parents and the others in the graveyard and, eventually, in the forest in Book 7, Harry's looks are long, his yearning to touch is deep; but in all cases he must say goodbye—at least for the present—to all those so well loved and so painfully lost. Yet Dumbledore, of course, gives us the lines that keep us going back to

Prisoner of Azkaban—not going back for more, but for the same, the same comforting words for perhaps readers who, like me, can see thestrals; for readers who've lost loved ones; and yet for readers too who have not known that sorrow. The wise old headmaster's question is simply, "You think the dead we loved ever truly leave us?" (427). No, Dumby, I don't think so. Then he asks, "You think that we don't recall them more clearly than ever in times of great trouble?" Yes, Dumby, I know I do.

Re-Gobletted: Afterthoughts on *Harry Potter and the Goblet of Fire*

I find that matters of interest that emerge from my rereading of *Harry Potter and the Goblet of Fire* are in three general categories: words and phrases aptly chosen, miscellaneous facts great and small, and, as usual, foreshadowing elements. The first category includes Rowling's changing narrative voice, with both an increasingly sophisticated vocabulary and syntax, her choice of words for special or dual meanings, and her use of alliteration.

We learn in Chapter 1 of Book 4 that Frank Bryce was sometimes seen "pottering" around in the flower beds at the Riddle House (5). Though it's typical for the British to use this word instead of *puttering*, as most Americans would say, it's appropriate that as Rowling's character is pottering, the author is Pottering a fourth book in the series. You may recall, incidentally, all that potting and repotting of Mandrakes in *Chamber of Secrets*, and in *Goblet of Fire* the kids are pottering around Herbology class repotting Bouncing Bulbs (293). I'm surprised that Rowling the wordsmith and punster didn't do more potting, repotting, and pottering in 4100 pages.

We re-readers know how fond Rowling is of alliteration, such as in many of the book titles (those by Lockhart and others). In Book 4 we have alliterative passages in the narrative on a considerable number of occasions. In Chapter 2 the last two sentences of the paragraph which discusses Harry's not being able to live with Sirius contain twelve words beginning with an *h* (23). In fact, almost one-third of all the words in this entire paragraph begin with an *h*. Similarly, when wizened wizards and walrus-mustached wizards look at Harry from their portraits, we see that Rowling has used nine *w* words in three lines (273). In still another nicely wrought alliterative passage, this one as Fleur leaves the tent to meet her dragon for the first task, we find eleven words beginning with *h*, this time in barely over two-and-one-half lines (352). Here's one further matter with regard to words starting with a certain letter: notice that Bulgarian Viktor's spoken *w* words are sounded as *v*'s and that Russian (?) Karkaroff's aren't. I vonder why; perhaps we vill never know, as with Hagrid's *ter*'s and *teh*'s.

I appreciate Rowling's humorous effects from some aptly chosen words and phrases in Book 4 as well. Reminiscent of all the "normal" emphases early in *Sorcerer's Stone* with regard to Vernon are the many neat little ironies revolving around "normal" and "normally" in *Goblet of Fire.*

Molly requests that Harry answer her letter in the "*normal way*" (30), which is definitely a not-normal way to send a letter in Uncle Vernon's world (32-33). Further, Vernon hopes the Weasleys will "have the decency" to dress in "normal clothes" when they come to his house (40), and we're reminded that "[n]ormally" he judges other men by what kind of cars they drive (41). Another example of humor revolving around a word or two comes as the kids are off to fetch some water at the campsite and they see wizards from various countries. A group of American witches have displayed a "spangled banner" (82) on their tents. All we need is a star or two on that banner. I wonder if the Salem Witches' Institute is a school like Hogwarts. If so, absenteeism may have run high in the early 1690s. By the way, Rowling much later in Book 4 uses "star-spangled" to describe the sky (624).

Another possible verbal wink comes as Rowling has Ludo Bagman compare Bertha Jorkins's memory to a "leaky cauldron" (89). This is just as Percy hands Ludo a cup of tea. Remember Percy's all-important report on the standardization of cauldron thicknesses to stop those leaks? More in the nature of puns—though not quite obvious ones—are two additional examples of word choices by Rowling. Do you recall Eloise Midgen? She tried to curse away her acne and had to have a Madam Pomfrey version of a rhinoplasty afterwards (195). Later Ron tells us that Eloise's repaired nose is "off-center" (394); so maybe it's just a *smidgen* out of line. The other bit of wordplay, or perhaps a more-than-coincidental choice of a word, comes in the cave when Sirius/Padfoot/Sniffles has been living with Buckbeak. The hippogriff had enjoyed Sirius's leftovers and is "ferreting" around the floor of the cave for more bones (532), much like Rowling describes him "ferreting for worms" in *Prisoner of Azkaban* (413). I strongly suspect, if I know my hippogriffs, that Buckbeak would prefer another kind of ferreting which doesn't involve bones or worms, but *ferrets*—his food of choice when in Hagrid's care.

Now let's look at a few serious word usages and some very impressive passages stylistically in *Goblet of Fire*. As Frank Bryce listens to Lord Voldemort talking about killing Bertha, he is struck by Voldemort's doing so "without any kind of remorse" (12). Ironically, the lack of any remorse is noted here as we're about to witness another remorseless murder (that of Frank himself), and Voldemort will show no "remorse"—which would apparently be his only hope to save himself—hundreds of pages later before he attempts to kill Harry in the final book (*DH* 741-42). Check out the sophisticated and quite vivid epic simile Rowling employs to describe the lightning-lit face of the fake Mad-Eye (184). An epic, or Homeric, simile is an especially long and often complex *as* or *like* comparison. This simile is almost three lines long and qualifies nicely as epic. We've come a long way from Dudley's looking "like a pig in a wig" (*SS* 21).

The vocabulary in general is changing in the Potter books as well. For example, the Hufflepuffs' coolness toward Harry is "exacerbated" by their house seldom basking in glory (293); Crabbe and Goyle laugh "sycophantically"(294); and Fleur gives Harry a "patronizing look" as he "desisted" what he was doing (309). I can't imagine any of these word choices in, say, *Sorcerer's Stone*—though there Crabbe and Goyle *were* sycophants (a word young readers would surely not know, nor would Crabbe and Goyle at any age). Another of Rowling's interesting word choices occurs as Ollivander is examining Fleur's wand. He twirls it between his fingers "like a baton" (308). Since the word *Beauxbatons* could reasonably be rendered "beautiful wands," this is a nice link or reminder of the beaux Fleur's beaux baton. We re-readers also find a rather interesting choice of an adjective in a brief exchange between Harry and Hagrid. The latter asks about Harry's progress in solving the egg clue; and, when Harry lies and says he's doing great, Hagrid's expression is a "wide, watery smile" (456). Water might be involved here, all right. Impressive too is Rowling's use of the word "apparently" in Sirius's eye-witness account of Barty, Jr.'s death in Azkaban and his mother's demise a short time later. Sirius says, "She died herself, apparently, shortly afterward" (529). Rowling even places the word in the middle of the sentence and surrounds it with commas almost as if she anticipated re-readers appreciating the irony. Mrs. Crouch only "apparently" died after her son, who didn't die at all. By the way, whether Rowling is aware of Ambrose Bierce's classic shocker "The Boarded Window" or not, Bierce places an "apparently" very similarly in his story about a dead woman who wasn't really dead; check it out and look for the "apparently."

Next let's take up a few miscellaneous matters I believe you'll find of interest on rereading *Goblet of Fire*. Lord Voldemort tells his servant in Chapter 1 that Wormtail's devotion to him is but cowardice, bitterly adding that he could not survive without Peter's help with the milking of the snake and the feedings. This causes me to wonder how Voldemort *has* survived before Peter's return. Before Wormtail wormed his way to Albania, maybe Voldy could have placed an ad in the *Daily Prophet*: "Wanted: snake-milking companion to strengthen Dark Lord for future return to power. Pays nothing. Should be able to work well with reptiles. Parseltongue not necessary. Right hand may be required."

Four miscellaneous matters in *Goblet of Fire* are Quidditch-related. Since Molly tells us there hasn't been a Britain-hosted World Cup in thirty years (30), we can assume that the wizarding games are, like Muggle Olympics and World Cups, not annual affairs (since twenty-nine other countries would have to have hosted previously); yet the Quidditch World Cup is not held every four years (since thirty isn't divisible by four). On the other hand, if the World Cup Harry attends is the four hundred and twenty-second one to be held (102), they would almost need to take place annually; after all, a tournament every three, four, or five years would have its origins before Quidditch even existed. Kennilworthy Whisp will answer some, though not all, of these Qudditch queries in his book, which we will discuss later. The fact that a member of the Bulgarian team in *Goblet of Fire* is Ivanova (105) indicates that both men and women (or at least one woman) constitute the team (*-ova* is a gender-linked name ending), as the feminine pronouns indicate that the Irish players Mullet and Moran are women (109, 111). These professional teams, along with the many references to the players at Hogwarts, could mean that the Slytherins are the only all-male Quidditch team in the Potter books. It seems appropriate that Rowling chooses the Wimbourne Wasps for Ludo's former Quidditch team. Wasps sting their victims, as do welchers on bets or those who pay off with fake gold. Kennilworthy Whisp tells us that supporters of Ludo's team are known as "Stingers" (*QA* 38). Just ask Fred and George if they got stung by an old Stinger. I suggest in *Repotting Harry Potter* that Harry is wrong about Krum's motivation to catch the Snitch (144), and now that I have reread the passage yet again, I'm even more convinced that Krum didn't choose to end the game "on his terms" (114). What I see is that poor, bloodied Viktor just couldn't see the scoreboard (or much else) after being hit in the face (112-13) and instinctively caught the Snitch.

Here are a number of other miscellaneous matters I found of interest while going back through *Goblet of Fire*; I hope you will as well.

§ When Harry and Hermione join all nine Weasleys for dinner, this marks the first and only time in the Potter books that these eleven people dine together (60-61). Soon Percy will be among the missing from family activities, and Fred's death will come all too soon as well.

§ At the start-of-the-term feast, I work out that Professor Sinistra (Italian for *left*) is sitting with Professor Snape on her left (175, 185), which means that sinister Snape is to Sinistra's sinister (Latin for *left*) side. Is that enough lefts for you?

§ The point in *Goblet of Fire* at which we first fully see Barty Crouch, Jr., as the fake Moody is in Chapter 13, thus adding to our unlucky number of occurrences that are linked to this traditionally unlucky number.

§ The only nice thing that anyone says about Blast-Ended-Skrewts comes when Ron says that at least they're small (198). Yeah, *now* they are, as Hermione quickly points out. So, Hagrid's hybrid critters grow from six inches (196), to six feet (368), to ten feet (625) in length (somewhat like the unabated growth of Book 4). From what Newt Scamander tells us of the two creatures that Hagird has bred the skrewts from—the manticore and the fire crab—we find that the former has "the tail of a scorpion" (*FB* 28), and the latter "shoots flames from its rear end" (*FB* 17). Who but Hagrid could create the worst of both creatures—an experimental breeding which *ended* badly indeed.

§ Rowling is still not always matching dates and days of the week with those in the Muggle world, nor is she being consistent between books. According to Rowling's calendar in *Goblet of Fire*, October 30, 1994, when the visiting students arrive at Hogwarts, is a Friday, and Halloween is a Saturday (237, 258); yet, these dates actually fell on a Sunday and Monday. Recall that Halloween is on a Saturday in *Chamber of Secrets*, the setting of which is 1992. Halloween day being on a Saturday again in only two year's time? No way. But, poetic license? Of course. When an author needs a Saturday, she makes it a Saturday.

§ The exchange between George and Hermione about the happiness of house-elves (239) is quite reminiscent of Jonathan Swift's definition of happiness: the state of being *well deceived*. George tells Hermione that the house-elves are "*happy*. They think they've got the best job in the world."

§ Hermione's bristling at the laughing Beauxbatons girl (who is Fleur, but we don't know that yet) is an appropriate first encounter between these two (251). Hermione and "Phlegm" have a long way to go before becoming friends.

§ If Rita Skeeter's fingernails are two inches long (303), shouldn't Mary GrandPré depict them a bit longer than they are in the illustration beginning Chapter 18 (288)?

§ When Rowling wrote that the Krum "fan club" will find him in the library and will soon be "twittering away" (339), she couldn't have imagined how appropriate the word "twittering" would be today.

§ Beyond the good humor of Dobby's love of mismatched socks, note that he makes his own and they're made of wool (409). Perhaps if Dobby at this point, now that he's free and can help Harry, were to gaze into a certain mirror, he really would see himself simply holding a pair of woolen socks.

§ To return yet again to one of the most often-asked unanswered questions in the Potter books—how many students attend Hogwarts—check out the table arrangements for the Yule Ball (415). Some readers think estimates of eight hundred students are too high (based on Quidditch crowd numbers), but the twelve hundred to be seated at the ball seems a *really* high number—especially since the non-Hogwarts guests are few and only fourth-year students and older can attend.

§ As Harry dreams in the library just before Dobby's pokes and shouts awaken him, consider the nature of that dream (489). The portrait mermaid from the prefects' bathroom has taken his Firebolt away, holding it over his head and poking him with it. Frustrating? Emasculating? I don't know, but Rowling seems to like to let us play Freud every now and then; and the next time a woman takes Harry's Firebolt, he is disempowered if not, indeed, emasculated at that *dolorous* moment.

§ Throughout the latter part of *Goblet of Fire* Harry and Cedric are *really* even, tied with each other in a number of ways: they have the same number of points after the second trial (507); they run across each other in the castle and walk to the Quidditch field together (550); they enter the maze simultaneously for the third task (621); and, of course, they touch the trophy together. Cedric and Harry are two equally fine boys—one fated soon to die, and the other, the Chosen One, destined to live and triumph in the end.

§ Not only do the Death Eaters' curses hit the Muggle gravestones as Harry flees the graveyard scene with Cedric's body; the shield he uses is "a marble angel" (668). That is, his guardian angel is a marble angel; then follows Harry's summoning of the Portkey and the return to Hogwarts from, essentially, a trip to hell.

§ I find it significant and quite touching that Rowling has Cedric's parents react to his death in distinctly different ways. Amos weeps while Harry talks with the Diggorys, and Mrs. Diggory's grief is "beyond tears" (716). The one of Cedric's parents, Amos, who has done all the talking (and, at times, plenty of bragging) heretofore is now silent. And the one who has been silent up to this point speaks enough words here for us to speculate that Cedric truly was his mother's son. This is apparent earlier, in fact: before the third trial when Amos brags on his son, Cedric tells Harry to ignore his father, and a silent Mrs. Diggory lays her hand on Amos's arm "and he merely shrugged and turned away" (617).

Finally, I'd like to share still more foreshadowing elements in *Goblet of Fire*—beyond those I previously discussed in *Repotting Harry Potter*. The first couple are brief, though perhaps not minor. When the group is traveling to the World Cup by Portkey—Harry, Hermione, five Weasleys, Amos, and Cedric—only the two men, Arthur and Amos, and one other traveler is "still standing" when they land at the campsite (74). This is, ironically, Cedric, who is perhaps stronger and more mature or has traveled by Portkey more often than his Hogwarts mates. Of all nine of these characters, Cedric alone will not survive the events of the coming year, though he is "still standing" in our memory long after. Did you notice this time through *Goblet of Fire* that Rowling drops the name of Mrs. Figg (79-80)? The author reminds us that Mrs. Figg babysat Harry a lot and that Perkins's tent is reminiscent of Arabella's house. I wonder if first-time readers of Book 4 even recall Mrs. Figg. Should they? Will she be important later? Hundreds of pages later her name comes up again among the "old crowd" who will need to be alerted that the Dark Lord has returned (713). Do readers wonder what Harry's cat-loving, smelly-housed old babysitter has to do with confronting Voldemort? Rowling doesn't leave us wondering about these things for long, though, since dementors are about to take to the suburbs in Book 5.

One very deftly written passage in *Goblet of Fire* occurs just as Harry embarks on his first task, confronting the dragon. It's noteworthy for Rowling's rare use of "miraculous" to describe a frightened fourteen-year-old mounting into the air, leaving "not only the ground behind, but also his fear" (354). As Harry soars aloft on his broom, so does his confidence replace his fear, as he does what he does best to succeed at a seemingly insurmountable task. This passage foreshadows one in Book 7, for there too in the forest scene something essentially "miraculous" occurs: Harry is able to rise above a fear even of death, to recognize the significance of "I open at the close," and to accept that for him the game is over and it is "time to leave the air" (*DH* 698). To confront the dragon, he leaves the ground and his fear below; to defeat the Dark Lord, he is willing to leave the air and life itself behind.

I find other interesting examples of foreshadowing of later events in Book 4 as well. On Christmas Eve Hermione encourages Harry to work on the egg clue, but he and Ron play a chess game instead. Why would Rowling give us further details about this throwaway detail—that the boys played chess when Harry should have been working? Notice that the game ends in a checkmate resulting from actions of "a couple of recklessly brave pawns" and "a very violent bishop" (407)—perhaps suggestive of how two brave pawns will unwittingly play their part in an evil and violent game with a violent bishop a few months later in the graveyard. The last time I reread *Goblet of Fire* I was also struck by the potential foreshadowing intended when Harry brings Ron up out of the water ending the second task (503). Hundreds of pages later Ron will bring Harry up out of the frigid water just before another Horcrux is destroyed in *Deathly Hallows*. Another link between *Goblet of Fire* and Book 7 is apparent when we look at Harry's thoughts regarding those who have suffered from Voldemort's evil: Neville's parents and, so Harry thinks, Mr. Crouch's son. Harry realizes that it is Voldemort "who had torn these families apart, who had ruined all these lives" (607). Similarly, when Dumbledore tells Harry what may occur if he leaves King's Cross not to go "on," but to return to the forest, the headmaster says, "you may ensure that fewer souls are maimed, fewer families are torn apart . . ." (*DH* 722). Still another link between Book 4 and Book 7 is the phrase "to conquer death"—words used by Voldemort as he tells the Death Eaters in the graveyard scene of *Goblet of Fire* that this is his goal (653). No wonder Harry is troubled three years later about the inscription on his parents' graves: "The last enemy that shall be destroyed is death" (*DH* 328). The Dark Lord's graveyard speech and the words St. Paul wrote to the Corinthians, as Hermione surely makes clear to Harry at Godric's Hollow, refer to two vastly different kinds of victories over death—one living on in a horrible body and the other living on in an eternal soul.

Lastly, near the end of Book 4 we find two more examples of foreshadowing. Notice how desperately and how long Harry clutches the body of Cedric as he returns to the maze (671). He lets go of the trophy, "but he clutched Cedric to him even more tightly." Fudge can't pry his fingers away; Dumbledore has to remove Harry from his friend. Harry's reactions to the essences of his parents, before and after this incident, and his reactions to the loss of Sirius and others are nicely anticipated here. It is hard for Harry to let go. The other, later example of foreshadowing involves Severus Snape. As Harry looks at Snape at the Leaving Feast, he recalls what he's learned in the Pensieve and wonders why Dumbledore is so sure that Snape is on the right side (720-21). Harry even wonders if whatever "job" Snape did when Voldemort was in power has been "taken up again." Has Snape contacted the Death Eaters trying to convince them of his loyalty to the Dark Lord and of his treachery against Dumbledore? Harry's "musings" on these matters are interrupted by Dumbledore rising to speak, but I have the distinct feeling that even if Harry had continued to muse on them, he would have concluded that Snape was a traitor to Dumbledore and is pure evil. The supreme irony here is that Rowling gives us, in Harry's musings, the role Snape *will* play in Books 5, 6, and 7, but since Harry "didn't have a clue" and was wrong about a few dozen other things up to this point, these musings are surely wrongheaded too, or so we think as we first read *Goblet of Fire*.

Harry stops thinking about Snape when Dumbledore starts talking about Cedric Diggory, whose loss, as many readers feel, is such a dramatic turning point in the Potter books. Maybe Rowling's rendering of the first of Dumbledore's last words to the students in *Goblet of Fire* is written with future events clearly in mind. She writes the following: "'The end,' said Dumbledore, looking around at them all, 'of another year'" (721). In a book that frequently mentions the headmaster's growing old and looking so weary, a book ending with a death that will result in Harry's seeing thestrals, a book in which evil rises to power again, this is indeed the end of far more than just another school year.

Re-Ordered: Afterthoughts on *Harry Potter and the Order of the Phoenix*

I would like to begin with a few "I wonder" moments in *Harry Potter and the Order of the Phoenix.* I wonder why Uncle Vernon cannot hold on to Harry when he feels pain like an "electric shock" as if "some invisible force" seems to have run through Harry (5). I wonder if this is part of Dumbledore's enchantment for Harry's Privet Drive protection or, maybe just as likely, it's an example of Harry's magic "coming out" in him during highly emotional moments (as when he found himself on the roof at school). I wonder why Harry is holding his wand in his left hand in Mary GrandPré's book cover illustration (as he is also on the covers of Books 4 and 6). I wonder why Harry doesn't get in trouble for Tonks's use of magic to help him pack (53) since Dobby's magic had caused Harry's letter from Mafalda three years before. I wonder why Harry closes a door that Hermione has already closed (166—this double closing was corrected in the paperback editions).

I wonder, but not much, why Rowling's 1995-96 days and dates, once again, don't match up with reality. The reason for one such discrepancy is that the author needed for Valentine's Day of 1996 to come on a Saturday Hogsmeade visit (528); Valentine's Day was a Wednesday that year. Again, this is a matter of poetic license. I wonder why Lee Jordan can't identify whether Fred or George beat a nice Bludger when we've earlier learned that the Gryffindor players have their names on the backs of their uniforms (276), and surely, as in Muggle sports, there would be "F. Weasley," "G. Weasley," and now "R. Weasley." I wonder why Harry refers to Dobby's coming to Privet Drive as "two years ago" (504—this was changed to "three years ago" in the paperback). And finally I wonder what Parvati and Lavender are doing with "their pencil cases" (710). I know they're "practicing basic locomotion charms" with them, but why do they have them in the first place? Magic folks use quills and ink, not Muggle pencils, right? That shop in Hogsmeade isn't Scrivenshaft's Quill and Pencil Shop. In short, though it's too late for that, there is much *to wonder at* in this biggest of all Potter books; but there's much more that's downright *wonderful* about it. As I've said in *Repotting Harry Potter* and in various lectures I've given, I didn't think I liked Book 5 very much initially. As time has passed, however, I find that I am very much moved by this the longest of the Potter books.

One aspect of *Order of the Phoenix* that's worth another look or two is Rowling's use of a considerable number of fantastic beasts, most of which she has described in *Fantastic Beasts and Where to Find Them.* There are dead puffskeins under the sofa in the house of Black (101), along with doxies all over the place. In addition, Professor Grubbly-Plank teaches a lesson on bowtruckles (259-60). The first syllable of these tree dwellers' name, I would guess, should be pronounced so as to rime with *now* rather than *low* in order to create a pun on *bough*. Surely Rowling, of all people, has thought about *how* it's nice to *know* which way to say an *–ow* word. Grubbly-Plank's upcoming lessons are on creatures Newt Scamander discusses as well—porlocks, kneazles, crups, and knarls (323). Book 5 also contains references to chimaeras (442). Significantly, Rowling's "new" creatures in *Order of the Phoenix* Newt discusses quite briefly, along with the "Winged Horses"; these are the thestrals. I'll say more about this impressive invention of Rowling's later.

Book 5 also contains several references to matters discussed in *Quidditch Through the Ages.* Seamus Finnigan has a poster of the Kenmare Kestrals (217); Cho is a Tutshill Tornados fan (and Ron is not) (230); and Oliver Wood now plays for the Puddlemere United team (264). Kennilworthy Whisp discusses all these teams and many more. In addition Whisp describes the Sloth Grip Roll, which Angelina has planned to teach the Gryffindors at practice one night (351) before the evil toad-woman disbands theirs and all the others' Quidditch teams.

I suspect some puns I had previously overlooked in Book 5. I believe Rowling has chosen her word with care when she has Sirius tell Molly that maybe Mad-Eye should "have a shifty" at the boggart in the desk (102). Have a "shifty" at a shape shifter? Or how about Neville's plant-giving great uncle, Algie? Maybe Algie would find algae interesting. The last first-year student to be sorted is "Zeller, Rose," and, less than two lines later, "Dumbledore rose" to make his remarks at the opening feast (208). Admittedly, these close uses of "rose" are probably coincidental, not an intended pun, but, if nothing else, maybe a future husband or wife in the crowd of older students thought, "Rose—that's a nice name for a baby girl." I suspect one more bit of wordplay. First, you'll need to recall how and why Dumbledore came across the Room of Requirement, as he tells Harry about it in Book 4—that he happened upon it one night when he needed, as the euphemism goes, to relieve himself. In *Order of the Phoenix* when Harry tells Hermione about the room where Dumbledore's army may now meet, he says the headmaster told him about the room "Just in passing" (388). Dumbledore's full bladder, a room with urinals, "just in passing"? (I know; I probably should have passed on this possible pun). On a much more somber note, it could be that the last word of this very long Potter book has double significance. Harry "led the way" away from King's Cross with his uncle, aunt, and cousin "in his wake" (870). Harry is still in the midst of a private wake of sorts, still grieving over and missing his godfather, yet buoyed by Mad-Eye, Tonks, and the others who've come to support him and to intimidate the Dursleys.

In a book as long as *Order of the Phoenix*, even this time as I reread, I noticed still more "little things that mean a lot." Here are a few:

§ The name Scrimgeour is just mentioned casually (122), so Rowling prepares us for this character with a now-throwaway name to become a main (and maned) player in the books yet to come.

§ The Ministry of Magic is essentially an underground high rise, mirror imaging such Muggle structures as skyscrapers, with Ministry floors numbered in *ascending* order from top to bottom. So Harry and Arthur go *down* to levels eight and nine, and the lift takes them *up* to level two.

§ Similarly, the ups and downs seem oddly opposite of what we're used to when points are taken from or given to one of the houses at Hogwarts. When the kids lose points, the stones don't fall; they "flew upward" (626), defying not only gravity, but the logic of loss being linked with falling downward or away—which is what happens to the stones in the hourglass when the kids *gain* points. When we Muggles try to conceive of magical matters, think of looking in a mirror or standing on your head; that's a Mark Twain allusion I'll explain later.

§ Notice that Fudge is without his usual bowler hat at Harry's hearing (138), yet he later swears by his hat (148), which lets us know how much Fudge's oath is worth.

§ Speaking of Fudge, when we see his full name on the proclamation, we wonder about Rowling's choice of "Oswald" (624) for the minister's middle name. American readers may be reminded of Lee Harvey Oswald, and British readers may know of Oswald Mosley, British fascist and anti-Semite whose associations with Hitler resulted in his being interned in Great Britain during World War II. In addition to Fudge fudging on the truth, I wonder if Rowling recalled "Fudge Motors, Inc." from W. H. Auden's poem "The Unknown Citizen."

§ At Harry's hearing still, do you think Mrs. Figg is fibbing? Has Dumby brought in a perjured witness (143-45)? I figure Figg fibs about *seeing* the dementors, but did indeed feel the effects of them, as well as see Harry's Patronus. So if a Squib can feel but not see dementors and can see a Patronus, the witness tells the truth twice, and two out of three's not bad in Harry's case anyway.

§ Mary GrandPré's drawing of Professor Umbridge (221) would seem to make the toad-woman left-handed. Though the text of Book 5 doesn't bear this out, she is later "smiling in sinisterly sweet fashion" (630); and in the case of the High Inquisitor, the etymological links between sinister as left and sinister as evil work for me.

§ When Ron tells Hermione that Seamus thinks Harry is lying about Voldemort's return, Hermione adds that Lavender "thinks so too." Hermione then tells Harry that she has told Lavender "to keep her big fat mouth shut . . ." (222-23). It won't be long before Hermione may wish she could get Lavender's big fat mouth out of Ron's.

§ As I've mentioned several times before, Rowling seems to associate some bad matters with the traditionally unluckiest of numbers from time to time. For example, Harry first meets Cho in Chapter 13 of *Prisoner of Azkaban*; the fake Mad-Eye's first class is in Chapter 13 of *Goblet of Fire*; and thirteen people come to the Dursleys' for the ill-fated seven Polyjuiced Harrys mission in *Deathly Hallows*. In *Order of the Phoenix*, when Harry receives his letter from Mafalda Hopkirk expelling him from Hogwarts, notice that he has violated "section 13" of the Statute of Secrecy (27). Moreover, the unlucky chapter in which Umbridge first punishes Harry is Chapter 13. The number of Death Eaters at the Ministry in Book 5 may be thirteen as well. This would be the case if Lucius Malfoy is not counted among the "dozen lit wands" held by the hooded figures who appear (781). Lucius does hold out his presumably wandless hand to receive the prophecy, so he could well be the thirteenth Death Eater. On the other hand, it could be a total of twelve against Harry and his five friends—and two-to-one odds are unlucky enough.

§ It strikes me that *pride* (in a good sense of the word) keeps Harry from telling McGonagall about Umbridge's bloody punishment of him, and *pride* (in the bad sense of the word) keeps him from telling Dumbledore about it (272-73). Rowling doesn't even use the *p* word, but it is a matter of pride, as in *honor* or *integrity*, not to let Umbridge know she's "got to" Harry; just as it is a matter of pride, as in *wounded vanity*, that keeps Harry from seeking help from the headmaster since Harry feels Dumbledore has been ignoring and neglecting him.

§ Rowling does some nifty things with the healing power of murtlap essence. Hermione uses it to give a helping hand to the back of Harry's hand (324); Harry recommends essence of murtlap to Lee Jordan after Umbridge has taken a hand in disciplining him (551); and, on Lee's recommendation, Fred and George use the solution as the solution to their unseen boils (574).

§ Looking back at the moment involving Harry, Luna, some seen mistletoe, and some unseen nargles (453), I suspect Luna really wants to be kissed. Harry's sudden movement to get out from under the mistletoe seems to prompt Luna's compliment of his caution, especially in light of the possible nargle infestation. Luna's comment is, I believe, to save face since said face won't be kissed according to the Christmas tradition. I base this, in part, on Luna's delight (and willingness to dye an eyebrow) when Harry asks her to Slug's party "just as friends" and on the fact that Luna was "so excited" to be going with Harry (*HP* 311-12).

§ We learn from McGonagall that five N.E.W.T.s are required to enter into Auror training (662). If we imagine, as Rowling herself has said, that Harry does become an Auror, we must also assume McGonagall's comment means that he returns to Hogwarts after the defeat of Voldemort and that he did some serious N.E.W.T.-ing in his final year—ditto for Ron, even more so.

§ Notice that when "that part of [Harry's] mind" that makes him feel guilty about his shoddy efforts at Occlumency speaks to him, it speaks "in Hermione's voice" (682). Her voice is indeed Harry's conscience with regard to this matter and many others. In fact, at times the voices and actions of Ron, Harry, and Hermione respectively seem to parallel the id, ego, and superego of Freud's tripartite mind.

§ When Gryffindor has won the Quidditch championship, Ron, riding on the shoulders of the others, holds the silver cup aloft and, in the chaos of the celebration, bumps his head on the door lintel (702). Check out A. E. Housman's poem "To an Athlete

Dying Young" wherein the winner of the town race is borne on the shoulders of his townsmen, and notice this line from the poem: "And hold to the low lintel up/ The still-defended challenge-cup." The situations in *Order of the Phoenix* and in Housman's poem are quite different, but I suggest Rowling is echoing this well-known poem a bit here.

§ In case you've ever wondered about the half-way point in the Potter series—or even if you haven't—it occurs in *Order of the Phoenix* on page 231. Once you finish reading that page where Ron and Hermione are "bickering" and the kids enter Snape's dungeon for Potions class, it's 2050 pages down and 2050 pages to go. And hasn't getting there been *more* than half the fun?

Book 5 is unusually rich in its foreshadowing elements. Consider with me that the eventual life mates are foreshadowed when Hermione sees Harry—with Ron's prefect badge in his hand—and she thinks that she and Harry are the *prefect couple.* Harry clarifies for Hermione: "It's Ron, not me" (162). Think about how all those readers who wished for different "shipping news" must have felt about that line. Also in *Order of the Phoenix* we have the same six people in a compartment on the Hogwarts Express (188) who will, much later in the book, go back to London on thestrals to fight as a sextet in the Ministry of Magic. It's significant too that Binns's lectures this school year are on "giant wars" (229, 355). This little detail is nicely in keeping with Hagrid's upcoming first-person minor participant narrative of current giant wars (if Hagrid can be considered "minor") and long before we meet Grawp and witness Hagrid's warring with his own little giant half brother.

A few more brief foreshadows are noteworthy as well. The first involves Rowling having Dumbledore state all five of his names at Harry's hearing (139); this is, in part, I believe, so we'll have no doubt later about the identity of the "A.P.W.B.D." to whom Trelawney spoke her prophecy. Secondly, when Harry is feeling terrible and is convinced that he is "the weapon" and that he in essence attacked Arthur Weasley, he decides he will leave his friends for their own safety and return to Privet Drive (494). Just before concluding this, Harry, riding on the London Underground, "stared up at an advertisement for home insurance" (493). Though always miserable at the Dursleys' home, at least Harry is protected there from Voldemort, and, so he thinks, his friends would be protected from him—home insurance indeed.

Here's one more example of foreshadowing I see in *Order of the Phoenix*: Do you remember Fred and George's Headless Hats? I mention in *Repotting Harry Potter* how Fred's demonstrating them might foreshadow his demise (211). I'd add here too that when Hermione is impressed with the magic the twins used to create the hats, she reflects, "I'd imagine the charm wouldn't have a very long life though . . ." (540). Fred's life is charmed and charming, though, of course, is not a very long life. Regarding these Headless Hats for a moment, I'd like to cite a literary parallel to Henrik Ibsen's *A Doll's House*, a late nineteenth-century play often described as a "feminist manifesto." Dr. Rank, a character in the play who is suffering from a terminal illness, in the last scene in which he appears, indulges in a bit of graveyard humor, saying that at the next masquerade ball he will be "invisible." He will wear "a big black hat" that makes the wearer invisible. He asks, "have you never heard of hats that make you invisible? If you put one on, no one can see you." Like so many other echoes of and parallels to classic literary works in the Potter books, the invisibility hats may be coincidental rather than a conscious influence. The similarities between those hats are interesting, nevertheless, especially since I'd be amazed if Rowling isn't familiar with this classic play. If you've never read *A Doll's House*, I highly recommend it.

In rereading *Order of the Phoenix* I was struck by a couple of other examples of foreshadowing I had not previously noticed. First, when Voldemort utters the killing curse in the Ministry and just before the unseen Dumbledore causes the headless statue to protect Harry, Rowling writes this description: "Harry had not even opened his mouth to resist. His mind was blank, his wand pointing uselessly at the floor" (813). This resignation and willingness to die, in fact these very words, could apply to the upcoming forest scene in Book 7 just as well as they do here. Another foreshadow I find upon returning to Book 5 involves a game of chess. It's often worth a second look at what's happening in wizard chess in light of what's happening around the players, as we have seen in *Goblet of Fire* in the two pawns and the violent bishop. Such is the case again in the final chapter of *Order of the Phoenix* when Ron has just found out that Ginny has broken up with Michael Corner. Ron "looked highly delighted" and encourages his sister to "choose someone—better—next time" (866) while looking at Harry in an "oddly furtive" way. Meanwhile, in the chess game, Ron is "prodding his queen forward toward Harry's quivering castle."

Most impressive with regard to foreshadowing in Book 5, however, is how Rowling handles one of her most powerful and poignant inventions: thestrals. Harry sees the creatures for the first time as they carry the returning students to Hogwarts (196-99). The wonderful contrasts of Ron's not being able to see thestrals and the fact that Luna *can* see them heighten the mystery of the scene for first-time readers. What *are* these creatures, and why can some people see them and others can't? And why do those, like Harry, who can see them find it hard not to watch them (200)? Harry next sees thestrals when he's in the Owlery, just before Cho enters and he thinks of Cedric, who is the reason Harry can see thestrals (282-85). Rowling gives us the name of the creatures for the first time in an off-handed way, when Professor Grubbly-Plank speculates on Hedwig's injury, saying that thestrals will "sometimes go for birds" (358). Next we have Hagrid's wonderful lesson when we, like the members of the class that day, are "at last going to understand the mystery of these horses" (445). Three students—Harry, Neville, and an unnamed Slytherin boy—have seen death and can thus see thestrals. Not only does Hagrid dispel rumors about the creatures; he calls them "dead clever" (446), an ironic phrase since, if you can see thestrals, you've become, in a sense, dead clever, or clever about death. Notice how Neville angrily states that he is not scared of thestrals/death (449) and how bookish Hermione unthinkingly (and atypically) is insensitive enough to tell Harry that she wishes she could see the creatures (450). Overall, the thing that strikes me, with regard to future books, is how many of Hagrid's students that day—far more than three—will be able to see thestrals in just over two years' time when Voldemort has returned to power and a major battle is waged on Hogwarts grounds.

Finally with regard to thestrals, we have Rowling's wonderful scene with Harry and Luna, two who can see thestrals and who, in a sense, have both lost something far more valuable than Luna's stolen possessions. What a well-chosen phrase Rowling employs for Luna's notice she has pinned on the board regarding her missing items; it's a "plea for their return" (862)—something that Harry feels about his lost loved ones throughout Rowling's saga. Once we discover that Luna's great loss occurred when she was only nine years old, it's rewarding to go back to Harry's first conversation about thestrals with Luna at the end of Chapter 10. She tells Harry that he's not going mad and that she too can see the creatures; and Harry "could see the bat-winged horses reflected in her wide, silvery eyes" (199). Eventually, we know that thestrals are not only reflected in Luna's eyes, but that her eyes have seen them since her first days at Hogwarts.

I'd like to revisit just one more scene before we move on to Book 6: the one-on-one shouting match/apologia/tutorial involving Harry and

Dumbledore in the headmaster's office just hours after the death of Sirius Black. Dumbledore confesses that he is guilty of "an old man's mistakes," of "the failings of age" (826). He then adds, "Youth cannot know how age thinks and feels. But old men are guilty if they forget what it was to be young . . . and I seem to have forgotten lately." I have spent most of my professional life, to use Yeats's title of one of his greatest poems, "among school children." I am in my sixties now, and the country of eighteen-to-twenty-one year-olds is, perhaps, as Yeats says in "Sailing to Byzantium," "no country for old men." Yet this passage near the end of *Order of the Phoenix* prompts me to confess to my students that I have one advantage over them: I can clearly recall what it's like to be eighteen and just starting college, but they can't know how it feels to have grown children or be a grandparent or to have said good-bye to aged parents who've had to leave, to pass through the veil. I remember one day a few years ago when I read Dumbledore's line aloud to the class—"But old men are guilty if they forget what it was to be young"—and I added, straight from the heart, that I think the worst teachers any of us ever have are those who've forgotten what it was to be young or, maybe, like poor Snape, those who remember how awful things were when *they* were young. One reason I have so thoroughly enjoyed my almost three decades at Pepperdine University is that I'm confident students there will encounter few if any such teachers. Plus—I get to read and reread and talk about great books with good people in a clean, well-lighted place, and they *pay* me for this.

Re-Princed: Afterthoughts on *Harry Potter and the Half-Blood Prince*

Many readers of *Harry Potter and the Half-Blood Prince* quickly took note of Dumbledore's uninjured hand in Mary GrandPré's cover art. You might wonder too, before you even open the book, about Harry's being left-wanded yet again. And, speaking of art work, and of left-wandedness, notice that in the illustration beginning Chapter 8 (155) Tonks is wielding her wand from her left and that in the drawing beginning Chapter 21 Hermione is siphoning up Ron's spilled ink with *her* left hand (447). Do we re-readers have any previous references to Tonks or Hermione as southpaws? I can't find any, so with which hand do these witches do wandwork, we wonder (alliteratively)? All that's *left* for me to conclude is that Mary GrandPré herself must be left-handed, as certain photographs on various web sites would indicate. Before we leave the subject, check out the moon in the illustration that opens Chapter 26. That's a full moon shining over Dumby and Harry (555), yet Dumbledore later that night mentions to Greyback that the werewolf is attacking at times other than on full moon nights (593), and still later we find a reference to "the light of the crescent moon" (602). Overall, GrandPré's illustrations are good and Rowling's words are great; they just don't always match up, do they?

Back to Hermione the ink siphoner for a moment: if she is siphoning the ink into her wand, surely it's to be put back in Ron's ink bottle. Earlier in Book 6, Slughorn's supply of dragon blood gets off the wall and back into a bottle during the magical clean up (65); and Bill waves spilled gravy back into its container with his wand (340). Yet there's still Harry's spilled essence of murtlap that can't be put back in the container to soothe his Umbridged hand in *Order of the Phoenix* (329). Maybe the difference is that the ink bottle, the dragon blood container, and the gravy boat didn't break whereas the murtlap bowl did—though Harry *Reparo*'s it "good as new." I can't seem to get this genie back into the bottle, so here are two more little puzzlers: just how many Defense Against the Dark Arts teachers did Hogwarts have before Harry arrived, and why is Harry clueless when he's wandless? First, the teachers: since the early events in *Chamber of Secrets* take place in 1992 (based, at that point in the series, on that year's Halloween marking the five-hundredth anniversary of Nearly Headless Nick's 1492 death and later verified by other chronological details), then Tom Riddle would have been born in 1926, making him sixteen years old when the Chamber of Secrets was opened fifty years before the events of Book 2. So, if Tom then finished his studies at Hogwarts in 1944, worked at Borgin and Burkes for a year or two, then ten years after that claimed he wished to teach the Dark Arts at Hogwarts, his meeting with Dumbledore that Harry witnesses in the Pensieve took place about 1955 or 1956. We learn that no D.A.D.A. teacher has lasted for longer than a year since the time Voldemort "applied" (446), so by the time Harry and his fellow first years study under Quirrell, there have been maybe at least thirty-five teachers of the class in as many years. Weird that not more is said about *that*, and it gives new meaning to a "dead end job." The other "little" thing (although the previous one turned out not to be so little) has to do with Harry's wand—though not with which hand he wields it. When Snape blasts Harry's wand away (604-05) and is almost beyond the Hogwarts grounds and near Disapparating, why does Harry grope around among grass and twigs in the dark looking for his wand rather than saying *Lumos* or *Accio Wand*? I'd say it's because Rowling needs for Harry *not* to retrieve his wand in a timely fashion because Snape must get away at this point.

Beyond, far beyond all this quibbling, *many* minor elements enrich a re-reader's return to *Half-Blood Prince*. For example, who, indeed, *is* the "other" minister that the title of Chapter 1 invites us to consider? If your perspective is Muggle, then Fudge and, later, Scrimgeour are the "others." If your world is magic, then any British Prime Minister—real or fictional—from Thatcher, to Major, to Blair, to Brown, to Cameron, and to the former and current fictional PMs in Book 6—all *these* are the "others." With all due respect to Abbot and Costello, who indeed *is* on first at 10 Downing Street? By the way, a classic feminist manifesto of 1949, *The Second Sex*, by Simone de Beauvoir, gives us a great perspective on the significance of being viewed as an insignificant "other"—such as a man's wife.

Other miscellaneous matters from *Harry Potter and the Half-Blood Prince* include the following:

§ After all of Rowling's references to Fudge's lime-green bowler hat in the books preceding Book 6, it's only appropriate that the vanquished Minister of Denial stands in the Muggle minister's office as lame duck, awaiting Scrimgeour with his "hat in his hand" (4).

§ I assume Rowling intends a little humor at the expense of the office of the Chancellor of the Exchequer when she mentions all who had tried unsuccessfully to remove the portrait that announces visitors from the magical world (7). Carpenters, builders, an art historian, and the Chancellor himself have all tried in vain; is that list in ascending or descending order of efficiency and probability of success? Maybe this is reminiscent of old jokes about U. S. Vice Presidents' jobs including making sure water pitchers are full and ash trays empty for cabinet meetings. I said "old jokes"; there were once ashtrays aplenty.

§ The first paragraph of Chapter 2, "Spinners End," describes Shape's shabby neighborhood (19). The description bears a close resemblance to Charles Dickens's account of little Nell and her grandfather's view of the mills of Birmingham in *The Old Curiosity Shop*.

§ Snape welcomes Bellatrix and Narcissa into his house, then closes the door "with a snap" (22). In *Order of the Phoenix*, when Snape leaves Umbridge's office following Harry's attempt to communicate that "He's got Padfoot," Snape "closed the door behind him with a snap . . ." (746). I offer this snap/Snape matter, with some trepidation, as yet one more of Rowling's couplings of words that echo names, like the almost countless *serious/Sirius* and *Harry/harried* examples in earlier books.

§ Rowling writes that Bellatrix was as "[d]ark as her sister was fair . . ." (23). Bellatrix is dark in every conceivable way beyond hair color, but "fair" seems a fair assessment of Narcissa—especially by the end of Book 7 when this fair-haired sister is surely fair to Harry and freely exchanges a chance to see her son alive again for the crucial lie she tells Voldemort, that Harry is dead. American Romantic writers like Poe, Hawthorne, and Melville—following much older literary traditions—often linked fair-haired with shallowness or goodness and dark-haired with complexity or evil. This was discussed decades ago in a seminal *New England Quarterly* article by Frederic I. Carpenter entitled "Puritans Preferred Blondes." At least in the case of Rowling's two sisters, it's safe to say that Potterites Prefer the Blonde. Here's one more literary link: Shakespeare's Venetian Duke says that Othello is "far more fair than black" (I.iii.289). Though taken completely out of that context, the same words, nevertheless, could be said of Narcissa, especially considering her maiden name. Narcissa is indeed far more fair (pun intended) than she is Black.

§ Book 6 contains a couple of references to the Holyhead Harpies (71, 280). This is the only all-female professional Quidditch team, which Kennilworthy Whisp discusses briefly in *Quidditch Through the Ages* (34-35).

§ Not only does Dumbledore pun on O.W.L.s and owls (79), but his wizard version of the Muggle cliché "Don't count your chickens before they're hatched"—"Don't count your owls before they are delivered"—also indicates to re-readers that Dumby knows Harry may not have to deal with Snape's rigorous Potions standards. Recall that at this point Harry doesn't know he'll be Potioning (with plenty of Half-Princely help) with Slug, not Snape.

§ A few of Newt Scamander's beasts are referenced in Book 6. Ginny is attracted to a miniature, or pygmy, puffskein (121), and Cormac and his uncle have been hunting nogtails (144). Moreover, Slughorn later mentions, much like Newt reports, that he has heard "rumors" that acromantulas inhabit the forest (480; *FB* 2).

§ Harry's clockwise stir at intervals during the counterclockwise stirring directions (191)—much to textbook-bound Hermione's horror—is reminiscent of saying or thinking things in a classroom that are counterintuitive or are antithetical to what the text or the teacher is teaching. This is, to use the well-worn phrase, *thinking outside the box*—a phrase, I'm afraid, sometimes used by those who *don't*.

§ Merope Gaunt's name is rich with mythological and astronomical associations. In Greek myth, Merope married a mere mortal and later hid herself in the skies for shame. Thus Merope was the name chosen for the dimmest star in the Pleiades, not visible to the naked eye. Consider the parallels involving pure-blood magical Merope Gaunt and her ill-fated marriage to Muggle Tom Riddle.

§ When Harry and Scrimgeour have their frosty conversation in the frosty garden, the gnome Harry is watching is "leaning against the bottommost branches of the rhododendron bush" (347). In traditional flower symbolism the rhododendron symbolized caution and wariness. I'd say Harry in this scene doesn't beat around that bush since he's pretty cautious in what he says and quite aware of what Rufus is up to.

§ When Dumbledore gives Harry his "homework," to get Slughorn's memory (372), Harry will finally complete this assignment 119 pages, or three months of book time, later—after much Draco guessing and Draco watching and a prolonged failure to recognize this assignment as the highest of priorities. Good thing Dumby doesn't take off for lateness.

§ Here's another brief day-watch: Ron's birthday, March 1, is on a Saturday in Book 6 (395), which does indeed correspond to the day/date in the Muggle world of 1997. Likewise, the date of the kids' Apparition tests is April 21, which would need to be a Monday (based on Ron's birthday), which it is in *Half-Blood Prince* (469).

§ As Harry, Hermione, and Hagrid walk the corridors of Hogwarts following Ron's hospitalization, they talk of who might be behind the necklace and poisoned mead (404). Between Hagrid's concerns about recent and coming events, "the ghost of a long-haired woman drifted serenely past." Wow, that was quick and seemingly irrelevant. Wonder what Rowling reminds us of *her* for? The Grey Lady ghost with the "waist-length hair" (*DH* 614) will play a major role soon when it's diadem-hunting time at Hogwarts.

§ Appropriately Quidditch in Book 6, the last in which the game is played, gradually becomes for Harry less and less important and more and more anticlimactic and irrelevant. Preoccupied with Draco and becoming, eventually, convinced of the vital quest to find and destroy the Horcruxes, Harry essentially, in the words of St. Paul, comes to realize that it's time to "put away childish things" with regard to Quidditch. Harry's interest in the Gryffindor team is minimal following Ron's being poisoned (408); "Harry had never been less interested in Quidditch . . ." (409); he wishes the game with Hufflepuff will end quickly so he can find out what Draco is up to (413); and he later wishes he had followed Draco instead of playing a "fiasco" of a match (417). All this is in stark contrast to the Quidditch-playing Harry of Book 3, who is motivated to cast a Patronus and combat dementors because they have ruined his Quidditch game. When Harry was a child, he spoke as a child. Now he has almost become a man, and he will play out a far different game in Books 6 and 7, all the way to the close, until it's time to "leave the air." And the ultimate victory at the end of *Deathly Hallows* will be far different and vastly more important than winning the silver Quidditch cup.

§ Just for the record, and it's a long one, let's remember what all happens to the well-traveled locket referenced in Book 6 (437). In the Pensieve memory of Tom Riddle we learn that the Slytherin locket once worn by rightful (but not too brightful) heir Merope Gaunt was sold to Borgin and Burkes, then bought by Hepzibah Smith, then stolen by Tom Riddle. Later we will learn said locket was made into a Horcrux, was stolen by "R.A.B.," was stolen by loyal Kreacher, was stolen by petty thief Mundungus, was passed on as a bribe to unpretty toad Umbridge, and was taken back by Harry, Hermione, and (stretching things a bit) Ron in the Ministry caper—only then to be taken all over Great Britain before being whacked into insignificance, but not before torturing a good young Weasley boy with images of his beloved Hermione snogging with the Chosen One. That is a whole lot for one little locket to do, is it not?

§ Notice how nicely Rowling, through Slughorn and Hagrid, contrasts the differing attitudes toward and interests in various beasts (484-87). Slug sneaks some serious giant spider venom as Hagrid thinks he's appreciating the beauty of the beast. Then Slug's eye catches the unicorn hair of which he knows the great value and which Hagrid puts to everyday use. Eventually Slughorn the pseudo-mourner comes away with valuable vials of venom and the whole unicorn tail, toasting "To friendship! To generosity! To ten Galleons a hair!" (487). Little could Slug know that he's about to be the proverbial *biter bit* since Harry will momentarily get something from *him*—the memory that helps complete the tale of Riddle and Horcruxes, something far more valuable than any unicorn tail. (By the way, I knew a few guys at the University of Tennessee decades ago who would be interested in how Harry pulls off that Refilling Charm.)

§ It's perhaps more than coincidental that Slughorn, who can never seem to get Ron's name right, calls him "Rupert" (485) since Ron Weasley on film had been portrayed from the beginning by actor Rupert Grint. I'd say this is a Rowling wink for faithful readers and movie-goers.

§ Some Hogwarts student from the past has stashed in the Room of Requirement a creature whose "skeleton had five legs" (526).

The only creature this description might fit in *Fantastic Beasts and Where to Find Them* is the Quintaped. And, unless your name is MacBoon, you couldn't possibly have hidden one at Hogwarts. Come to think of it, you couldn't have hidden one there no matter *what* your name is (see *FB* 34-36).

§ Maybe there *is* (and long-since has been) something between Irma Pince and Argus Filch, as Harry and Hermione have speculated earlier (308). After all, they stand side by side in their grief over Dumbledore later in Book 6 (640).

§ In a rich tradition of literature featuring the superhero living and acting alone for the good of the many, Harry tells Ginny in Book 6 that, alas, she cannot be *his* nor he *hers* in any traditional boyfriend-girlfriend sense (646-47). This resonates, I believe, especially well with American readers of fantasy literature and superheroes. After all, Superman cannot woo and wed and settle down with Lois Lane in the suburbs of Metropolis. There can be no Mrs. Batman with a Gotham City zip code; Spiderman must, at least for the present, forswear Mary Jane. That superheroes must, at least for the time it takes them to complete their quests, fly solo begins, in American literature at least, with James Fenimore Cooper's frontier hero Natty Bumppo, aka Deerslayer, aka Hawkeye. In Chapter 27 of *The Deerslayer*, Cooper has Hawkeye (after whom the *M.A.S.H.* antihero is named) say tellingly: "I may never marry; most likely Providence, in putting me up here in the woods, has intended I should live single, and without a lodge of my own . . . ." Harry's literary predecessors must give up "females" (as Cooper almost always calls women) for a lifetime or for a long time—until the quest is finished or until the last daring deed is done. Superhero Harry, happily, must painfully give up Ginny only for a year, only until those awful Horcruxes are found and destroyed and the most evil of all wizards is done with forever.

With regard to foreshadowing, I was pleasantly surprised as I *re-Princed* myself once again. Note, for example, that in Snape's first lecture as D.A.D.A. professor, he's trying to impress the students with the hydra-like, multi-headed-monster nature of the Dark Arts. In fighting such a beast, Snape says, "each time a neck is severed, sprouts a head even fiercer and cleverer than before" (177). What a choice of words from one whose "neck is severed" in a sense in Book 7 and whose name echoes "sever his nape."

Also noteworthy is that Harry runs across a cooking-sherry-fortified, card-reading, muttering Trelawney on his way to a private lesson with Dumbledore (195). Three cards indicate "conflict," "an ill omen," and "violence," and the knave of Spades suggests to Trelawney "a dark young man, possibly troubled, one who dislikes the questioner" (195). These words seem to foreshadow both our discovery of Tom Riddle's seeking a professorship from Dumbledore many years ago and Draco's confrontation of the headmaster on the tower in the immediate future. Both are dark young men (technically, Draco is a light dark young man), one "troubled" with making a Hogwarts Horcrux and the other "troubled" with having to kill Dumbledore to save himself. Moreover, both young men, for different reasons, dislike the headmaster's questioning of them.

Other neat foreshadowing elements in Book 6 relate to Snape's considerable abilities to prevent a victim from suffering further harm from a serious curse. After Katie Bell's encounter with the potentially deadly necklace, Dumbledore tells Harry that Professor Snape, not Madam Pomfrey, treated Katie since he knows more about the Dark Arts and "was able to do enough to prevent a rapid spread of the curse" (259). What the skilled Snape therefore does for Katie, he had done for Dumbledore some months earlier. Later in *Half-Blood Prince* Dumbledore tells Harry that if it had not been for his own skills and Snape's quick aid following the curse from the ring/Horcrux, "I might not have lived to tell the tale" (503). Recall that in Snape's first lesson in *Sorcerer's Stone* Snape had told the students that one who masters Potions can even "stopper death," as surely he has done for the fatally wounded Dumbledore in Book 6. The choice of words here is telling too: Dumbledore does *not* say that without Snape's help, "I might have died," but "I might not have lived to tell the tale." Given all that he leaves unexplained, we might conclude that he both did and didn't live long enough to tell the tale.

One last statement of Dumbledore's that I think both foreshadows what's to come and serves as a commentary on the entire Potter series occurs in the dialogue between the headmaster and Harry in the "Horcruxes" chapter, Chapter 23. While Harry feels inadequate to the task ahead, while he shows he's tired of hearing about the power of love, and just before he wonders if he's a mere pawn in a deadly game and is void of any free will in the matter, Dumbledore says, "You are still too young to understand how unusual you are, Harry" (509). This foreshadows the more mature, acquiescent, even transcendent Harry in the forest willing to undergo the sacrificial death in the latter part of Book 7. And, too, Dumbledore's words here serve as a commentary on Rowling's extraordinary books when they were originally (and still are today) read by millions of young readers who are the same age as Harry, Ron, Hermione, and the others—readers too young to understand how unusual these *books* are. Yet, as Harry will some day understand, so will the youngest of readers who, we assume, all have a great power in common with Harry: they can love. Even though Harry, having heard all this before from Dumbledore, is tempted to say, "Big deal," it *is* just that, isn't it? It's a big deal indeed to be able to love people and at least to forgive those whom we can't quite yet love. After all, Dumbledore says to Harry, "you remain pure of heart" and have "a soul that is untarnished and whole" (511); yet, among his last words, he also says to Draco, the desperate young man who seeks to kill him, "I can help you . . . ," "Come over to the right side," and, most importantly, "you are not a killer" (591-92).

Later in the Potter books, in "The Prince's Tale" chapter of *Deathly Hallows*, we learn that the dying Dumbledore does not wish to be killed by Draco because "[the] boy's soul is not yet so damaged . . . I would not have it ripped apart on my account" (683). Reminiscent of Jesus' admonition to "love your enemies," Dumbledore's words here and those he speaks on the tower show his concern for the yet untarnished soul of another and his ability rightly to discern the still young heart of one who has come there to kill, but who is *not* a killer.

Re-Hallowed: Afterthoughts on *Harry Potter and the Deathly Hallows*

I regret to begin, yet again, with disconnects between words and drawings, but look at Mary GrandPré's cover illustration for *Deathly Hallows*. Why are Harry and Voldemort wandless? The text indicates that when they're circling each other in Chapter 36, they're both wanded, so I see no reason Harry is depicted empty handed as well as You-Know-Who without *his* you-know-what. Further, at the beginning of Chapter 9, we see Harry *as Harry* (complete with glasses) on Hermione's left (160), yet it's not until the trio enters the café that Harry, with the "last vestiges of Polyjuice leaving him" (164), resumes his true appearance and puts his glasses back on.

Curious too are the drawings at the beginnings of Chapters 10, 22, and 28. First, do I see a *full moon* behind Wormtail, Padfoot, Prongs, and Moony in the photo taken when the four were at Hogwarts (176)? If so, three of this foursome had better be distancing themselves from Remus asap—or at least getting on with some serious Animagusing. Next, the illustration beginning Chapter 22 depicts Hermione and Ron tuning in to *Potterwatch* on the radio (424). That sure looks like a Muggle electric lamp on the table—with a raven (?) sitting on top of it. Arthur might be looking for a plug in that tent, and Poe might be looking for his bird Nevermore. The other problematic chapter illustration shows a staircase somewhat close behind Ariana (554), though the narrative twice indicates a long tunnel painted in the background behind Albus and Aberforth's sister (569).

I find no inconsistency between art and literature, but *do* find of interest three additional chapter illustrations. First, you might agree with me that Voldy could *really* use a manicure (638); maybe Rita Skeeter could recommend a good nails person to the Dark Lord. In the second of these drawings, young Severus seems to be pointing out something to young Lily rather demonstrably with his left hand (659), but several times in the Potter books he seems to be right handed— such as when he right-wandedly tries to help the injured Dumbledore in "The Prince's Tale" (680) or when he confronts Sirius, wand in right hand, at a serious moment in *Order of the Phoenix* (516). It *would* be appropriate if double agent Snape were ambidextrous, though, wouldn't it? Thirdly, the figures in the illustration beginning Chapter 36 of *Deathly Hallows* almost look as if either Hagrid has grown or Harry has shrunk (724). Wouldn't an upright Harry come to just above Hagrid's knees in the drawing?

Now, happily, from illustrations back to words: I invite you to consider the significance of certain word choices Rowling makes in Book 7. Naming Voldemort's first victim in *Deathly Hallows* Charity Burbage is an interesting choice. Charity's having shown charity toward Muggles results in the Dark Lord's having no charity for Charity. Burbage reminds me of Richard Burbage, the Shakespearean-era actor who first played the roles of Hamlet, Othello, and Lear. I have nowhere to go with that, however, except to say that those Burbage characters, like Charity, don't make it to the end of the play. In poor Professor Burbage's case, she doesn't make it to the end of the first chapter. Another name, one which seems to suggest a pun, is Betty Braithwaite, the woman who touts Rita's book and seems to be waiting with *baited breath* for the publication of *The Life and Lies of Albus Dumbledore* (22-23). "Braithwaite" is a name Jane Austen uses in Rowling's favorite novel *Emma*, by the way. There's also an interesting juxtaposition of sound-alike words which I don't think is coincidental when Rowling says, "Harry hesitated" before joining Hestia (36). Nor do I think it's accidental that she describes "a ghostly moon [Latin *luna*] hanging behind . . . Luna's house" (397).

There are five other word-related matters I find of interest in Book 7. When Ron cleans his handkerchief by saying *Tergeo* (94), he's using the Latin verb for *wipe*, *scour*, or *clean*, which forms part of the English word *detergent.* Rowling appropriately names Fleur's mother Apolline, a feminine form of Apollo, a Greek god renowned for his beauty. Thirdly, I have no idea why Xenophilius calls Hermione "Close-minded" (410 and later remembered by Harry on 434) instead of *closed-minded.* Maybe it's a Britishism linked to *narrow* or *limited* and different from having one's mind *closed* to possibilities. For what it's worth, "Close" did not become "closed" in the paperback edition of *Deathly Hallows.* Fourthly, I noticed in my most recent rereading of Book 7 that there is a "peculiar grinding noise from above" just before Dobby crashes the chandelier on all below (473). In *Repotting Harry Potter* I suggest that this scene is reminiscent of Poe's "Hop-Frog" (324), and now I'm even more convinced of parallels since Poe's diminutive character, before he wreaks havoc on his victims below, makes a "*grating*" sound. The fifth word I find of significance is simply Dumbledore's name when Harry says it "without thinking" as the stone gargoyle asks for the password to the headmaster's office (662). Of course with Dumby no longer alive, the password is unlikely to be the name of some sweet treat. Yet, Harry's unwittingly correct guess at Headmaster Snape's password gives us a preview of where the Half-Blood Prince's loyalties lie in what was, I presume, both Snape's password and his sweet tribute to Dumbledore—though I can't help but imagine how Snape would glare at me for using the word "sweet" in connection with him.

There are also a few interesting matters related to Polyjuice in *Deathly Hallows.* Apparently, the appearance and taste of the potion sometimes matches the personality of the one who is Polyjuiced. For example, when Harry's hair is added to the mixture before the embarking of the seven Harrys, the potion becomes "a clear, bright gold" which, Hermione says, looks "much tastier than Crabbe and Goyle" (50). Surely this potion seems appropriate for our *gold*-hearted hero on what is, eventually, a *clear* mission. Similarly, Malfalda Hopkirk's potion turns "a pleasant heliotrope color" (238), fitting for the Ministry messenger of bad tidings who signs her "you-might-be-expelled" warnings with good wishes and pleasant salutations. Incidentally, the blossoms of the heliotrope in traditional flower symbolism suggested devotion or faithfulness, and it seems safe to say Mafalda is a devoted Ministry minion. Also fitting is that when Hermione Polyjuices herself into Bellatrix, the potion tastes "*disgusting*, worse than Gurdyroots!" (523). Although Hagrid cannot Polyjuice himself into the form of another since the potion is for humans only (70)—something furry-faced Hermione once found out the hard way—we see again in the seven Harrys caper that Polyjuice Potion is not gender specific. Hermione and Fleur can assume Harry's form—female to male—just as Crabbe and Goyle can assume the little girl shapes in Book 6—male to female. Here's one more Book 7 Polyjuice matter, this one with regard to the re-formed person being recognizable: Luna knows "Barny" is Harry by his expression (140); Ron (as Reg Cattermole) tries not to look directly into his father's eyes to avoid detection (254); and Bathilda Bagshot seems to know the Muggle Christmas shopper is really Harry as her eyes are "fixed upon" his (338). So I suppose the next time we Polyjuice ourselves into someone else and we're among those who know us well, we'd better look down at our shoes a lot.

Several references to various beasts in *Deathly Hallows* are worth comparing to Rowling's beastly descriptions in Newt's *Fantastic Beasts.* According to Scamander, ghouls usually live in wizards' attics and moan a lot, as does the Weasleys'; the skin of a moke makes good moneybags and purses, such as Hagrid's gift to Harry; and billywigs' wings act as propellers, giving Xeno Lovegood's bust of Rowena Ravenclaw "an elevated frame of mind" (404). Newt's account of the billywig, incidentally, includes the mention of young witches and wizards who like to be stung by the creatures because of the effects: "giddiness followed by levitation" (*FB*

4)—as in laughter and being a bit "high"? Speaking of parallels between Muggle and wizard (if, indeed, we were), how about Rowling's subtle account of the "golden-jacketed band" members who've come to play at Bill and Fleur's wedding sitting under a tree as Harry sees "a blue haze of pipe smoke issuing from the spot" (137). Are the band members' pipes filled with tobacco or with certain parts of billywigs, I wonder?

Now here are some miscellaneous matters I noticed in Book 7 which I had either missed or somehow not previously thought of as significant:

§ You may recall how often Rowling uses the number thirteen in some unlucky or unfortunate contexts. Here's still one more: Betty Braithwaite's article on Rita's new book is continued on "page 13, inside" the *Daily Prophet* (23).

§ Harry's difficult conversation with a very concerned Molly is made more difficult when Harry notices that her eyes "were precisely the same shade of brown as Ginny's" (88). Thus both Harry and Ginny have their mothers' eyes; this may also foreshadow Snape's final look into eyes he surely sees as Lily's.

§ Just a few pages after Hermione tells us that if Voldemort feels "[r]emorse" he could possibly reverse the effects of his soul splitting (103), Harry feels "remorse" for "the inconvenience and the pain" he is causing Molly (110). Harry is remorseful because he knows his birthday party, the upcoming wedding, and Molly's concerns about him and his fellow Hogwarts drop-outs have all burdened his mother figure, Molly. By stark contrast Voldemort feels no remorse for having repeatedly killed and severed his soul.

§ The differences in both denotation and connotation between *pathetic* and *pitiful* come to my mind when I reread Kreacher's tale and visualize him huddled up on the floor, rocking back and forth, and weeping as he relates his story (192-97). The dirty, ill-clad, hateful creature we first meet in *Order of the Phoenix* is *pathetic*, as we sometimes use the word in derision, perhaps synonymous with *disgusting* or *repulsive*. But the grieving, keening creature of Book 7 is *pitiful*; in fact, "Harry had never seen anything so pitiful" (197); this word is now perhaps synonymous with *heartbreaking* or *forlorn*.

§ I wonder if Rowling made Hermione's Patronus an otter (263) because otters have four long canine teeth, because they are such hard workers, or maybe because they're members of the weasel family. Isn't Ernie MacMillan sometimes a bit of a bore? His Patronus is a boar (649). Luna sometimes seems as mad as a March hare; her Patronus is a hare (649). And Seamus Finnigan's Patronus is a fox, and I have no idea why; Rowling has outfoxed me on that one.

§ After the countless times when Harry and Ron have been wrong and Hermione has been right in their theorizing and mystery solving, Rowling surprisingly reverses the norm in Book 7. Ron's strong feelings about saying You-Know-Who's name comes from his being convinced that the name is jinxed (273). Ron is *right.* Harry has a strong feeling that there's a Horcrux at Hogwarts (289), and Harry is *right.* Hermione then sighs at Harry's shortsightedness since she still feels strongly that there's not a Horcrux there, and she is *wrong.*

§ Another miscellaneous matter revolves around the word "chivalry." As Harry thinks about how Gryffindors are to show daring, nerve, and chivalry (368-69), he wonders where the latter comes in as, with daring and nerve, he prepares to go into the frigid water and retrieve the sword. A bit later, rescued by Ron, Harry wants his friend to destroy the Horcrux. Since Ron got the sword, "it's supposed to be" Ron who uses it to destroy the locket (374)—which would seem a chivalrous act on Harry's part—not unlike Ron's chivalrous insistence later that Hermione destroy the Hufflepuff cup Horcrux (623). Harry also shows Gryffindor chivalry when he Crucios Amycus Carrow, who spat in McGonagall's face (593-94)—an act McGonagall calls "*gallant.*"

§ Three matters involving Hermione are worth noting as we go back through Book 7. Her convincing argument (convincing *to me*, if not to Harry) that *people change* in an effort to reconcile the young Dumbledore and the headmaster Harry knew (361) reminds me of Saul of Tarsus/St. Paul. History shows us that it is possible for people to change into the antitheses of what they once were; and, later in Book 7, we'll see Ariana's death as Dumbledore's Damascus Road experience. Secondly, notice the good humor of Hermione's harsh body language upon Ron's return (381); we haven't seen arms and legs crossed so tightly since the Patil sisters sat rigidly (and frigidly) at the Yule Ball. Thirdly, Rowling once again gives Hermione statue status, as she does in Book 1 when the petrified Hermione is "still as a statue" (*SS* 243) and when she is petrified statue-like in *Chamber of Secrets*. Here in *Deathly Hallows*, following the explosion in Xeno's house, Hermione is covered in dust "like a . . . statue" (420). As I mention in *Repotting Harry Potter* (33), Rowling may be linking Hermione to Shakespeare's statue-like character Hermione in *The Winter's Tale*.

§ Since Harry uses the shorter and more comfortable of the two wands in his pocket when he inscribes Dobby's gravestone (481), this is the hawthorn-and-unicorn-hair wand of Draco Malfoy (493). And since Harry's taking of Draco's wand will mean that he is the "true master of the Elder Wand" (743), Dobby's inscription is written with one important wand indeed—a fitting instrument to write fitting words for this free elf.

§ I wonder about a bit of wandlore not taught us by Gregorovitch or Ollivander: does Rowling have some traditional flower or tree symbolism in mind with regard to whose wand is made of what? Harry's wand is made of holly, and the tree and its blossoms traditionally symbolized protection; he becomes protector of all in the end. Voldemort's wand is made from the yew tree, which was associated with both power and sorrow. Wormtail's wand in Book 7 is made of chestnut; this tree suggested "do me justice," or the idea that justice will be done; think of Wormtail's demise—he who lives by the chestnut dies by the chestnut. Most interestingly, Draco's wand, which becomes Harry's during crucial scenes in Book 7, is a hawthorn wand, and the hawthorn tree, according to almost all sources, symbolized hope. Through the magic of the power won over the Elder Wand, this wand Harry wields in the final battle is, indeed, the hope of all.

§ Don't you like Rowling's considerable (double) irony in Bill Weasley's words of warning to Harry: "All I am saying . . . is to be very careful what you promise goblins, Harry. It would be less dangerous to break into Gringotts than to renege on a promise to a goblin" (517). As Maxwell Smart might say, "Would you believe *both*, Bill?"

§ The longest of the several long days in the Potter series (it's not a single calendar day, but a period from dawn to dawn) is 228 pages. It begins on the morning of the Gringotts caper and ends after the defeat of Voldemort. This is a day in May (522), which is appropriate since it will be filled with many a "May Day! May Day!" moment. In addition, the final drama plays out within a "single revolution of the sun," the taut time period that Aristotle, in the *Poetics*, claims is best for a high tragedy to unfold. Rowling is in the good company of tragedians from Sophocles to Shakespeare to Arthur Miller in her day-long high drama.

§ When I see Mary GrandPré's drawing of the scruffy young Snape and the lovely young Lily (659) and then read of their relationship in childhood and during their time at Hogwarts, I realize the power and poignancy of this part of our story and of the Prince's tale. This is an old plot line: the ugly character who loves the beautiful woman, who loves him not in return—or who loves him not as he loves her. Snape is to Lily as the beast is to the beauty, as the Phantom is to Christine, as Quasimodo is to Esmeralda, or even as King Kong is to Ann Darrow. And in the end what is said about the giant gorilla in one way or another is true of all: "'Twas beauty killed the beast." It was the loss of Lily—her love and her friendship and later her life—that killed Snape's capacity for love, warmth, and compassion. Though "always" devoted to Lily in his heart, Snape never was to be close to her again once the Sorting was done.

§ In this regard, note that twice in Snape's memories—once as a child and once as a man soon to die—he demonstrates his love for and loyalty to Lily. He affirms to Lily that being Muggle-born "doesn't make any difference" (666), and he chides Phineas Nigellus Black not to use the word "Mudblood" (689). That doesn't sound like a Death Eater to me—as boy or man.

§ It's curious that of all whom Harry has loved and lost to death, Rowling chooses James, Sirius, Lupin, and Lily to walk with him to his sacrifice. It's tempting to identify them, though I don't intend this as a one-to-one allegorical interpretation, as corresponding to Father (James), Son (Sirius), Holy Spirit (Lupin), and Holy Mother (Lily). I say this not entirely arbitrarily because in the scene (698-703) James offers encouragement and praise, Sirius offers comforting words about dying, Lupin talks of the transcendence of death when it's to make a better world, and Lily, whose "smile was widest of all," looks at her son "as though she would never be able to look at him enough" (699). They are all, indeed as Harry's father says, with him "[u]ntil the very end" (700).

§ In addition to all of the other *three*'s Rowling employs in earlier Potter books, here in Book 7, following Harry's "death" in the forest, he is thrown "three times into the air" as Voldemort screams "*Crucio!*" at what he thinks is Harry's dead body (726-27). Not only is this scene parallel to the torture and mockery of Jesus before his crucifixion (Harry knew his body "must be subjected to humiliation"), but it's also suggestive of Jesus' three days in the tomb prior to resurrection. After Voldemort's three curses directed at the boy "dead by my hand" and the subsequent events at Hogwarts, Harry emerges from beneath the Invisibility Cloak—resurrected in a sense—to the shouts of "HE'S ALIVE!" (737) just before the sun dawns on a new day for all.

§ Lastly, I appreciate the symmetry, the sense of completion, the coming full circle that Rowling achieves by having Hagrid take the "dead" body of Harry into Hogwarts. This is the complement and the counterpart of the first scene in which we see this giant figure of a man with an even greater heart carrying infant Harry to the Dursleys' doorstep in *Sorcerer's Stone* as our saga begins. On *that* next morning baby Harry awoke to his decade-long nightmare life on Privet Drive. By the time *this* new day dawns, Harry will return from what all thought was death itself to vanquish the Dark Lord forever. And we're assured in the Epilogue that Hagrid is still serving tea nineteen years later (758)—as well as probably both drinking and talking more than he should.

Understandably there aren't many foreshadowing elements in the last book of the Potter series. I find it impressive that as early in *Deathly Hallows* as the Elphias Doge article on Dumbledore, Rowling employs the phrase "for the greater good" (20). Whether verbatim or in paraphrase, this concept permeates Book 7. The ways in which the phrase is understood, intended, and applied vary from its applications to the young and to the mature Dumbledore, to Grindelwald, to Harry, and to Voldemort and the Death Eaters. It's a phrase used both to justify killing others and to explain why one would die for others. Another nice foreshadowing in this final book is of the (then) soon-to-be-published *Tales of Beedle the Bard* as Ron tries to explain the "old kids' stories" he grew up with to Harry and Hermione (135), naming what would turn out to be three of Beedle's five tales. Even more deftly foreshadowing something to come in this book, however, is at the end of Chapter 7 when Ron "clicked the Deluminator once more as Hermione left the room" (136). Here Hermione leaves as

Ron clicks out the lights; much later, after Ron has left Hermione, the Deluminator will light his way back to her.

Finally, by way of the significance of the present in light of the future, Rowling writes somewhat anticlimactically of how Harry "wrestled the three wands from Draco's grip" (474) during the chaos at Malfoy manor. I say "anticlimactically" because not only does Harry now have the power over the Elder Wand in having won Draco's; he here has possession of all three Hallows. Yet, more importantly, he has much, much more to do and to endure before the last Horcrux is destroyed. The contrasting climactic nature in which upcoming Horcrux scenes are related—from the Gringotts raid to the death of Tom Riddle—are testimony to Rowling's plan, which is one *without* a flaw. From the beginning Harry and others will be tempted by and impressed with powerful objects, Hallows and Hallows-like things that can bring might, communion with the dead, invulnerability, and invisibility to those who possess them. Yet Harry, eventually, knows that true power and a kind of immortality come from intangibles, from sacrificial love that knows not even the limits of the grave. So in the later part of Book 7, in the final pages of the 4100-page saga, Harry redirects his quest from seeking Hallows to destroying Horcruxes. He keeps the rightful Hallow, his inherited cloak, which will surely serve his heirs in ways it once did his father and his forbears. For we readers know that in the end Harry has done just what Dumbledore hoped for him when he passed the father's cloak on to the son in Book 1: Harry has used it well, proving himself worthy indeed of the name "The Chosen One."

Chapter 2: A Return to Fantastic Beasts

An Introduction to Rowling's Fantastic Beasts: Rehearsed, Rehashed, Re-formed, and Recherché

I thoroughly enjoyed going back through Newt Scamander's *Fantastic Beasts and Where to Find Them*, and I hope you will too. Pervasively, it's a good satire on textbooks with their matter-of-fact tones and their inevitable *Why* [insert subject matter here] *Matters* sections (see *FB* xx-xxi). And, after a delightful "brief" introduction, which, along with the other prefatory elements, makes up more than one-third the length of the entire book, Newt gives us one-by-one the *whats*, *whys*, and *wheres* of those wonderful beasts. Along the way, Rowling shows her usual deftness with words as she splices and combines and creates delightful hybrid and original names for some of her creatures—resulting in puns aplenty (sometimes bi- and tri-lingual ones). As any re-reader of Rowling knows, she doesn't write too many pages without coining a remarkable new word or phrase. So plentiful are her wordplay and neologisms, Rowling is fortunate the Ministry never passed a Ban on Experimental Word Breeding; she is quite an accomplished word breeder and an unrepentant and flagrant one at that.

When we get into our discussion of the beasts themselves, and in the spirit of this *Re-* book, we'll point out some examples of creatures that are *rehearsed*, *rehashed*, *re-formed*, and *recherché*. By *rehearsed*, I mean those beasts Rowling describes through Newt's scientific eyes, but which she will treat more fully later in the Potter books to come after *Fantastic Beasts*—that is, *Order of the Phoenix*, *Half-Blood Prince*, and *Deathly Hallows*. The creatures are rehearsed here to take center stage later (Doxies and Ghouls, for example). Other beasts are *rehashed* as we get Newt's views on some we've already seen in action (such as the Basilisk and the Hungarian Horntail dragon). In a few cases, Rowling seems to *re-form* her ideas about a creature—changing its appearance, whereabouts, eating habits, or essential nature (as with Bowtruckles and Thestrals). These cases are very rare, understandably, given Rowling's characteristic consistency and her careful planning. Finally, we will see in *Fantastic Beasts* that sometimes Rowling's beasts' qualities or behaviors are so wacky and wildly humorous, so Thurber-like (I'll explain that later), and eccentric and esoteric that I use the term *recherché* for those humorous elements in *Fantastic Beasts.* Examples would be what happens when the Jobberknoll dies or how we can ward off a Kappa attack. I apologize if using a word like *recherché* seems pedantic (or, for that matter if using "pedantic" seems pedantic), but it does seem to fit well here—and it starts with a *re-*.

Newt's Long Introduction and the Kids' Textbook Graffiti

The fun begins with *Fantastic Beasts* before we even open the book. Did you notice the "ripped" left lower corner of the cover? Undoubtedly, this is damage inflicted by some fantastic beast's talons, fangs, claws, or who knows what other sharp beast body part. While you're there, take a look too at Harry's signature, especially the letter *y*. I don't think we encounter another *y* quite like that one anywhere in the book. Notice that Harry writes his *y*'s differently in the name "Weasley" to the left of the "Contents" page and at the bottom of the "Contents" page ([v]). For that matter, I'm not always sure whose textbook graffiti I'm reading, are you? I wish there were more differences in Harry's and Ron's quillmanship, yet it seems safe to read the comments written larger as Ron's and smaller as Harry's (compare either to Hermione's, the smallest writing inside the front cover). On a related matter involving a single letter, you may recall in *Deathly Hallows*, as Harry reads Lily's letter to Sirius, he notices that she makes her *g*'s as he does. The *g*'s that can surely be attributed to Harry in *Fantastic Beasts*—at the bottom of page 12 in the word "kidding" and at the bottom of the "Contents" page in the word "change"—don't look that unusual, however. Ron, by contrast, seems not to close the loop at the bottom of his *g*'s, as in "Hagrid" on page xxii. Yikes, enough handwriting analysis already—on to other matters like the games people play in the margins of textbooks, Newt's nature, Dumby's foreword, and that long "brief" introduction to the beasts.

Let's look at some matters on these preliminary pages—and their accompanying marginalia. If you can't figure out the word that stumps Ron in the game of Hangman he and Harry have played ([iv]), the beast Newt describes first alphabetically provides the answer (1) and is surely the reason for Harry's artwork pointing to the hanging man. Let's hope too that Moaning Myrtle hasn't seen this page or she'll be in tears; actually she'll probably be in tears whether she sees her name marked through or not. In the tic-tac-toe game, we don't know who "O" is, but Ludo would probably have bet on him.

In "About the Author," we learn that our "author" has quite a name: Newton Artemis Fido Scamander. When does Jo *ever* give us a throwaway name or one not fraught with possibilities? Newt is no exception. *Newton* is reminiscent of Sir Isaac, and *newt* is an amphibian in the Muggle world, as is a sound-alike to Scamander, a salamander (one of which, a newt, I'd guess, is wrapped around the giant letter *N* in the author's bio (vi). Incidentally, that reminds me of the old adage, "All newts are salamanders, but not all salamanders are newts." Admittedly, that's not really much of an adage and may not be all that old; but it could be useful to break the silence in a Jiffy Lube waiting room or to interject at a boring committee meeting (which is, perhaps, a redundant phrase). Artemis is a female deity in Greek mythology (the Roman Diana) and a versatile one at that—goddess of the hunt, virginity, and forests, among other things (such as, I assume, the hunting of virgins in forests). Fido is a generic name for a Muggle "man's best friend," always faithful, as the shortened form of *fidelis* indicates. Have you ever known anyone with a dog actually named Fido, or, for that matter, a horse named Dobbin (ask Trelawney about the latter)? Skamandros (Greek) is the ancient name of a river known in Latin as Scamander, named for Scamander (or Xanthus), the river god. It flowed on the plains of what was once Troy. I can't find any links to beasts—either Trojan (or otherwise Muggle) or magical—in the name of the river or god or Newt. I suspect Rowling just liked the sound of Scamander, and I hear *scam* and *meander* in the word, which is somewhat appropriate since the beasts are imaginary (a scam) and since our "author" meanders a bit (as do I at this point). One last name-related matter: do you think when Newt was a young boy his parents called him Eft?

Rowling tells us in "About the Author" that Newt's first job at the Ministry involved "House-Elf Relocation." When *Fantastic Beasts* first appeared, house-elves were probably much on Rowling's mind—given Dobby and the others' roles in *Goblet of Fire* and her eventual treatment of Dobby in Book 7. This is the only reference to house-elves in *Fantastic Beasts*, however, which seems a bit odd considering how much Newt will say about various talking, two-legged creatures in his "What Is a Beast" section. Also in "About the Author," we learn how far back the ban on experimental breeding of potentially dangerous creatures goes—in fact, almost thirty years before somebody whom we won't name brought Blast-Ended Skrewts into the world. Moreover, the names of Newt and Porpentina's pet Kneazles are interesting: with a fellow pet named Mauler, should Hoppy and Milly be concerned? Mrs. Scamander's name, Porpentina, reminds me of *porpoise* and *porcupine*; but, then, a book like Newt's puts animals always in the back of your mind or on the tip of your tongue (neither place you'd want a real beast to be).

In Dumbledore's "Foreword," we find that the "noble publishing house" that has made *Fantastic Beasts* available to magic and Muggle folk alike is "Obscurus" (vii)—in fact, the publisher, "Obscurus Books," is located, understandably, in Diagon Alley ([iii]). I think we can assume they specialize in little known authors and titles, as well as publishing the fifty-two editions of Newt's book. Note in Newt's "Introduction" that the person who first got Scamander's book underway is "Mr. Augustus Worme of Obscurus Books" (ix); surely he was an august book worm. We also learn in Dumby's "Foreword" that the 250 million dollars raised by Comic Relief U.K. equates to just over thirty-four million Galleons, thus making a Galleon equal to a little over seven dollars, about $7.35, as I mentioned in my afterthoughts on *Sorcerer's Stone*. This amount is interesting to use for magic-to-Muggle monetary conversions throughout the Potter series. For example, it seems appropriate that the Triwizard prize is about $73,500—enough to enable Fred and George to get their business going. What Dumby says next assures us the master headmaster hasn't lost his sense of verbal irony as he refers to Harry, Ron, and Hermione's marginal notes as "informative" ([viii]). Sure, they're as informative as a cerebral game of tic-tac-toe and about that complex. I find it interesting too that Dumbledore says that wizards who wish to contribute to Comic Relief at Gringotts should "ask for Griphook" ([viii]). This is an example of what I call a *rehearsed* element in *Fantastic Beasts*, for, even though readers have met Griphook briefly in *Sorcerer's Stone*, Rowling has much more in store for her goblin character in *Deathly Hallows*. The author has here *rehearsed* Griphook for major duty later. Moreover, by having Dumbledore end his foreword with the Latin motto of Hogwarts school, Rowling has *rehashed* an important phrase and concept from the Potter series.

In his "About This Book" section of the introduction, Newt makes us almost travel weary as he mentions going to over one hundred countries on five continents to learn of the beasts he describes in his classic text. Notice that the first edition was nine years in the making (ix). The first of Scamander's FAQs is predictable: what is the definition of a "beast"? Yet, that's a rather problematic matter, isn't it—especially with uncooperative goblins and recalcitrant centaurs complicating things. It's curious that Rowling coins the term "Magizoology" (x) for Scamander's chosen field of study since it's not a part of the Potter canon and not a part of the Hogwarts curriculum. It would seem to be a good companion word with Herbology, but Rowling has Hogwarts students taking Care of Magical Creatures instead of Magizoology. Burdock Muldoon, whose first name is a sticky thistle said to have inspired the invention of Velcro, has the proverbial idea whose time has not come: bipeds are *beings*, and more-than-two-peds are *beasts* (x-xi). Simple, Burdock, but not smart. Goblins and a bunch (flock?) of wild bird-like creatures, as Bathilda Bagshot tells us, caused trouble aplenty. (Readers of *Fantastic Beasts* could not have guessed in 2001 how much more we would hear about batty old Bathilda and her history.) So the first attempt to delineate between *beings* and *beasts*, perhaps captured best in the phrase "a biped is its own excuse for being," ended in a fiasco, and Burdock was left without a leg to stand on—his own biped status notwithstanding.

As time went by, according to Newt, others attempted in vain to classify. Elfrida Clagg's criterion fared no better than Burdock's (xi-xii), again at least in part because of goblins. This is nicely anticipatory, neatly *rehearsed* if you will, for Griphook and matters in *Deathly Hallows* involving the treatment and behavior of goblins. The central points of distinguishing between *beasts* and *beings*, as decreed by Grogan Stump (xii), sound something like a Muggle lawyer or, worse, a politician might have come up with; but it does leave us with the three-fold classification setting the stage for Scamander to describe his beasts and leave the beings and spirits for others to figure out. Minister Grogan Stump, incidentally, may have been on *grog* as he *stumped* around wizard communities trying to convince magic folk of his decree, or maybe not. The uncooperative and prideful nature of the centaurs is nicely *rehearsed* here for the yet-to-be-written Potter books as well. I also like the reference to "extremists" of the wizarding world who would like to classify Muggles as beasts (xiii). This humor is reminiscent of some of Mark Twain's misanthropic observations, including classifying humans as the "lowest form" of life in his essay "The Lowest Animal." I recommend Twain's satire there, or anywhere else for that matter.

In Newt's account of Muggle awareness (or lack thereof) of fantastic beasts, his "Brief History of Muggle Awareness of Fantastic Beasts," I appreciate Rowling's irony and inversions: medieval Muggle artists long ago depicted the "real" creatures that contemporary Muggles are now convinced are "imaginary" (xiv). Don't you smile too at Brother Benedict's account (or maybe his *accouynte*) of encountering the talking Ferret (xiv)? I love the Jarvey's jargon too: calling a tonsured monk "baldy." I'm not sure I can imagine drinking "Turnip Wine"; I've not yet tried the "dandelion wine" referred to in Tennessee Williams's *The Glass Menagerie*.

Rowling's rich humor directed at Muggles permeates Newt's discussion of "Magical Beasts in Hiding." Especially effective are poor Dodgy Dirk, who can't convince people a dragon once flew over Ilfracombe, and proud "Nessie" (as we Muggles call her) who likes being the subject of Muggle sightings in Loch Ness (xvi-xvii). Old Dodgy's pub tales involve a claim that a "'dirty great flying lizard' . . . punctured his lilo" (xvi, footnote 7). When I first read this, I wondered if the lilo was anywhere near the kidneys or lungs, but later discovered it's an air mattress—which, if you're going to have anything punctured by a dragon, is better than a body part. The title of Professor Mordicus Egg's book (his publisher is "Dust & Mildewe") is quite descriptive of Muggles who would much rather believe even lame non-magical explanations of strange things that happen, preferring not to know about anything magical: *The Philosophy of the Mundane: Why the Muggles Prefer Not to Know* (xvii, footnote 8). This is in keeping with Rowling's earlier comments in the Potter books about Muggles not seeing the Knight Bus or ignoring shrinking keys. When a Muggle does try to convince someone he's seen a magical creature, Newt explains, he is "generally believed to be drunk or a 'loony'" (xvii). With Luna, dubbed so often "Loony," coming up in Rowling's next Potter book after *Fantastic Beasts*, I find Newt's phrase interesting. Luna is loony to most of the magical world for all her talk of nargles and Crumple-Horned Snorkacks, suffering the same fate in the wizarding world as Muggles do in theirs when they've seen something that others haven't or can't or won't. By the way, Rowling has said that Luna's husband is Rolf Scamander, Newt's grandson; that's only fitting, isn't it?

Also in light of the upcoming Potter books, Rowling, for whatever reason, does not mention thestrals (discussed briefly under "Winged Horses" near the end of *Fantastic Beasts*) among the creatures that Muggles won't spot because they're invisible (xvii-xviii). We can perhaps assume that Muggles who've seen death could, like wizards who have, see thestrals; but I suspect that Rowling had not worked out all the thestral details at this point or was being careful about not giving away the crucial fact about seeing thestrals. If it's a case of the former, then this would be a rare example of the author having *re-formed* a creature in later books. Another Rowling device is *rehearsed* here too, as Newt explains that the locations of certain beasts "have been made unplottable" (xix), nicely anticipating the unplottable number twelve Grimmauld Place. Newt's reminders of the "Controls on Selling and Breeding" (xix) call to mind someone whom, yet again, we won't name, but we'll just say: *dragon egg* and *skrewts* (good textbook graffiti here in *Fantastic Beasts*, right?). "Disillusionment Charms" Rowling debuts here, another element that is *rehearsed* and that will be of significance in Potter Books 5, 6, and 7. The time at which the "effects [of Disillusionment Charms] are apt to wear off" (xix) Rowling doesn't address later in the Potter books, leaving this charm, like Polyjuice, sometimes quite temporary and sometimes not. Finally, another element—this time actually a scene—that is *rehearsed* here for use later has to do with Muggle and wizarding worlds interconnecting.

Newt tells us that sometimes when the Muggles are affected by a magical-caused catastrophe or accident, a magical liaison will meet the Muggle Prime Minister (xx), thus anticipating the opening chapter of *Half-Blood Prince.*

So, having given us definitions of fantastic beasts, the history of Muggle awareness of said beasts, the methods of hiding beasts from Muggles, and a few other subjects, Newt ends his introduction with a paean to his profession and area of life-long study: "Why Magizoology Matters" (xx). Magizoology matters to Newt Scamander, whom we don't know well but who seems certainly to love these fabulous creatures—as does Rubeus Hagrid, whom we *do* know quite well and whom we come to love in the Potter books as much as he loves the most unlovable (and downright deadly) beasties.

The Seventy-Five Beasties in the Flesh (or Scales or Fur or Hide or Feathers or Bark or Whatever)

Although it is Newt's task to tell us the classifications of the dangerousness only of *beasts*, I find it of great interest that the Department for the Regulation and Control of Magical Creatures classifies *beings* and *spirits* as well (xxii). I figure Dolores should have an XXXXX rating, and Binns I've got down for an X. Now, for the beasts. Of the seventy-five that Newt discusses, forty beasts, according to my count, appear in the Potter books written before and after Newt's accounts here. One more minor matter: when Newt capitalizes a creature's name in *Fantastic Beasts* that Rowling doesn't capitalize in the Potter books, I use Newt's capital *T* or *B* or whatever in my discussions. Following each of my comments on the beasts that appear elsewhere in Rowling's works, I will give you book and page references so you might revisit scenes involving your favorite creatures elsewhere in the Potterverse.

Acromantula

The *A* beasts begin with a *rehash*—a reminder of the giant spider Aragog and of Harry and Ron's forest encounter in *Chamber of Secrets*. In addition it *rehearses* a dying and, eventually, dead Aragog in Book 6 yet to come. Not only can Ron and Harry confirm the existence of Acromantula in Scotland, Rowling essentially confirms the location of Hogwarts at the same time (2). Given that Hagrid hatched his Acromantula when he was at Hogwarts fifty years before Harry's days there and given Newt's account of the creatures' prolific breeding habits, the Forbidden Forest of Harry's time must have been (sorry) crawling with giant spiders.

CS 275-79; *GF* 631-32; *HP* 480-85; *DH* 639, 646-47

Ashwinder

I can imagine the Ashwinder winding its way out of the fire and through the house, leaving its ash behind on its way to lay those dangerous eggs. The very odd life cycle (complete with the fiery eggs) of this beast in one sense serves as a fable not to leave fires unattended—whether magical or Muggle fires. That seems like sound advice; after all, who wants to be responsible for this creature making an ash of itself and laying eggs that can burn down the house "within minutes" (2)? As we will later find out in *The Tales of Beedle the Bard*, the use of an Ashwinder in dramatic productions is ill-advised to say the least, though Victor Fleming might have employed some of the creatures for the burning of Atlanta scene in *Gone With the Wind*.

BB 37-39

AUGUREY

The Augurey is well named since an *augur* predicted future events in ancient Rome, and *augury* means prophesying or telling future events, based on signs and omens. This bird is vulture-like, flies in rain, has a tear-shaped nest, and makes a cry that is "heart-rending" (3). When compared to the wonderful qualities and abilities of a phoenix, this "Irish Phoenix" doesn't come off too well (nor does Ireland by implication). The fact that hearing the Augurey's cry does not augur well and could even mean death is reminiscent of a Grim being associated with impending death or believing that seeing thestrals will result in bad luck. In all cases, Rowling seems to be reminding readers of the logical fallacy *post hoc ergo propter hoc* (again, that's *after* this, therefore *because* of this). Augureys don't deserve the bum rap or the bad press. Gulliver Pokeby is right: we won't die from the cry (and we learn that Gulliver traveled a good deal and was poked by many an Augurey in doing his "Patient research" (3, footnote 4). From footnote 3, I conclude that poor Uric the Oddball, though concussed, was blessed with a sympathetic biographer in Radolphus *Pitti*man.

BASILISK

The Basilisk was bred by Herpo, and the Greek word for *reptile* just happens to be *herpeton*, and why do we feel Rowling knows this? This foul Herpo was an ancient herpetologist (one who studies reptiles and amphibians) who used a toad to produce a giant snake, though I'm not sure how the chicken or the egg it laid fits into this picture (or which comes first). No wonder "much experimentation" was involved (3). It's good that Herpo spoke Parseltongue, or he could have become a wizard Dr. Frankenstein. The Basilisk's fangs are "exceptionally venomous," and we'll bet they can destroy Horcruxes (even five years after they're extracted from the Basilisk). But that yellow-eyed stare of the snake that will result in "instant death" (4) for the stared-at is another matter. As I point out in *Repotting Harry Potter* (84), you'll be all right if you're near a puddle of water or a ghost, or have a camera or a mirror on you, which is to say that Tom Riddle's pet was pretty inefficient at killer stares.

CS 290-91, 317-20; *DH* 623

BILLYWIG

The Billywig looks like a Christmas tree ornament, flies like a helicopter, stings like a bee, and provides young witches and wizards with an enjoyable high (after a spell of giddiness). Hmmm. That last part rings a distant bell. Rowling locates Billywigs in Australia. I can imagine some magic Aussie lad wearing a billycock (a derby hat), wielding a billy club, and petting his billy goat while cooking Billywig stingers in a billycan to make a potion (and that's about all I *can* do with *billy* words—but Rowling started it with this creature's silly billy name). Billywigs come up in *Deathly Hallows* as having improved Xenophilius Lovegood's statue of Rowena Ravenclaw. Moreover, as I suggest in my *Re-Hallowed* section, I suspect Billywigs may have affected the quality of the music at Bill and Fleur's wedding since maybe some dried Billywig wings might be in the pipes the musicians are enjoying before their gig.

DH 404, 513

Bowtruckle

In one sense, the idea of trees needing guarding seems ludicrous, but deforestations, in other contexts, are serious matters; and trees have been felled in great numbers because they had no guardians. I don't see how we can assume Bowtruckles are ecologically sensitive, "green" creatures, though, since they seem to be guarding trees from woodcutters and pruners because they *live* on that block. Notice that while the would-be wood wand worker gathers enough wood for the wand, the woodlice must woo the Bowtruckle's attention away from the "wand-wood" (5). To go from the ridiculous to the sublime, I wonder if Rowling is echoing one of the best-known neologisms in all of English poetry in "wand-wood"; Gerard Manley Hopkins's beautiful short poem "Spring and Fall: To a Young Child" contains the word "wanwood." (You might check out Hopkins's poem; if you do, you might see why I use the word "sublime" to refer to it.) One more Bowtruckle matter: Rowling will later add that the beasts eat fairy eggs (*OP* 259) and, apparently, doxy eggs as well (*DH* 560)—a rare example of Rowling's having *re-formed* one of her beasts, changing its diet a bit (or, at least, adding a few more foods to the Bowtruckle's fare).

OP 259-60, 759-60, 717; *DH* 560; *BB* 85-86

Bundimun

Having Bundimuns in your home would be a bummer. These "creeping" pests "infest houses" and can even cause them to collapse (5-6). They surely seem like the termites of the wizarding world, and, like Muggle termites leave their droppings, Bundimuns ooze secretions which cause the rotting of wood. If these pests don't leave after a wizard yells "*Scourgify*!" maybe magic folk need to call Orkin or Bundimex.

Centaur

Scamander seems a bit apologetic about giving centaurs an XXXX classification, though Dolores Umbridge or Sybill Trelawney might go for XXXXX (for different reasons). These creatures, like the Basilisk, Rowling borrows from ancient myth, art, and literature. Sagittarians know Newt has accurately addressed centaurs' knowledge of divination, archery, and astronomy. Rowling's centaurs, especially Firenze, are nicely developed in the Potter series to illustrate Scamander's generalizations here. After writing *Fantastic Beasts*, Rowling is about to continue her applications of centaur lore in *Order of the Phoenix* and *Deathly Hallows.* Just as there are good and bad wizards and Muggles in Rowling's world, Firenze and the hostile Bane demonstrate antithetical qualities. Firenze sheds his centaur blood in the Battle of Hogwarts, though Bane and the others centaurs in the forest seem, with Hagrid's chiding, to come through in the end as well.

SS 252-59; *OP* 597-605, 697-99, 753-59; *HP* 644; *DH* 608, 661, 728, 733-34, 745

Chimaera

Still another creature from ancient myth is the chimera (Rowling uses the Latin spelling with the *ae* in the middle). Speaking of the middle, this fabulous Greek beast was depicted as having the head of a lion, the midsection of a goat, and the tail of a serpent—as does Rowling's creature. This is a strange image to me—a hybrid monster made up of one more body part than usual with its goatness in its middle; I wonder if an AREMIHC would have a serpent head, goat body, and lion tail? Such a creature would still be mainly a goat and would perhaps be of interest to Aberforth and, I suppose, Capricorns. As you may know a chimera can also be an illusion or nightmarish-like image in the mind. The American poet Wallace Stevens seems to be using the word thusly in his poem "Sunday Morning," in the line containing "any old chimera of the grave." Rowling uses the word, with her *ae* spelling, to describe one of the shapes of "fiery beasts" the Fiendfyre is forming as it pursues Harry and the others (*DH* 632). Greek chimeras, incidentally, were all females—she monsters—which makes you wonder where future generations of chimeras, or chimaerae, came from.

OP 442; *DH* 18

Chizpurfle

The word "Chizpurfle" looks like a cross between *cheese puffs* and *chutzpah*, and these tiny creatures seem to have a lot of the latter. I like the comic juxtaposition regarding their size: "a twentieth of an inch high" (7), which is, let's face it, not all that high. Like Bundimuns (and Muggle termites) Chizpurfles are pests, but Rowling makes them pests in *both* worlds—ruining wands and spoiling cauldrons, as well as causing even new Muggle electrical devices to malfunction. We unknowing Muggles think our new laptop has a virus or the GPS has a few bugs to work out or there's a glitch in the rewinding of a DVR program; but, no, it's all a result of a Chizpurfles infestation of our electronic gadgets and gizmos. I told you these 1/20 inch-"high" creatures had chutzpah. By the way, these tiny creatures, these "small parasites," have large fangs, look like crabs (let's not go there); and, flea-like, they "infest the fur and feathers" of furry and feathery beasts (not unlike fleas and lice do Muggles' doggies and budgies).

Clabberts

You would think that Clabberts would have something to do with curdled, sour milk—clabber—but no. You would think that "a cross" between a mammal and an amphibian would be a bit tricky; maybe such a mixture of monkey and frog would be clabbered and scarier than simply having the head of a monkey and the body of a frog (or vice versa). You would think I could explain why these beasts originated in the American South, but I can't (even though I originated there). And you would think that Christmas trees wouldn't be decorated and flashing red in June, and that is precisely what Muggles thought, isn't it? I especially like the wackiness here, the *recherché* nature of the beast: it's a mottled-green, web-footed, long-armed, short-horned, wide-mouthed, sharp-toothed tree dweller with pulsating red pustules. What a sight to see in a tree on a calm summer night—*recherché* indeed.

Crup

In creating the Crup, Rowling achieves another effective comic juxtaposition: a Jack Russell terrier with a forked tail. The terrier is not exactly a terror, but creatures with forked tails tend to be. I wonder if this beast's name rimes with *hoop* or with *pup*—much like we once wondered if a certain author's name rimed with *howling* or *bowling*. Since one meaning for *croup* is a disease and the other is the rump of a horse, I'd like to think this creature's name rimes with *pup*, which is, after all, all it is after its magical owner makes sure it has been de-tailed. The range of a Crup's diet—"from gnomes to old tyres" (8)—surely qualifies it for omnivorous status. I really like Newt's tale of the pup with the forked tail, which is a rare end for a fish or a bird, but which is, again, *recherché* for a canine (and one named after clergyman Jack Russell at that).

OP 323, 552

Demiguise

The Demiguise is well named. The prefix can mean "half" or "less than usual" or "lesser." This hairy herbivore can be less than *there* if it chooses, hiding by the guise of invisibility to escape its enemies. Those "skilled" wizards trying to capture the invisible Demiguise remind me of the Three Amigos (in John Landis's wacky film of the same name) and their efforts to summon the Invisible Swordsman, a scene which ends badly for the invisible one. One further Demiguise-related thought: we might first assume, as Xenophilius Lovegood seems to, that one of Harry's ancestors spun that Invisibility Cloak we readers know so well with Demiguise hair. But, no, Harry's cloak is far beyond the best of Demiguise cloaks. It's like the handkerchief in *Othello*: "there's magic in the web of it" (III.iv.64).

DH 410-11

Diricawl

Any Muggle should know what a Diricawl is; it's just that we've thought they've been extinct for over three hundred years. Now Newt tells us the creatures have instead vanished into the hidden (to Muggles) world of fantastic beasts. The Diricawl can do an animal version of Apparating, and the hybrid look does approximate what Muggles once knew as the "Dodo" or "Dodo Bird," which did indeed exist on Mauritius where Newt tells us the Diricawl still lives. The Muggle Dodo too, like the magic Diricawl, was/is flightless. (By the way, there's a good line about the Dodo in Mark Twain's wonderful "The Diaries of Adam and Eve," a work I'm sure Rowling readers would thoroughly enjoy.) Rowling's explanation of the reason for allowing the Diricawl to remain unknown to Muggles (9-10) is, in essence, an effective barb at hunting a creature (real or imaginary) to the point of endangerment or extinction (real or apparent).

Doxy

Rowling has big things in store for the little pest known as a Doxy in her then upcoming *Order of the Phoenix*. Molly wants number twelve Grimmauld Place to be a Doxy-free zone, Fred and George want to experiment with Doxy venom, and everybody gets elbow deep in Doxycide. I love the Doxy drawing here in *Fantastic Beasts* (10), and I can see there's a fairy in there somewhere, albeit a hirsute and hostile version with extra limbs. I wonder if there's a *good* Doxy somewhere out there who would give an arm (and an arm) and a leg (and a leg) to be a fairy some day. In British slang of a bygone era, by the way, a "doxy" referred to a promiscuous woman or a prostitute—which sheds a whole new light on the Doxy's bite.

OP 85, 102-05

Dragon

Once known to Muggles as well as to magic folk, the dragon is arguably the highest profile fantastic beast that ever existed or, in the wizarding world, exists. Rowling surely doesn't short change us in this section of Newt's accounts of beasts, giving us ten sub-species—a delightful deca-list of dragon descriptions (to use a Lockhartian phrase). Notice that Rowling emphasizes the size and ferocity of the females, understandably so in light of the four dragons in *Goblet of Fire* viciously and maternally guarding their eggs. You may recall that Rowling's Book 4 dragons are the Chinese Fireball, the Common Welsh Green, the Swedish Short-Snout, and the dreaded Hungarian Horntail, Harry's challenge. As far as other *rehashed* dragon matters are concerned, remember that Rowling includes a reference to the two British dragons in *Sorcerer's Stone* (231) and several references to the Norwegian Ridgeback in Book 1 as well. Norbert (later to be renamed Norberta) is of this latter breed—hatched, typically illegally, by you know who.

The Antipodean Opaleye is from New Zealand and Australia, known to the British as the antipodes (places on the opposite side of the globe), and it has opal-like eyes. This creature's eggs can be mistaken for fossils by "unwary Muggles" (11), which Rowling may very well intend as a redundancy. The Chinese Fireball shoots a "mushroom-shaped flame" from its nose, which is reminiscent of the mushroom-shaped cloud that follows the detonations of Muggles' ultimate weapons, nuclear fireballs far more deadly than any dragon's fire. I like the manner in which Rowling juxtaposes the Fireball's preferred foods: "pigs and humans" (12). This, it seems to me, is a Swift-like snipe perhaps intended as comic misanthropy, for these two creatures taste the same to this dragon, though, since listed first, pigs may be tastier. And is that meant as a *compliment* to *homo sapiens*?

The Common Welsh Green is the breed of dragon responsible for the Ilfracomb incident Newt tells us about early on in *Fantastic Beasts* (xvi). Taken together, the descriptions of this Welsh dragon and the other from Great Britain, the Hebridian Black, surely contain some in-jokes. The Welsh Green comes from a plush, green land, is not very "troublesome," wants no part of humans, and its eggs are "earthy brown, flecked with green" (12). The black dragon from the Hebrides (islands off the western coast of Scotland), however, is "more aggressive," takes up a great deal of space, and has features that are "razor sharp" and "rough scaled" (12). These British dragons are under the responsibility of the MacFusty wizard clan. *Fusty* can mean musty- or stale-smelling, out-of-date, old-fashioned, or very conservative. There's surely some British social satire going on here, it seems to me, though I am not qualified (or foolish enough) to try to say what it is. I will leave it to the green Welsh and the fusty Hebridians to draw their own conclusions.

Let's now examine more dragons in light of the Potter series. The Hungarian Horntail, as we know from *Goblet of Fire*, is the worst possible draw underdog Harry could have made since this is one darn dangerous dreaded dragon. This beast "feeds on goats, sheep and, whenever possible, humans" (13). And we might add, if it had been "possible," a certain momma Horntail would have had a human named Harry for a light snack in the first Triwizard trial. Since Rowling had earlier treated us to the charms of a baby Norwegian Ridgeback in *Sorcerer's Stone*, the description of this dragon by Newt is richly ironic. Note that the breed will attack "most kinds of large land mammal," like maybe a very large land mammal who calls himself "Mommy"; and note too that Newt says the Norwegian Ridgebacks breathe fire earlier than most breeds of dragons (13). This is an especially convenient detail for Rowling since she can have newborn Norbert scorching his/her mommy Hagrid almost right out of the egg.

With just four more dragon species to go, Jo doesn't lose her comic touch. For the sound effects alone, I appreciate the smallest of Rowling's dragons, the Peruvian Vipertooth. The venomous fangs of this beast give it its name, Vipertooth; and since Rowling gives us a word with the prominent consonants *V* and *P*, she makes the creature Peruvian—with an appropriate *P* and *V* sound. These Peruvian Vipertooths (or Viper*teeth*; Rowling never answers that grammatical plural puzzle) *really* like us humans—so much so that they could just eat us up, which they have so often done that dragon exterminators have had to intervene (calling Dragonix?).

Rowling makes quick work of her final three dragon species. The Romanian Longhorn might be a crowd favorite in Austin, Texas, and we assume Charlie Weasley has studied it and other dragons at that "important dragon reservation" (14). The Swedish Short-Snout doesn't kill many humans, but, then again, since they live in "wild and uninhabited mountainous areas" (14), they're not often close enough to get a good chomp in, are they? Finally, Newt tells us that the Ukrainian Ironbelly has been under "constant observation" (15) since a certain boat incident a couple of centuries ago (14-15). Somehow, logic seems to tell us that a beast weighing "six tonnes" would not be all that difficult to observe, constantly or even occasionally.

SS 64-65, 231-41; *GF* 325-29, 351-56; *HP* 65; *DH* 120, 535-36, 541-46, 548

Dugbog

Newt's next beast, the Dugbog, has one of those Rowling names that might be just as good backwards: *Gobgud* works pretty well, doesn't it? Plus, we've got both *dog* and *bug* among the letters, whichever way we spell it. Yet, Rowling's letter order is, as always, best; for, after all, in the case of the ruined Mandrakes, the Dugbogs (creatures of *bogs*) have *dug* beneath and destroyed the all-important Mandrake plants. And, given the Dugbog's fondness for Mandrakes, it's a good thing Professor Sprout kept her growing medicinal Mandrakes Dugbog-free during those crucial times in *Chamber of Secrets*. I like the concept too of this fantastic beast, this Dugbog, having "finned paws" (15)—a crazy kind of fish-bear image, totally Rowling *recherché*. One more Dugbog-related thing: I suppose the ankle biting these beasts inflict on "human walkers" comes as a result of humans walking through *bogs* as a Dugbog has *dug* its "very sharp teeth" into said human (Muggle or magic) ankles.

Erkling

Rowling's Erkling is a beast originating in Germany; it is elf-like (15). With a switch of consonants we have Erlking, the legendary king of the elves in German lore, a character who worked mischief and evil directed especially at children. In fact, Der Erlkönig is the subject of a Goethe poem and a Schubert *Lied*. An Erkling Newt tells us about tried to attack a tough *sechs Jahre alten* boy named Bruno, but it picked on the wrong kind of *Kind*, didn't it? Young Bruno hit the Erkling "very hard over the head with his father's collapsible cauldron" (15). Death by "collapsible cauldron" concussion would be a tough way to go, whether your *k* or your *l* comes first.

ERUMPENT

Readers of *Deathly Hallows* will surely recall the Erumpent horn in the Lovegood home—the one correctly identified by Hermione as extremely dangerous. In the name of this beast, I hear echoes of *erupt* and *trumpet*; and when the Erumpent's horn explodes, it erupts like a loud note bursts from a trumpet. Of course the name is a sound-alike too for a creature we Muggles know, if only from circuses. Imagine asking a wizard *and* a Muggle this riddle: "What do you call a 'large grey African beast' with 'great power' and weighing about a ton—and, as a hint, the answer starts with an *e* and ends with *nt* and has eight letters?" Naturally, the wizard/Muggle would yell out, "An Erumpent!/Elephant!" I suspect that at least figuratively speaking male Erumpents aren't the only species of male animals who "frequently explode each other during the mating season" (16).

DH 401, 419-20, 511

FAIRY

If Muggles find fairies dear, cute, cuddly, and lovable, often depicting them conversing "in a nauseatingly sentimental fashion" (16, footnote 7), yet if fairies themselves are of "little intelligence"—what does that say about Muggles? Newt doesn't speculate as to why fairies are the recipients of "the best Muggle press" of any magical beasts, even lending their name to Muggle "fairy tales." These creatures in Muggle lore wave wands and solve problems and dry up tears and turn an abused scrubgirl into the belle of the ball. In magical reality, these mute, wandless, not-so-distant cousins of butterflies are decorations *at* balls (like the Yule Ball in *Goblet of Fire*). Professor Flitwick also decorates his classroom with fairies for Christmas in *Prisoner of Azkaban*. Newt surely explodes the fairy tale of fairies.

PA 189; *GF* 413

FIRE CRAB

If a creature has either "fire" or "crab" in its name, I'm not sure I want to be close to it, so the fire crab I'm staying even farther away from. Hagrid, on the other hand, did a little experimenting with one or more of these beasts (does stinging on one end and shooting out fire on the other ring a bell?). By the way, if a fire crab rates an XXX classification and the other Blast-Ended Skrewt mixture, the manticore, rates an XXXXX, would the Blast-Ended ones be XXXX (the danger ratings of the two bred beasts *averaged*) or XXXXXXXX (the danger ratings *combined*)? Hagrid apparently never considered this question.

GF 438; *OP* 717

Flobberworm

Going from fire crabs to Flobberworms alphabetically is about as anticlimactic as Hagrid's class going from studying Hippogriffs to Flobberworms after Draco is "attacked" in *Prisoner of Azkaban*. This is one of Newt's briefer creature descriptions in *Fabulous Beasts*, and the creature has the lowest M.O.M. classification: a single X, which means "Boring" (xxii). Poor worms, we can imagine them flobbering around in their own flobber, hoping to score a little lettuce for lunch and aspiring some day, by their mucus, to make some potion maker's potion thicker.

PA 142, 220, 317

Fwooper

How many times do English speakers get to make a *fw* sound? Maybe Elmer Fudd would say, "The bird fwoo away" or "I'm fwightened"; but Elmer is not your average English speaker. This is why I love Rowling's *recherché* name *Fw*ooper. If you have a set of felt-tip highlighters, you might want to color the drawing of the Fwooper since you should have a highlighter for every color the Fwooper comes in: "orange, pink, lime green, or yellow" (18). Maybe his mood will improve if he's pastel-ed; the Fwooper in the drawing appears to be a worried or, maybe more likely, an angry Fwooper. As far as the caution about Fwoopers singing us out of our wits, I'd be sure I had the Silencing Charm clearly in mind. We wouldn't want to end up like Uric the Oddball (18, footnote 8) with a dead badger on our heads, would we—or, arguably, even worse, a *live* badger on our heads? This is the same Uric the Oddball who had a run-in with Augureys, you may recall (3, footnote 3). Dare we readers of *Hamlet* say, "Alas, poor Uric"? One more question: did you think of Muzak or your local "easy listening" radio station when you read about the Fwooper's song: "at first enjoyable," but a song that "will eventually drive the listener to insanity" (18)?

Ghoul

The ghoul in the Weasleys' attic has indeed become, as Newt says, "a talking point or even a family pet" (19). That particular ghoul's specialty is *moaning* and making noises with pipes (*piping*?). I wonder if Rowling already had the more serious role in mind for the Weasley ghoul (in *Deathly Hallows*) when she wrote Newt's ghoulish commentary. Ron might appreciate his family ghoul a bit more than we thought since Newt tells us they eat spiders. Do you think young witches and wizards lie in bed dreaming of someday becoming a member of that "Ghoul Task Force" in the Department for the Regulation and Control of Magical Creatures at the M.O.M. (18-19)? What an exciting job description: "to remove ghouls from dwellings that have passed into Muggle hands" (19). Which might be more delightful for a witch or wizard—de-gnoming a garden or de-ghouling an attic?

CS 41; *GF* 154; *DH* 97-98

Glumbumble

Rowling gives us another of Newt's brief, six-line descriptions in the account of the Glumbumble, but it's as rich as honey. This *bumble*bee-like insect produces a *glum*-inducing treacle useful to bring someone down from an Alihotsy leaf high—and we've all been *there*, I'm sure. "Treacle," incidentally, can mean both a sweet liquid like honey or molasses, and an antidote—both of which fit nicely here. Nettles, Glumbumbles' food, are prickly plants with stinging hairs—a fitting food for any Bumble, even a glum one.

Gnome

When I see the drawing of the gnome, I can't help but wonder about its score on the cephalic index. I like the fact that Rowling draws (pun intended) such a contrast between real magical gnomes and those silly things Muggles like to put on their lawns and in their gardens. However, at least Muggle gnomes don't ruin the lawn; Muggle moles do essentially what magic world gnomes do, and de-mole-ing is comparable to de-gnoming. If the Erkling is about three feet high (15) and a gnome a mere foot tall (19) *and* if these creatures could talk, they might have a saying like "gnome-high to an Erkling"—used much like the Muggles' "knee-high to a grasshopper." Rowling's gnomes, along with the family "pet" ghoul, provide a contrast within the magical world between the affluent Malfoys and the much poorer Weasleys, a contrast with parallels, of course, within the Muggle world. The Weasley ghoul is perhaps comparable to an inexpensive Muggle pet parakeet, rather than say, an albino peacock. Moreover, I doubt that Draco had to de-gnome the lawn at Malfoy manor. Newt explains the de-gnoming process Harry and the others use in *Chamber of Secrets*, and he seems relieved that most wizards are too humane to de-gnome with Jarveys. The disorienting process seems to work, and the Jarveys might be overkill—they surely would be to the gnomes. Long after Rowling provides us our first gnomes in *Chamber* and our gnome description in *Fantastic Beasts*, she has Xenophilius give the creatures good press and sing the praises of *Gernumbli Gardensi* in *Deathly*

Hallows (140). Xeno couldn't be happier that his own daughter has been bitten by one of the foot-high gnomes.

CS 35-37; *GF* 60; *HP* 329-30, 344-47; *DH* 140-41.

Graphorn

The Graphorn has two horns, and Rowling has said that this beast is the rune symbol for the number two. Newt describes this beast's relationship with mountain trolls: the trolls like to ride Graphorns, but Graphorns do not want to be ridden and "do not seem to take kindly to attempts to tame them" (20). It would seem safe to assume that it will be a long while before trolls are playing polo on Graphorns. Apparently, when a Graphorn walks, it is all thumbs.

Griffin

With the griffin, Rowling once again has Newt's list of beasts include an ancient classic: a creature that is part eagle and part lion. Rowling's griffin usage seems more significant in name than in the flesh. Harry's house at Hogwarts suggests the image of a *griffin d'or* (or a griffin "in a field of gold"), and the *griffin* on the headmaster's *door* comes to mind as well. The banner Gryffindor displays in *Goblet of Fire* has a gold lion in a field of red (237). The lion, of course, is the symbol of Gryffindor throughout the Potter novels, and a griffin is indeed more lion than eagle. Besides, the Ravenclaws need the front part of the griffin, the eagle, for *their* house symbol.

Grindylow

Remember the Grindylow from a visit to Lupin's office in *Prisoner of Azkaban*? And, of course, these creatures present an aquatic hazard for Harry in the second trial in *Goblet of Fire*. Grindylows seem creepy, kind of an animated seaweed that won't keep their bony pale green fingers to themselves. When merpeople "domesticate" Grindylows (20), I wonder what they *do*—fetch the merpeoples' merpapers in the morning?

PA 153-54, 318; *GF* 495-96, 498

Hippocampus

The hippocampus also goes back to ancient Greek myth. Notice that merpeople, having caught a "blue roan" (I love *that* oxymoronic color) hippocampus, "domesticated" that creature too (21). Merpeople do a lot of domesticating for folks who don't seem all that domesticated themselves—at least based on some of their actions in *Goblet of Fire*.

The hippocampus is an odd horse-fish combo (not on *anyone*'s fast-food menu I hope) and has a Muggle ocean parallel in the sea horse. *Hippos* is Greek for *horse*; and *kampos* is Greek for *sea monster*, though the word *hippocampus* also denotes an area of the brain. Rowling's one-word original contribution to the fish/horse lore and vocabulary is classic: inside the hippocampus's eggs are "Tadfoal" (21). How does she come up with these? (Consider "Buckbeak" and "Witherwings"—horses buck and birds have beaks; horses have withers and birds have wings.) I know, tadpoles aren't "fish" (though they're in the same water); but horses do have foals. Love that word "Tadfoal," which is spelled with a capital *T* though the grown hippocampus has the lower case *h*; remember, Rowling capitalizes (or not) as she pleases in her word world.

Hippogriff

Speaking of which, in *Prisoner of Azkaban* this eagle/horse creature's name is not capitalized. Yet in *Fantastic Beasts* hippogriffs have become Hippogriffs (and, though they have been elevated to capital-letter status, the Thestrals of Newt's book will be downgraded to the thestrals of *Order of the Phoenix*). Newt's description of the Hippogriff's behavior and attitude toward humans is "right out of the book"—Book 3 of the Potter series, that is. And if Draco were writing Newt's book, he'd probably add two more X's to the classification of these creatures. This is one of Rowling's rare borrowings of beasts from other literary works, usually taking them from the lore of the centuries or inventing new ones herself. Sixteenth-century Italian epic poet Ludovico Ariosto introduces the Hippogriff in *Orlando Furioso*, a poem which is a mere 38,736 lines long. Ludovic Bagman almost has the same first name as the poet, but I'm *betting* he hasn't read the other Ludo's poem. Here in Newt's book, as always, the Hippogriff-related graffiti is good. For those of you whose interest I've piqued in Hippogriffs, you may want to read *Orlando Furioso*; if so, I'll meet you back here on this page year after next.

PA 113-18, 331, 400-05, 413-15; *GF* 521, 523, 532; *HP* 53, 227-28; *DH* 733-34

Horklump

It seems that the Horklump forms clumps on your horticultural efforts. To no one's surprise, I'm sure, *hortus* is Latin for garden, and *klump* is Greek for clump. Notice that gnomes love to chomp on Horklumps, and Horklumps chomp on worms (22). The Weasley gnome near Harry and Scrimgeour in the "Frosty Christmas" garden scene in *Half-Blood Prince*

(Chapter 16) is eating a worm, so maybe the gnome wrestled the worm from a Horklump before eating the Horklump he wormed out of the worm *and* before being eaten himself by a Jarvey. This is all theoretically possible given the Jarvey-gnome-Horklump-worm food chain. In Dumbledore's notes to "The Warlock's Hairy Heart," he tells of a broken engagement between his aunt and one rumored to be a Horklump fondler (*BB* 60). More about that later.

BB 60

Imp

An imp has a "slapstick sense of humour" (22). Rowling thus gives a magical creature characteristics that lead to Muggle comparisons—such as someone having an impish sense of humor or a pixie-like personality. It's good to know that imp "breeding habits" are similar to those of the fairies; though I can't help wondering just what *are* those habits that lead to all those fairies' and imps' eggs and babies, respectively. One of Edgar Allan Poe's oddest stories (and that's saying something) is "The Imp of the Perverse"; you might find some good impish "humour" there too.

Jarvey

Newt has already had Brother Benedict tell us of the attack of the talking ferret (which sounds like a 1950s B movie title), which turned out to be a Jarvey mugging, complete with verbal insults (xiv). The rudimentary as well as insulting nature of Jarvey talk may be a bit of social satire directed at *jarveys*, who were, in Irish slang, coachmen—probably not renowned for extensive vocabularies and witty repartee. If Newt hadn't added rats to the preferred diet of Jarveys ("moles, rats, and votes"), I would have concluded that they eat only creatures whose names have a long *o*—though note that Jarveys eat only monosyllabic food. That could be the next Muggle weight loss craze: *The Monosyllabic Diet—Lose Weight Eating Only Foods of One Syllable*—a sure bestseller.

Jobberknoll

With regard to the strange beast known as the Jobberknoll, let's change a vowel or, even better, two—kind of like when we switch a couple of consonants in the Erkling. Imagine Jobberknoll as *Jabberknell.* To *jabber* is to talk uncontrollably, and a bell *knells* at a funeral or to announce a death (actually, *knoll* is a variant spelling of *knell*). So, when a Jobberknoll dies, it jabbers what all it has heard its whole life as the death knell tolls. No wonder the Jobberknoll's feathers contribute to magic folk "fessing up" and calling memories back to mind (23). Do you remember the sound of rewinding an old reel-to-reel tape recorder? All that high-pitched screeching and squawking may be like what Newt describes as the Jobberknoll's swan song. Given the choice, I'd sure rather hear a swan's swan song, than a Jobberknoll's, wouldn't you?

Kappa

In her creation of the Kappa, Rowling reaches further heights of absurdity. I especially like the way we humans might ward off a Kappa attack: throw the beast a cucumber with our name carved in it (23). This may make the cautionary and circumspect among us want to travel to Asia with a named-carved cucumber at the ready should we venture too close to Kappa-infested waters. This humor is *recherché* it seems to me, and it is reminiscent of the animal-related humor of James Thurber (who also loved beasties). Thurber wrote "The Pet Department" as a satire of a daily pet column in the *New York Evening Post*, writing both questions and answers about various pet problems with accompanying illustrations. Thurber's work is similar to much of *Fantastic Beasts*: one question begins, "My husband's seal will not juggle, although we have tried everything." Warding off Kappas with carved cucumbers is matched in Thurber by his advice on getting a horse out of the house by yelling "Roogie, roogie!" or "Whoosh!" (*The Thurber Carnival* 349). The anti-Snape graffiti in the margin across from the Kappa's XXXX classification refers to the fact that Rowling has Snape tell Lupin's class that Kappas are commonly found in Mongolia (*PA* 172). The fact that the Kappa is a "Japanese water demon" makes Snape's certainty problematic. Land-locked as Mongolia is, though, I suppose some Kappas could find their water way there. The graffitist here, Harry, would of course be hypersensitive to any Snape mistakes. The way a Kappa may be conquered is richly humorous too and almost as absurd as the cucumber bit. If an attack is imminent from this beast that "feeds on human blood," the endangered witch or wizard should "trick" the Kappa into bowing, thus spilling its water-trough-source-of-strength on its head. This begs the question, "Precisely what trick would make an attacking Kappa bow?" One last question, "What's a Japanese (or Mongolian) creature doing with a Greek letter for a name?"

PA 141, 172

Kelpie

Rowling uses a name from Scottish folklore for the water demon—with etymological origins that *don't* seem to have anything to do with *kelp.* Newt has already warned us that a certain showboating, photo-op-loving Kelpie has caused trouble for many years at Loch Ness (xvii). Rowling accounts for the difference between the serpent-like appearance of Nessie and the usual horse-like look nicely here by making the beasts shape shifters. So here, with the Muggle sightings of Nessie, as with the malfunction of Muggle electrical devices and the appearances of the yeti, Muggle mysteries are explained by the perfectly normal "facts" of the wizarding world. Pesky Chizpurfles get in computers, and Nessie and the yeti aren't at all careful about who sees them, with the former being a downright publicity hound (or publicity sea serpent, though, technically, it *could* be a hound). That Loch Ness Kelpie is the Lockhart of the Kelpie world. By the way, the "Placement Charm" (23) used to get a bridle over a Kelpie's head is a charm I can't recall being used or mentioned in the Potter books. Rowling may have misplaced the Placement among her charms.

CS 114-15

Knarl

The Knarl looks just like the European hedgehog, which is the same as the American porcupine (or close to the same, and you don't want to get too close to *any* of these spiny creatures). In *Order of the Phoenix* Harry's O.W.L. exam for Care of Magical Creatures includes distinguishing a knarl from among several hedgehogs (717). Consistent with Newt's account here, offering food is the deciding factor. As Newt explains, once the Knarl has refused the offered food (which, for hedgehogs and porcupines is insects) and once it has messed up the garden plants and "ornaments" (24), you might say it has left the Muggle garden *gnarled.* If there had been Muggle gnomes in the garden planted with, say, knotgrass, and said garden has been gnarled, we might conclude that the Knarl was offended by some proffered gnats and then gnawed and gnashed both knotgrass and gnomes in its knavery. And an innocent Muggle child gets blamed for the last of these silent initial-consonant words.

OP 171, 323, 717

Kneazle

The Kneazle is the chosen house pet of Newt and Porpentina you may recall; they are the owners of Hoppy, Milly, and Mauler (vi). When we learn that these cat-like creatures are "occasionally aggressive" (24), we figure that for every happy Hoppy and mild Milly, there's a mauling Kneazle like Mauler. It seems that the Kneazle's "uncanny ability to detect unsavory or suspicious characters" might have been useful to smell out a rat like Peter Pettigrew or to keep an eye on Polyjuiced Barty Crouch, Jr. Likewise, these beasts are useful in leading their lost owners home—though, in Mauler's case, perhaps, not gently home. Rowling has said on her web site that some famous cats in the Potter series—Mrs. Figg's smelly pets and Hermione's Crookshanks—are Kneazles or mixtures of cats and Kneazles. That might explain Crookshanks's attitude toward Scabbers beyond just the usual cat-and-dog antipathy. I wonder if some magic folk say *KUH-neezul* instead of *NEE-zul*, like Muggles who aren't sure about how to say *Knopf* publishers or *Knute* Rockne.

OP 323

Leprechaun

The leprechaun, a familiar and recurrent creature in Irish folklore, Rowling makes a mere six inches high. This is a wee bit more wee than we often see for these little fellows. In myth, they are usually exclusively male, which makes reproduction, as Newt says, by live birth (or by any other means, for that matter) problematic. In Irish folklore, leprechauns are linked to many a pot of gold, but I assume Rowling invented the matter of Leprechaun gold vanishing. Don't the leprechauns in *Goblet of Fire* seem larger than half a foot high? Could fans in the cheap field-level seats even see their aerial antics? Newt says this beast "enjoys attracting Muggle attention" (25)—especially in South Bend, Indiana, Newt (where Knute is well known, with or without sounding the initial *k*).

GF 104-05, 111-12

Lethifold

The effects of the Lethifold, as well as its eventual defeat, seem closely parallel to Rowling's dementors. The cloak feels "clammy" and wraps its "coldness" around its victim (26). Nothing repels it until the victim of the attack recalls a happy memory, like being elected president of the local Gobstones Club, and who among us *wouldn't* be cheered by that thought? Then the victim feels "fresh air" on his face, and the "deathly shadow" is gored by the horns of his Patronus (27). Thus we know the potential victim's Patronus was a stag, a bull, or some other horned animal or, perhaps, a dilemma. Our account of this dementor-like experience is from Flavius Belby, so the surname may be here *rehearsed* for use in *Half-Blood Prince*; there Marcus Belby appears for the first time, presumably a descendant of Flavius of Gobstone fame. The creepy nature of the Lethifold, which is "found solely in tropical climates" (25), is reminiscent of scenes we've probably all seen on the screen wherein someone is sleeping in a tropical climate and a creepy tarantula is creeping up the sleeping person's arm or leg or over the face. As regards this beast's name, *Lethe* is the River of Forgetfulness in Hades of Greek myth; but it's similar to a Latin word for deathly, *lethalis*, and we English speakers think of death when we hear *lethal*. So Rowling's *fold* of cloth, her cloak-like creature, can be *lethal* as it seeks to en*fold* its sleeping victims. Belby's compelling narrative in *Fantastic Beasts* is comparable to some of Poe's terrified and paralyzed narrators' middle-of-the-night accounts, like that in "The Tell-Tale Heart." In fact, I think Eddie Poe would have loved the Lethifold.

Fortunately for us, the fun's not over when Belby's tell-tale narrative is done. The attempt by Janus Thickey to fake his death by Lethifold attack is richly humorous (27, footnote 9). This "victim" leaves a bedside note that's a bit like the scrawled schoolchild's note to teacher asking for an excuse from something unpleasant and unfortunately signed "Yours truly, My Mother." Thickey's note may even contain the run-on sentence to heighten the sense of hastiness in which it was written. Janus was a *two-faced* liar (Google *Janus* if you need to), leaving his family to grieve and taking up with a (Green) Dragon Lady. At St. Mungo's, you may recall, there's a ward named in Janus's memory; it's the place where magic folk go who have suffered "permanent spell damage" (*OP* 510-11). So I think we may assume that Mrs. Thickey did some serious damage to Janus even if the Lethifold did not. And this is not to mention what the Dragon Lady may have done. So, here again, Rowling has *rehearsed* a name in *Fantastic Beasts* for her minor usage of it in *Order of the Phoenix* to name a hospital ward; the Thickey ward is permanently damaged Gilderoy's permanent home at St. Mungo's, by the way. One final thought: since the Lethifold, when it *is* successful, "digests its food there and then in their bed . . . leaving no trace of itself or its victim behind" as it exits (27), *that* is one tough CSI, is it not?

Lobalug

If something is ten inches long and found at the bottom of the North Sea, it's a pretty good guess, I'd say, that it is a "simple creature" (27). And so it is with the Lobalug. We can safely assume the beast (stretching the term *beast* a bit) has few wants, few needs, and, what's more, no complexes, complexities, complications, or dilemmas. It's only purpose in life seems to be to serve as a kind of merpeople handgun. The extract of the Lobalug poison is "strictly controlled." Think of that: say a young witch or wizard has just finished Hogwarts near the bottom (not of the North Sea, but of her or his class). Said witch or wizard then lands that first job at the Ministry and writes home telling the folks that she or he will be working in the Department for the Regulation and Control of Magical Creatures, Sea Creatures Division, North Sea Assignment, Lobalog Venom Control Group. Well, it's a start, and Mum would still be proud. Freud, incidentally, might find some subliminal submarine symbolism in the Lobalog (carefully reread Newt's second and third sentences about this beast).

Mackled Malaclaw

Newt tells us that the Mackled Malaclaw looks like a lobster, but "should on no account be eaten" (28). So for openers, put away the drawn butter and don't uncork the champagne if you've come upon a Malaclaw. *Those* claws are *bad* (*mal*!) not succulent—and these beasts are mackled, which can mean *blurred* (as in, easily confused with the delicious crustaceans) or *spotted* (which they are). Once bitten twice afflicted are this creature's victims: first the fever and green rash, then a week of bad luck. So no "bets, wagers, and speculative ventures" for the Malaclaw bitten. I wonder if Ludo Bagman lived near a coven/nest/pride/school (?) of these beasts and was bitten regularly.

Manticore

The manticore is the other half of Hagrid's fire crab combo, the lovable Blast-Ended ones. In *Prisoner of Azkaban*, Hermione researches a case of a manticore attack in her efforts to help Hagrid defend Buckbeak. Though Persian myths include such a creature as the manticore and though the Greek word *mantikos* means soothsayer or prophet, Rowling chooses not to do much else with this beast than let it be the front (or rear?) end of the Hagrid hybrid.

PA 222; *GF* 438

Merpeople

Weren't those merpeople so nice to Harry in *Goblet of Fire*? These beings/beasts chose, like the centaurs and unicorns, beasthood. Again, as with the yeti and Nessie, I like the way Rowling melds magical "facts" and Muggle (in this case) literature. Homer's sirens were merpeople, and Muggles have long known of mermaids. Though we encounter mermaids in literature and in the other fine arts far more often than mermen, Søren Kierkegaard's *Fear and Trembling* (a book I refer to a couple of times in *Repotting Harry Potter* and in this book as well) contains a somewhat elaborate passage dealing with a merman. Having read the passage numerous times, I have no idea as to precisely what it means, or even approximately what it means. Notice that Rowling writes of the "selkies of Scotland and the Merrows of Ireland" (29). The selkies of Scottish lore are seal/human in form; they can shed their sealskin to assume human form for a limited time. Once they've sealed the deal, they can put the skin back on and be a seal again. The Merrow in Irish legend is physically more like the merpeople (part fish, part human), and, typically, Rowling arbitrarily makes Merrows capital *M* beasts and selkies lower-case *s* beasts. Meanwhile, merpeople exist both here and in the Potter books not only under water but with a lower-case *m*.

GF 497-503, 505; *HP* 642-43

Moke

A mokeskin pouch would be a good thing for a Muggle to receive as a birthday present, right? But a mokeskin pouch is a *really* good thing for a certain Seeker to receive from his favorite Magical Creatures teacher as he heads for parts unknown looking for Horcruxes. So Rowling, in introducing us to the Moke in *Fantastic Beasts*, as well as to the virtues of mokeskin money bags and purses, prepares us for Hagrid's gift to Harry for his seventeenth birthday in *Deathly Hallows*. The device is well *rehearsed* here. Moreover Rowling actually *re-forms* mokeskin matters slightly from the concept that a mokeskin pouch (let's say) will "contract at the approach of a stranger" (29) to allowing only the owner being able to extract something from it, as Hagrid explains to Harry in Book 7. I assume Hagrid tells Harry that mokeskin pouches are rare because Mokes, which have "the ability to shrink at will" (29), may shrink out of sight before they can be caught, skinned, and pouched.

DH 120

Mooncalf

Though Rowling's Mooncalf is a specific creature in *Fantastic Beasts*, the word in the English language has long meant an idiot, a born fool, or a lunatic. This is all derivative of the ancients' assumptions that moonlight caused insanity or mental instability. Rowling's Mooncalf, like the lycanthrope, only comes out on full-moon-lit evenings and dances on its hind legs in wheat fields leaving "geometric patterns behind . . . to the great puzzlement of Muggles" (30). Thus we have still another example of Rowling giving us Muggle readers an explanation from the magical world for a Muggle mystery: crop circles. Who makes them, we wonder, and when and how? Aliens? Hoaxers? No way. It's just the mundane monthly moves of mating Mooncalves. Who knew? What a wacky detail we have about the Mooncalf's "silvery dung": it's quite a fertilizer *if* collected before sunrise (30). Wouldn't someone like the folks at Miracle Gro love to score some of *that* pre-sunrise silver dung?

Murtlap

The Murtlap has a growth on its back that looks like a sea anemone. My first thought is that I don't believe I've ever met anyone who seems to have marine life growing on his/her dorsal side; and if I do, I'll be circumspect about glad handing him/her and slapping him/her on the back. Let's say a witch or a wizard has pickled and eaten the growth on this "ratlike" beast (30). That magic person then has a heightened curse/jinx resistance level. But there are Murtlap caveats, so I issue these Murtlap alerts: (1)magic folk, don't OD on Murtlap pickles, for fear of purple ear hair; (2)magic and Muggle folks alike, don't step on a Murtlap; and (3)crustaceans, avoid all ratlike creatures with sea plants on their backs *at all costs*—you won't improve your jinx resistance; you are dinner. Recall that in *Order of the Phoenix* "essence of murtlap tentacles" (325), not unlike aloe, is helpful in relieving pain in Harry's and Lee Jordan's hands. It also alleviates the pain that Fred and George experience literally, which is, figuratively, what they *are* to Umbridge.

OP 324-29, 551, 574

Niffler

Remember when Ron has great success with a Niffler in *Goblet of Fire*? Where do you *get* one of these, poor Ron wonders. This is another example of a Rowling *rehashed* device from, in this case, the most recent Potter book prior to *Fantastic Beasts.* In the Niffler, Rowling kind of personifies (or, technically, beastifies) the human urge (magical and Muggle alike) for treasure hunting, for finding hidden or buried wealth serendipitously. If "it's" that easy, it probably isn't, right—like the old clunker that if "it's" too good to be true, it probably isn't. A *nifty* way to *sniff* out a fortune will most likely result in Leprechaun gold, not real gold (or dollars or Galleons). At the risk now of sounding schmaltzy, Ron's bringing a Niffler into the Burrow would not only wreak havoc with the shiny objects that are there; it couldn't possibly find the real treasures that are there: family love and loyalty. But it would be nifty for the Weasleys to have a few more Galleons too, wouldn't it?

GF 542-45; *OP* 677, 689, 715, 723

Nogtail

To ferret out (no Jarvey reference intended) a Nogtail and keep it from becoming a bully suckling to a mother sow *and* to keep it from bringing a blight to the farm where it suckles, a witch or wizard needs only one thing: a white dog. And, as usual, the Ministry of Magic is prepared, having within the Department for the Regulation and Control of Magical Creatures "(Pest Sub-Division)" (31) a dozen white-furred, Nogtail-chasing-on-the-ready bloodhounds to chase away the Nogtail from your sty. The job description of the witch or wizard assigned to *that* albino bloodhound dispatching would probably be even less impressive than that of the meager magical folks assigned to Lobalug venom control.

HP 144

Nundu

Whoa! Now we come to the "most dangerous" beast in the world, which, ironically, Newt discusses in just five lines. This "gigantic leopard," the Nundu, breathes a virulent breath that causes a disease so deadly as to "eliminate entire villages" (31). *None do* survive the Nundu's mere breathing on them, and, except in rare cases involving the efforts of a hundred magic folk, *none do* subdue the Nundu. The implications of the dangers and of the deadly effects of this most dangerous of beasts are more serious than comic, though, it seems to me. After all, there is many a Muggle disease that "moves silently despite its size" (microscopic), that is virulent and is often fatal, and that has "never yet been subdued" even by hundreds of scientists and researchers and Nobel laureates working over many decades. Incurable fatal diseases, in a sense, are gigantic leopards still moving silently among us, still breathing virulence, still unsubdued—much to the frustration and dismay of us all, including, as Ron says, those "Muggle nutters who cut people up" (*OP* 484).

Occamy

Rowling's Occamy leaves me at a loss, alas. An Asian creature with a plume and wings and a "serpentine body" of up to fifteen feet (31). Yet it *eats* fellow plumed and winged creatures: birds (and also rats, as a serpent would). On a good day, the Occamy will "carry off" monkeys—to eat or to elope? All we know for sure is that a momma Occamy will fight to protect its pure, soft, silvery eggs. So, who wouldn't? Interestingly enough (or not), the Occamy is a classification XXXX beast. Though it would seem humans are safe from it as long as they leave those silver eggs alone, we've probably all known people who'd risk life and limb just to point to an object on their mantel and say, "Now, *that's* an Occamy egg. Them's rare, they are."

Phoenix

Rowling taps into much ancient lore in the Potter books in her use of the phoenix. In several books of Harry's saga, the author draws on the myths of this creature's regenerative powers, its magical disappearances and reappearances, its extraordinary and transcendent songs, and its healing powers. Rowling's *Fantastic Beasts* inclusion of this creature, most notably represented in the Potter books as Dumbledore's beloved Fawkes, is both a *rehashed* reference to *Chamber of Secrets* and a *rehearsed* occurrence for *Order of the Phoenix* and *Half-Blood Prince* Fawkes scenes. This bird will definitely rise again.

CS 206-07, 315-22; *HP* 614-15; *DH* 104

Pixie

The first time I can recall hearing the word *pixie* was in connection with a pixie haircut (think of Judy Carne if you're old enough to remember *Laugh-In*). The coif may not have anything to do with the creature, but it's my first memory of the word, so, as Arthur Weasley sometimes says, "There you are." Rowling localizes our next beastie to Cornwall, and she colors them "Electric blue" (32), which I think of as a meta-pastel comparable to hot pink. Based on local folklore, Rowling's "very mischievous" pixies love to trick and play jokes on humans (magic and Muggle alike?), and they are Gilderoy Lockhart's idea both of an ideal introductory D.A.D.A. class and, we assume from his behavior, dangerous beasts (note the textbook graffiti). Since pixies only rate an XXX classification, our three favorite thirteen-year-olds deal with them even if our favorite toothy, photogenic fraud cannot. *Whatever* we need to say to rid ourselves of pixies, *Peskipiksi Pesternomi* is certainly not it, is it? Alas, poor Gilderoy.

CS 101-02

Plimpy

When I reread Rowling's description of the Plimpy, I recalled Xenophilius Lovegood's repeated claims that his beloved Luna was out gathering Freshwater Plimpies to make soup for a delicious repast for all. These beasts are *rehearsed* here in *Fantastic Beasts* for that important scene in *Deathly Hallows*; moreover, Luna mentions using a Gurdyroot for "warding off" Plimpies in *Half-Blood Prince* (425). I suppose we can assume that, as with bass, there are both fresh water and salt water

Plimpies and that when they are nibbling at us is when they need warding off. Notice in the drawing (33) that the Plimpy is rather plumpy, and, it seems to me, is an aquatic version of that plump aviary creature, the Snidget—depicted in *Quidditch Through the Ages* (11). Lips and beaks, legs and wings notwithstanding, fat fish and fat bird have some heavy things in common. Have you ever been floating in a lake and felt something nibbling at you? Now, as we learn from Newt, that nibbler could be a Plimpy perhaps trying to get his own webbed feet untied, a *feat* which would surely "take hours" (33). One final thought: do the merpeople, who consider Plimpies pests, *themselves* come in fresh- and salt-water varieties? Merpeople's prefix would suggest the latter, but they do dwell in the lake at Hogwarts apparently far from the sea.

HP 425; *DH* 402, 404, 418

Pogrebin

Since Rowling makes the Pogrebin "a Russian demon" (33), I can't help but think of Cold War politics and the paranoia of American or British Muggles thinking that they were being followed, spied on, tailed, taped, or otherwise surveilled by communists. The Soviet threat, once assumed to be gigantic, was, in the end, like the Pogrebin "barely a foot tall" with a head that was "oversized" though quite "smooth." Many hexes can repel this Russian beast (think of sabotage, subterfuge, codes, and counterintelligence); but "Kicking has also been found effective" (as in Muggle weaponry up to and including nuclear kicking). Forgive me for going so far with these Cold War analogies, but, again, Rowling *does* call the Pogrebin "a Russian demon," *and* the only entry in my Muggle dictionary beginning with *pogr* is *pogrom*—a demonic fact of Russian history a former Amnesty International employee like Rowling would be quite familiar with.

Porlock

Our last two beasts whose names begin with *P* seem not only harmless (both are classified as XX) but rather inconsequential in nature. The Porlock guards horses; in fact, a Porlock "lives to guard horses" (34). You may recall that Bowtruckles guard trees. All of which makes me wonder *why* horses and trees need guarding, not to mention *who* or *what* the Porlocks and Bowtruckles are guarding them from. Can you imagine a Porlock poring over the knots in the forelock of an equine, or can you see a Bowtruckle watching over the knots in a pine?

OP 323

Puffskein

Rowling's Puffskein is beloved by kids in the wizarding world partly because, like kids in the Muggle world, they like gross stuff. Puffskeins eat (British) bogies (34) or (American) boogers and drink from the toilet (vii). So what's not to love in a charming creature like the Puffskein? Newt tells us that when these beasts are "contented," they make a "low humming noise." Having held some happy cats, I can imagine the contented sound of the purring Puffskein. Rowling will later give us a Puffskein *re-formed* as a pygmy puff (*HP* 121), miniature Puffskeins that come in pink and purple (and lose their capital *P* in the Potter books). One cuddly purple pygmy puff appeals to Ginny and becomes a part of the Rowling canon as Arnold.

OP 101; *HP* 121, 123, 235, 300

Quintaped

In Newt's description of the Quintaped, Rowling actually writes a very effective "short short," a subgenre of the short story also known as "flash fiction." After a few lines of what this beast looks like and where it is found, Rowling gives us this humorous "legend" as to the origin of the five-legged, club-footed, human-eating creature. Typically, the author uses her strong background in Latin in naming this beast (*quint*-five; *ped*-foot), and notice too that she has *rehearsed* the unplottable geography matter again here (pre-Grimmauld Place). Quintius MacBoon was not a boon companion to Dugald McClivert, and the Isle of Drear was not big enough for both clans (note one family is "Mac" and the other is "Mc," just to add to their differences). If you're an avenging clan out to transfigure your enemy, it's probably not a good idea to turn them into creatures which are more ferocious than you and which will have a hearty appetite for you. Once all the McCliverts were eaten by the MacBoon-turned-monsters, what do contemporary Quintapeds eat on the isolated and dreary isle of Drear? Rowling says the beasts have a "particular taste for humans" (35), so I suppose they can't be as particular anymore and have had to settle for nonhuman fare over the years. In Rowling's temptingly suggestive conclusion, she tells us what life has shown us from time to time: that some humans turn hairy and are "quite happy to live out their days as beasts" (36). As I mentioned earlier, there is a reference to a creature whose "skeleton had five legs" in *Half-Blood Prince* when Harry is frantically looking for a place to hide his Potions book in the Room of Requirement (526). That five-legged creature, however, died in a cage inside a cabinet in the Room; so I assume it wasn't a Hairy MacBoon, though as to what it was or why it was there, I, like Harry so often, don't have a clue.

Ramora

Three fantastic beasts beginning with an *R* Newt dispenses with rather quickly. The Ramora is one vowel change away from a *remora*, which, like Rowling's beast, is a fish. The fish that Muggles know as a remora has a large sucker on the top of its head, and it latches on to larger fish, turtles, or even ships for a few leagues free ride. Come to think of it, the Muggle world *re-* fish may be more bizarre than Rowling's *ra-* fish. Newt's last sentence begs the question, "*Why* is the Ramora so 'highly valued' (36), and why would a witch or wizard want to *poach* one?"

Red Cap

The Red Cap is an interesting creation, a legend dating back centuries in Rowling's part of the world. These beasts live where blood has been shed, yet we assume they are bloodthirsty for more. Rowling here has *rehashed* Red Caps, having had Lupin teach the D.A.D.A. students about these beasts in *Prisoner of Azkaban* (141). On a somber note, no wonder Red Caps are "most prevalent in northern Europe" (36) since much "human blood has been spilled" there. By the way, if you've never read Carl Sandburg's brief poem "Grass," I highly recommend it to you. It's about places where much blood has been shed and about time turning those battle sites into places of peace once again.

PA 141, 318

Re'em

Remember the old saying, "Never get too close to an animal whose name is a contraction" or, in Canada, "Never trust an animal with an apostrophe in its name." All right, neither is an old saying; I just made them up. But Rowling's Re'em elicits whimsy just by its nutty name alone, it seems to me. Moreover, she makes us wonder just what letter or letters are left out of this beast's name and why. Try inserting a letter or two right between the *e*'s and see what you get. If you spend more than a few minutes doing this, incidentally, I wouldn't mention it to anyone. I figure Rowling wants the sound of *ream* (not the bundles of copy paper) since many meanings of that word have to do with enlarging an existing hole, boring it further, or even making a hole in a piece of fruit to extract juice (a juicer is also known as a reamer). In slang, to ream is to cheat or swindle or get the better of someone. So the wizarding world has found it is quite difficult to extract blood from these giant oxen (no surprise there). Magic folk can't ream the Re'em, and the beast reams them of its power-producing blood. The irony here, if any, could be that a wizard might need to drink Re'em blood in order to have enough strength to ream Re'em blood from a Re'em. Any way you look at, this is not a practical source of strength.

Runespoor

Rowling outdoes herself in creating the Runespoor. For starters, from now on when someone asks us, "What can be scarier than a two-headed snake?" we have an answer. Does Rowling's choice of a name for this beast suggest someone who's poor at runes? More likely, I'd say she wants the near-homonym to suggest a *pure* rune. I say this partly because Rowling has said the ancient rune symbol for the number three is the Runespoor. This beast, "orange with black stripes" (37) and thus always dressed for Halloween, is of three minds. I assume from the drawing—as I turn my copy of *Fantastic Beasts* sideways so as to be "facing" the serpent—that the left head, the planner, is, ironically, looking backwards; the middle head, the dreamer, is looking forwards; and the right head, the critic, is looking sideways, slightly southeasterly, with both eyes and with what I imagine to be a cynical expression on its face. Newt tells us that this right head has "extremely venomous" fangs, just as critics often do. Of course, all this is not only speculative but highly problematic because in trying to follow Newt's instructions to face the Runespoor, can we really be sure we're facing the right (that is, the correct) face when dealing with a three-faced creature? Just for fun, look back through the descriptions of the three heads with Freud's tripartite division of the mind in mind. How about the planner head as the ego, the dreamer head as the id, and the critic head as the superego? After all, when the heads are in conflict with each other, it's the critic head/superego/conscience that's often missing, bitten off completely in fact. Does that sound familiar, my fellow sometimes-two-headed friends?

Salamander

Compared to the dull salamanders that Muggles know, the magic world salamander is a ball of fire—or it appears in one anyway. Drawing on ancient myths about salamanders and fires, Rowling gives us here *not* a creature that can only survive for a brief time out of water (like a fish), *not* a creature that can only survive for a brief time without air (like a human), but a beast that can't survive for long without *fire*, though fiery peppers will suffice for a while (38). I feel a temptation for some cheap jokes at the poor salamander's expense. Think of what you could do with "You're fired," or "Are you burned out in your job?"; but I'm not going to touch that kind of humor with a hot poker.

CS 130; *PA* 235

Sea Serpent

Rowling's sea serpent reminds me yet again of that recalcitrant kelpie whom Muggles call Nessie since the sea serpent happens to be that shape shifting kelpie's favorite form to take. Rowling describes this beastie in terms that "hysterical" Muggles have used in their sightings of Nessie or "real" sea serpents for many years—a creature with a "horselike head and a long snakelike body that rises and humps out of the sea" (38). As I've suggested before, it's tempting to think that Rowling's juxtaposition of two words like "hysterical" and "Muggle" is intended as a redundancy.

Shrake

The Shrake is a rare example of a creature born of a conflict between magic and Muggle folk. Insulted wizards avenged themselves against Muggle "fisherfolk" by creating the spiny fish called Shrakes to tear up the Muggles' nets. Little did those early nineteenth-century Muggle fisherfolk know that neither they nor their fisherfolk descendants would be able to fish those Atlantic waters again. Not wanting to make this beast's name too easy to explain, notice that Rowling describes the nets as "ripped and empty" (38)—not *shredded* and empty. If Muggle fisherfolk *really* knew who ruined their fishing that day and forevermore, the headlines might have read: "Shrakes Shred Shrimpers' Nets."

Snidget

Readers of *Quidditch Through the Ages* will recall the Golden Snidget as the original, living object sought by the forerunners of Quidditch Seekers to earn the points and end the game. Notice in one footnote that Rowling footnotes herself and invites us to check out Kennilworthy Whisp's book published by Whizz Hard Books (39, footnote 13). It's hard to determine from Newt's description whether the Snidget's feathers and its "highly prized" eyes or its use (or, more accurately, its abuse) in the early days of Quidditch was the chief factor in its becoming endangered. Oliver Wood would be a good person to ask. Every reference to this beast, by the way, is to the "Golden Snitch," which makes me wonder why it's relegated to the *S* section of Newt's book instead of the *G*'s. After all, the fire crab is with the *F*'s, not *C*'s; and the Red Cap takes its alphabetical place with the lowly *R*'s rather than the rather high *C*'s. I'll get back to this fantastic bird when I comment on Kennilworthy Whisp's history of Quidditch. The Snidget I will leave up in the air until then.

QA 10-15

Sphinx

The sphinx Rowling had recently employed in *Goblet of Fire*, so the beast is *rehashed* here, and she adds nothing new to the human/lion riddler. Rowling draws on the Egyptian myths of the sphinx more so than the Greek, and reveals that magic folk have been sphinxing for "over a thousand years" (39). This is a long time indeed, but not as long as Muggles' history with this beast. The Greek sphinx, by the way, was a woman/lion combo who *killed* all whom she riddled who didn't get the answer right; luckily for Oedipus, he did—though he wasn't lucky for all that long. By comparison to some of the legendary human-sphinx encounters, let's face it, Harry got a veritable pussy-cat of a sphinx in the maze, didn't he? *Spy-D-er* indeed. Of course Fake Mad-Eye might have had something to do with that.

GF 628-30

Streeler

The "giant snail" called a Streeler, like chameleons in the Muggle world, changes color; but this magical beast does so on a time schedule not because of its background, changing its "colour" on an hourly basis (40). An odd detail is that the colorful (or colourful) Streeler leaves behind it a trail "so venomous that it shrivels and burns all vegetation over which it passes." I hear a bit of *stream* and *trailer* in the name of this Rowling beast. It leaves a *stream* of potent venom in its *trail*, its pretty colors notwithstanding. Those magic folk who enjoy the Streeler's "kaleidoscopic colour changes" (40) might send an owl to friends saying something like: "Come have dinner with us Saturday night, after which we can all watch our Streeler change colours till dawn." Sounds like fun, right? Guests had better be careful of their salads in light of that snail trail, though.

Tebo

Since this beast has "the power of invisibility," Newt tells us it is hard to "evade or catch" (40). With all due respect to this magical beast called the Tebo (and with no wish to offend), this creature's *dis*appearance may be an improvement over its appearance. There's something about warthogs—the snout, the tusks, the warts, or the overall *hogness*—that's just not that pretty to look at. The reason a witch or wizard would want to catch a Tebo is to obtain its valuable protective hide, but given that invisibility factor, the Tebo's prized hide is not hard for it to hide. Imagine magic folk tracking this beast, just about to get a bead on him, and *poof* it's gone; and there they are wondering Tebo or not Tebo—that is the question.

Troll

We've met trolls in the Potter books. The mountain troll caper is our dynamic trio's first big adventure together. The references to trolls as guardians remind me of their minor role in *Prisoner of Azkaban.* Do you recall that they specialize in grunting and comparing the size of their clubs (*PA* 269-70)? I'm glad too that Rowling has Newt mention river trolls hiding underneath bridges. Remember the tale of "The Three Billy Goats Gruff"? Newt tells us too that the troll is notable "equally" for its "strength and stupidity" (40). That's a nice alliteration, but not so nice a combination. With regard to another matter, Newt does not mention the stench of these beasts. Maybe, like Hagrid, Newt the magizoologist, doesn't see the warts of a Tebo or smell the foul odor of a troll. Rowling's trolls are *only* (!?) twelve feet tall, yet they weigh a "over a tonne" (40). Assuming a "tonne" is, like a ton, two thousand pounds, isn't Rowling a little heavy handed in making her trolls so huge? Or, is she just, as often, being a bit droll—this time about trolls?

SS 174-77; *PA* 269-70

Unicorn

All that Newt records about the unicorn is explained or illustrated in the Potter books: the changing colors as the beast matures, its preference of witches over wizards, and the value of its body parts—you may recall how Slughorn lusts over Hagrid's collection of unicorn hair. It is noteworthy too that it is one of these centuries-old, legendary creatures who is the first death on the pages of the Potter series (*SS* 255-56). All of the above is, as Newt says, "excellent Muggle press" for the unicorn indeed (41, footnote 15). Finally, and a propos of perhaps nothing Rowlingesque, the unicorn is Laura Wingfield's favorite figure in her collection, her *glass menagerie* in Tennessee Williams's beautiful play of that name—which, since I've mentioned it twice now, you probably infer correctly I recommend that you read if you never have.

SS 255-56; *GF* 436, 440

Werewolf

This beast is nicely named: he *were* a man and then he *were* a wolf (this is *not* the etymology). As the graffiti indicates, we readers of the Potter books see how the same affliction has resulted in a good man, Lupin, becoming, arguably, a better man—while another man, Fenrir Greyback, has become more monstrous than the most ferocious of wolves. Maybe when Rowling wrote *Fantastic Beasts* she hadn't planned to develop Greyback into such a despicable and evil creature—even when he's in his human form. Note that footnote 16 says, "When there is no full moon, the werewolf is as harmless as any other human" (41). Fenrir didn't get the memo, did he? It's a good thing Flavius Belby survived that Lethifold attack since his (probable) descendant Damocles Belby invented the wolfsbane potion that enables Lupin to function more like a normal person. Maybe many another despondent werewolf's life was changed as well. If that same anonymous author who, Newt says, wrote *Hairy Snout, Human Heart* (41, footnote 16) were to write a tribute to the wolfsbane potion, I have a title for him: *From Miserable Misanthrope to Coping Lycanthrope*. Maybe Whizz Hard Books would go for that. Not only here in Newt's account of the werewolf, but in all other descriptions of the creature I have seen, the werewolf is a man (the two Old English root words meant *wolf* and *male human*). So I suppose we can assume there are no female Muggle or magic werewolves out there; and perhaps if Remus and Tonks knew from an ultrasound that they were going to have a little girl, werewolf-father-to-be would have been less worried. I don't think ultrasounds are available at St. Mungo's, though. Back in the 1930s and 40s, moviegoers were treated to *The Wolf Man* and *Dracula Meets the Wolf Man* and other scary-movie gems, but no *The Wolf Woman.* By contrast, speaking of Dracula, a vampire's bitten victim of either sex becomes a vampire; female vampires aplenty *are* out there somewhere in the dark (or twilight?).

PA 171-73, 380-81

Winged Horse

Horses with wings consist of "many different breeds" (42); Newt discusses four of them. Only two of these turn up in the Potter books: the giant palominos that bring the Beauxbatons students to Hogwarts (*GF* 243) and, of course, Thestrals. I assume Hippogriffs are similar in size and nature to a winged horse, but with them (since the eagle is mixed up in there) the wings are the bird's not the horse's, so Newt discusses them separately. The word "Abraxan" reminds me of *Arabian*, but they're not palominos; the word "Granian" names the greys; and the word "Aethonan" reminds me of nothing. I did discover, however, that Ovid, Homer, and Virgil all have horses named Aethon in their works—and that the Greek root of that word could mean reddish brown in color; Rowling's Aethonans are chestnut. But what intrigues me about Newt's description of these beasts is that Thestrals have "the power of invisibility" (42). Would Newt not know when and why and to whom Thestrals are invisible? Hagrid seems to indicate that seeing Thestrals by having seen death is widely and long-since known about these creatures. Muggle-born Hermione knows this, which probably means it was written in *someone*'s book if not Newt's. Or did Rowling refine and *re-form* the visibility/invisibility factor of this beast between writing *Fabulous Beasts* and *Order of the Phoenix*? That is, perhaps Newt didn't know about "seeing death/seeing Thestrals" because Jo didn't know about that yet. Given Rowling's meticulously planned Potter series, I'd guess she knows more than Newt (after all, he doesn't debunk the belief that the beasts are unlucky either) and chooses not to reveal too much yet about the soon-to-be-important *t*hestrals (with a lower-case *t*). Whether speaking through the narrative voice of the Potter books or as Newt the magizoologist, Rowling knows her beasts to a *T*.

GF 243, 245; *OP* 196-201, 444-49, 762-68;
DH 53, 733-34, 757

Yeti

One last time, Rowling explains a Muggle mystery by a magic "fact." To vary (and internationalize) an old saying: "Yes, Rachita, there is an Abominable Snowman"; "Yes, Indira, there is a yeti"; and "Yes, Virginia, there is a Bigfoot"—though his name is not Harry and he didn't once live with the Hendersons. My favorite phrase from this final entry in *Fantastic Beasts* comes when Newt explains that theories that the yeti is troll-related have never been verified because no one has been able to perform "the necessary tests" (42). What, exactly, would a troll test consist of? Would the investigating wizards need to get a urine or blood sample, a strand of yeti hair? Of course, magic folk would not know about such Muggle scientific stuff, but would instead, I suppose, conduct simpler investigations and necessary tests—like seeing if the yeti smelled really bad, listening to its grunted words, or checking out the size of its club.

They're All Fantastic: Jo's Things That Go Bump in the Night

I have now written more words *about* Rowling's *Fantastic Beasts and Where to Find Them* than there are *in* Rowling's *Fantastic Beasts and Where to Find Them.* This is something I didn't have to worry about in my book on the Potter series. Yet this is sometimes a cardinal virtue, not sin, for the literary analyst—just ask someone who's written fifteen insightful pages on a haiku. I know, I'm rationalizing and self-justifying a long chapter on a short book, so I'll just plead guilty, your honors. I am in good company, though: Dumbledore's commentary on "The Tale of the Three Brothers" in *The Tales of Beedle the Bard* is twice as long as the tale itself.

I do have just a few more afterthoughts on Rowling's rich little book of beasts. Think of this: Newt Scamander's academic specialty is fictitious as well as fantastic. But his enthusiasm for his subject matter is real—reminiscent of Hagrid's emotional reaction to Buckbeak's imminent execution. That beast is fantastic too, and that book is fantasy, but Hagrid's grief over the imminent death of an imaginary creature is as real as rain, his mourning as deep as that of anyone who's ever grieved over losing a loved animal. So, I really appreciate Rowling's having Newt confide to us, as his long introduction ends, that he hopes witches and wizards in the future who read about these beasts will "enjoy their strange beauty and powers as we have been privileged to do" (xxi). Newt adds that he is pleased that past generations of magic folk "have grown to a fuller knowledge and understanding of the fantastic beasts I love through the pages of this book." As a professor of literature for over thirty years, I appreciate Newt's words from the heart, and I think I understand completely what he means: whatever we love, whatever we teach with passion and learn with enthusiasm, is a privilege and a pleasure that enriches our lives. Ideally, we are purveyors and receptors of not just information, but of wonder—whether what we pass on to others happens to be real books or imaginary beasties.

Moreover, the fabulous nature of Rowling's imaginary creatures reminds me of the fabulous nature of some real beasts. Fantastic is the march of the penguins; fantastic too are the migrations of whales, the annual arrival of Monarch butterflies in Mexico, the hummingbird beating its wings eighty times per second, the human heart pumping blood through vessels which end-to-end would be almost 100,000 miles long. I recommend that you read the title essay in Dr. Lewis Thomas's classic collection *The Medusa and the Snail* for even more fantastic stuff about some amazing creatures. If you love *Fantastic Beasts* and fantastic beasts, you will love that essay, I guarantee.

So, Newt's book reminds me of the wonders of the real world, as well as informing me of those of the magical world. Rereading *Fantastic Beasts* and writing about Newt's creatures and magizoology makes me appreciate zoology and renders it at times indistinguishable from magizoology; *Fantastic Beasts* makes me want to go to a natural history museum or to a zoo or to read more about our own Muggle beasts. As I said in my introduction to this book, "fantastic beasts" is a redundant phrase; for all creatures here below, magic and Muggle alike, are fantastic. Don't you get the distinct impression that J. K. Rowling has a pronounced fondness for, indeed a profound love of, animals? I think it's important to recall that the first time she gets Harry out of the dreaded Dursley house, she takes him to the zoo. And there Harry talks to an animal and frees a caged creature, who thanks him and calls him friend.

Still another nice thing about Newt's book is that Rowling can give us the scientific views of one who has devoted his life to the beasties in Newt, which is a nice complement to the emotional (sometimes blindly emotional) perspective on creatures that we get in the Potter books in Hagrid. Rowling shows us in the little beast book and throughout Harry's long saga all kinds of creatures, letting us view them with both head and heart, from both Newt's classic textbook accounts to Hagrid's illegal test breeds in his cabin.

Most of you are probably familiar with this traditional Scottish prayer. We don't know its origins—neither author nor time nor place. But it's a timeless and placeless plea for deliverance and safety from fantastic beasts.

From ghoulies and ghosties
And long legged beasties,
And things that go bump in the night,
Good Lord, deliver us!

You may recall in *Sorcerer's Stone*, that Peeves, hearing noises in the night, asks, "Are you ghoulie or ghostie or wee student beastie?" (274). So, as if there were any doubt, Jo Rowling surely knows the old prayer. As a life-long animal lover myself, I'd like to amend this prayer thusly, by way of tribute to J. K. Rowling's overall treatment of non-human creatures, both real and imaginary, in her books.

To ghoulies and ghosties
And long legged beasties,
And things that go bump in the night,
Rowling has delivered us!

And, as an afterthought in this book of afterthoughts, I think it's fair to say that, like all the authors who matter and who move us beyond ourselves, Rowling has rightly discerned that among all the creatures of the earth, the most fabulous of all may be the one designated as *Homo sapiens* (essentially, *wise being*). After reading all of Newt's descriptions, I couldn't help but wonder what he would write about this creature if he'd done a book on the beings as well as the beasts. So, if you'll be kind enough to forgive me and indulge me, here's my guess:

Human

M.O.M. Classification: XXXX

The Human is found all over the earth. When fully grown, it is usually between five and six feet tall. It comes in two sexes called male and female. Though the male was long thought to be stronger and wiser than the female, this is now thought to have no basis in fact or, by some, to be counterfactual. The Human is cruel and kind, heartless and compassionate. It loves to wage wars, but loves peace as well. It eats many of the plants and beasts with which it shares the earth, and is sometimes destructive of its own environment. It fears the unknown, the dark, and death. Its hide is thin, its powers are limited, its joy is contagious, and its eyes may sometimes let you see its soul. It is capable both of killing and of dying for its own kind. It is characterized, more than anything else, by its deep but somewhat inexplicable capacity for what Albus Dumbledore, long-time headmaster of Hogwarts, often calls "love." There are two forms of this being: magic and Muggle. Although we magic folk are quite aware of the non-magical others, on occasion some Muggles draw on a power unique to Humans and imagine that we too exist.

Chapter 3: A Return to Quidditch

Pre-game Matters and Dumby's Foreword

The first page of *Quidditch Through the Ages* lets us know who all has checked out this book before Harry. We recognize most of the names whether they are Hogwarts Quidditch players (like Oliver Wood, Marcus Flint, Cedric Diggory, Angelina Johnson, Katie Bell, and Fred Weasley) or non-players (like Ernie Macmillan, Millicent Bulstrode, and Hermione Granger). Notice that there's an unusually long time between when Oliver Wood checked out the book and when the next borrower did (and that Oliver was the first to check out *Quidditch Through the Ages*). Hermione, understandably, didn't seem to linger over the pages long. I noticed that she checked the book out the day after Ron's birthday (March 1), perhaps having increased interest in something Ron likes—but to attach significance to that may be more of a stretch than Harry has to make to catch a Snitch. The period during which these "borrowers" could check out *Quidditch Through the Ages* is just under a year, and I think we could assume that's 1994-95, the *Goblet of Fire* school year. Warrington's having checked out the book in November, 1994, would fit since he's on the Slytherin team in Book 4. What I can't explain is how at least four borrowers seem to have checked out the book during Hogwarts summer vacation.

Interestingly enough, four readers of *Quidditch Through the Ages* never make their way into the Potter books: B. Dunstan, K. Bundy, J. Domy (or Dorny), and S. Capper. I wonder if Rowling once had plans for them which, unlike Quidditch players, never got off the ground. (By the way, of all the would-have-been Potter-book characters who ended up on the proverbial cutting room floor, the three that I would most like to have read about are Su Li, Weasley cousin Mafalda, and Arthur Pyrites—

if interested, see what Steve Vander Ark has to say about them in *The Lexicon.*) Check out Madam Pince's warning to borrowers before you leave this opening page, especially the "consequences" for doing harm to the book; those consequences will be "as awful as it is within my power to make them," which is, let's face it, probably not all that awful.

As we turn to the title page, we see that the author of *Quidditch Through the Ages* has an unusual first name—Kennilworthy. It reminds me of our late dog Shelley, who stayed one Christmas holiday (with his fellow dog Keats) at a local kennel, had a few "incidents" with his keepers, and was thereafter not welcome to return for further stays. In short, he was no longer *kennel worthy.* I don't know what Rowling may have had in mind with her *Quidditch* author's funny sounding name, though an alternate meaning of *kennel* is a *gutter.* The author's last name, Whisp, is another matter altogether. The British say the similar sounding *whist* like we Americans say *shhh* or *hush*; and *whist* is an old card game, a forerunner of contract bridge. Further, Whisp is a homonym for the *wisp* in Will-o'-the-Wisp, a mysterious light appearing in bogs, swamps, and marshes in the lore of Britain and elsewhere. All of which leads me not all that close to an explanation of Rowling's *Quidditch* author's name; no closer than my dog Shelley's kennel rejection, a card game, a hushing sound, a swamp light, or the gutter. I found Newt Scamander's name much easier to deal with. But let us proceed. Moving from *Whisp* to *whist* to *wisp*, now we come to "Whizz." Kennilworthy's publisher is an in-your-face pun: Whizz Hard (Wizard). The Whizz Hard Books address is across the street and far away from the address of Newt's Diagon Alley publisher, Obscurus Books (numbers 129b and 18a respectively).

There's rich humor indeed on the "Praise for *Quidditch Through the Ages*" page. Rowling quotes Bathilda Bagshot, whose big moment (sort of) is yet to come in *Deathly Hallows.* Readers of the Potter books have also encountered the *Which Broomstick* publication before, such as in *Prisoner of Azkaban* when Harry is trying to decide *which broomstick* to order by reading *Which Broomstick* (190). Moreover, the match up of reviewers to the blurbs is classic, as we see Lockhart's conceit, Ludo's love of a good bet, and Rita's nastiness (she's not only "read worse," she's *written* worse). Noteworthy here too is Rowling's use of the name Brutus Scrimgeour, author of *The Beaters' Bible*, long before readers meet Minister Rufus Scrimgeour in *The Half-Blood Prince.* The Minister is perhaps Brutus's brother or some other relative. Like Lockhart and many another of Rowling's "authors," Kennilworthy likes alliterative titles, as evidenced by a couple of his other Quidditch-related books listed on the "About the Author" page. You may recall that the subject of Kennilworthy's *The Wonder of Wigtown Wanderers, He Flew Like a Madman*, "Dangerous" Dai Llewellyn, has a ward named after him at St. Mungo's (*OP* 487). The patients in the Llewellyn ward, like Arthur Weasley, are victims of bites, which makes me wonder just how dangerous wild flying Dai was.

Albus Dumbledore's "Foreword" would surely not make Madam Pince happy. Dumby is downright pleased that the book is in a thoroughly used condition. This tattered and stained copy of *Quidditch Through the Ages* reminds me of the words of Sir Francis Bacon: "Some books are to be tasted, others to be swallowed, and some few to be chewed and digested . . . ." Forgive me for making a metaphor literal, but I agree with Dumby that the condition of Kennilworthy's book is "a high compliment" (vii). Dumbledore also tells us about Madam Pince's displeasure at copies of *Quidditch Through the Ages* being made available to Muggle readers; here we find an interesting line in light of the headmaster's future roles in *Half-Blood Prince* and *Deathly Hallows*. Irma Pince suggested that they could claim the Hogwarts library burned, or that Dumbledore "had dropped dead without leaving instructions" ([viii])—which Harry might say a few years later is exactly what Dumbledore did. After Rowling's imaginary headmaster gives us Muggle readers real-life information about Comic Relief U.K., I love the transition from reality back to fantasy. In the last words of his Foreword, Dumby reminds us that Quidditch is "an entirely fictional sport and nobody really plays it," and then immediately wishes Puddlemere United well for the coming season. This seems comparable to someone saying at Christmas time, "There is no Santa Claus, and here's what I want him to bring me."

Sticky Business: Kennilworthy's Chapter 1

Ironically, the first fearless generalization we get from Quidditch historian Whisp will be proved wrong later in the Potter books: "No spell yet devised enables wizards to fly unaided in human form" ([1]). Snape's escape from Hogwarts in *Deathly Hallows* and You-Know-Who's flight through the skies on the night of the seven Harrys prove Kennilworthy's views wrong. Whisp also assumes that a witch or a wizard in bat form will not be able to think like humans, so he must be thinking of magic persons who have transfigured themselves, rather than Animagi. As Dumbledore tells us in his commentary on Beedle the Bard's "Babbity Rabbity and Her Cackling Stump," Animagi when in animal form "keep all their human thinking and reasoning" (*BB* 84), and Peter Pettigrew as a rat, Sirius Black as a dog, and Minerva McGonagall as a cat all seem indeed to think as the humans they are.

Moving on, Whisp is crystal clear about those crude early brooms that were flown by wizards who suffered "splinter-filled buttocks and bulging piles" (2)—not to mention the probability that there's a pun in the pain of riding on a broom made of "unvarnished ash." I think it's safe to say that the medieval broom in Figure A (3) is indeed a far cry from a Firebolt. Once brooms became "comfortable" and "aerodynamic," they were flown, Whisp tells us, "for pleasure rather than merely used as a means of getting from point A to point B" (3). The same could be said, to state the obvious, for Muggle trains, planes, and automobiles.

Dangerous Games and Bladder Matters: Kennilworthy's Chapter 2

The humor is rich as Kennilworthy gives us overviews of the predecessors of modern-day Quidditch. The winner of that ancient broom race from one barely pronounceable Swedish town to another was awarded a dragon-shaped silver trophy. This is not just any old dragon trophy, though, but one in the shape of the native species—the Swedish Short-Snout, a creature that is described by Newt Scamander in *Fantastic Beasts* and egg-robbed by Cedric Diggory in *Goblet of Fire* (350-51). As Rowling moves on to Stitchstock, I love her humor with what Mark Twain called "The Awful German Language," especially the "*ist der Gewinner*" phrase (4). Twain does innovative things with *geworden* and other *ge-* words, eventually suggesting that a German book may best be read while held up to a mirror or while the reader stands on his head. The use of the dragon bladder in Stichstock reminds me of early American footballs (inflated pigs' bladders). This pre-Quidditch game ends with someone sticks (or *stichs*) the bladder. Speaking of bladders, the Irish wizards and witches used a goat's gallbladder in Aingingein, and the Herefordshire Swivenhodge players "usually" used a pig's bladder (5-6). Apparently, no animal's bladder was safe from uses as sports equipment in the old days. This may seem strange to those of us with little or no experience with internal organs other than our own, but perhaps not so to folks used to chowing down on haggis.

Notice that Shuntbumps resembles jousting, as Whisp points out, and that Swivenhodge is tennis-like. My favorite among these precursors of Quidditch, though, is Creaothceann, which is surely a bit of a satire on the difficult-to-pronounce Scottish or Welsh names. The cauldron-strapped-to-the-head image is good, the Gaelic poem indicating a one-in-six survival rate for players is disturbing, and "Dent-Head" Macdonald's having "spearheaded" an unsuccessful revival of the game is good wordplay (which is a game Rowling likes to play and one that is considerably safer than Creaothceann). For those of you still trying in your heads to *pronounce* Creaothceann, you might consider Mark Twain's suggestion (in his hilarious essay "Fenimore Cooper's Literary Offenses") for pronouncing a character's name in *Last of the Mohicans*: "Chingachgook (pronounced Chicago, I think)."

The Game Marshes On: Kennilworthy's Chapter 3

Just as the place named Queerditch becomes Quidditch, so other telescoped or slurred words evolved over the centuries: the local *sheriff* was once the *shire reeve*, *bedlam* evolved from London's St. Mary of *Bethlehem* hospital for the insane, and *maudlin* comes from Mary *Magdalene*'s shedding copious tears. Our dear diarist, Gertie Keddle, is probably a pun on *kettle*, which Rowling obviously puns on with Professor Kettleburn's name (*PA* 93). I like the every-day-is-Tuesday silliness. Wimpy might have had some trouble using his "I will gladly pay you Tuesday for a hamburger today" line with Gertie (probably Google time for Wimpy, if you're younger than 90). I find it of interest that Gertie's friend's name is Gwenog, who's a player of the new game herself (7-8). Rowling will later name a star Quidditch player Gwenog Jones, who appears off the page in *Half-Blood Prince* (71, 280) and is a member of the all-female Holyhead Harpies team. Typically, Gertie's "disgust" at watching these "idiots" and "numbskulls" belies the fact that she watches the games and is surely one of the first fans of this queer Queerditch game.

Godwin Kneen, a Yorkshire resident with apparently Scandinavian ancestry, writes his Norwegian cousin about the new game (8-9). This cousin, like countless male Norwegians, is named Olaf. Godwin's wife is Gunhilda, and the surname probably sounds the *K*, as in *Knute* or *Kneazle* (?). Gunhilda, whose name has Old Norse origins meaning *battle maid*, is usually battling the opposition in the air, but is currently battling a case of dragon pox (9). Thus Rowling seems to be readying us for Elphias Doge's boyhood case of the disease in *Deathly Hallows* (16, 20) and Slughorn's reference to Draco's grandfather's death by dragon pox in *Half-Blood Prince* (189-90). Unlike those later cases, Gunhilda's pox was indirectly a pox on someone else—poor Radulf the blacksmith, who subbed for ailing Gunhilda and "got a Blooder in the head" in the game (9). Yet, I assume from the whopping victory of his team, Radulf left the pitch bloody but unbowed.

From *–idget* to *–itch*: Kennilworthy's Chapter 4

Whisp's history now progresses to the arrival of the all-important object that ends a game of Quidditch—first a live bird, the Golden Snidget, then a mechanical device, the Golden Snitch. Kennilworthy's description of the Golden Snidget here is consistent with Newt's account in *Fantastic Beasts*; and, given the "very great speed" and the "remarkable agility" of the Snidget, this creature is reminiscent of a certain bird in the Muggle world as well. In fact, Figure B (11) surely looks like a hummingbird that's been way too long at the feeder; part of the visual humor here is, I believe, the incongruity of an obese hummingbird, which must set world standards for metabolic rates and calorie burning. Rowling has Whisp get in a swat or two at hunters of "these peace-loving little birds in the name of sport" (11). Readers might even be reminded of pheasants, quail, or (speaking of "peace-loving") doves—though not endangered, they're killed for sport by Muggles using "a kind of metal wand that Muggles use to kill each other" (*PA* 38).

Alas, the poor Snidget's plight worsened when that barbarous braggart Barberus Bragge bragged that he would reward with one hundred and fifty Galleons the catcher of the Snidget (11-12). Here we see the origin of the inordinate number of points awarded to the catcher of the Golden Snitch. When I've asked my students, "What *don't* you like about Quidditch," the most common response is, "Catching the Snitch counts too much." What's worse is that if you check out footnote 1 (12), Bragge's one hundred and fifty is comparable to "over a million Galleons today"; so snatching the Snitch is like earning over a million points "today"—that may be flawed logic, but it's still *way* too many points for many of us.

There's a lot to learn from Madam Modesty Rabnott's letter to her sister Prudence (12-13). First, Modesty seems to have the finest penmanship in all of the Rowling books, whether she would admit it or not (and her name may not permit her to). Secondly, Modesty is relieved that she is "only fined ten Galleons" for saving the Snidget—*only*? That would be "only" sixty-six thousand, six-hundred and sixty-seven Galleons "today." Though the fine cannot be paid and she loses her home (but not her Hippogriff, thankfully), at least the Barberus one didn't turn her into a "horned toad," which would be worse than the heavy fine—except, perhaps, for some ardent TCU fans. Thirdly, I appreciate the irony of Modesty's threat that she would not have cast a vote for Chief Barberus Bragge "if I'd had one." If this is a subtle reference to women's suffrage matters, Modesty might be comforted in knowing that Muggle women in Great Britain would have full voting rights in *only* another six-hundred and fifty-nine years. I wonder if Modesty, in addition to Prudence, had a sister named Patience.

A later head of the Wizards' Council, Elfrida Clagg, is the witch who ordered the protected species status for the Golden Snidget. Elfrida's administrative position might indicate British magic folk approved universal suffrage a bit before the Muggles. The bird reservation was named in honor of Madam Modesty Rabnott, so future Barberus types would *rob not* the peace-loving bird for use in sport again. Given the comparative connotations of *hunter* and *seeker*, I think it's noteworthy that in the ancient games the "Hunter" pursued the live bird (13-14); yet when the mechanical Snitch is invented, it is captured by a Seeker. Speaking of which, as Snidgets would give way to Snitches forever after, the inventor who got it *right* was one Bowman Wright from a place we Potter readers know well, Godric's Hollow. Hermione informs Harry (and us) of this in *Deathly Hallows* as she reads from *A History of Magic* (319). *Wright* is from an Old English word meaning *maker*, as in *shipwright*, *wheelwright*, or *playwright* (often, understandably misspelled as *playwrite*). Ironically, and I know this is a bit of a stretch, Bowman put a permanent end to the actions of those bowmen and hunters who used to capture the poor, plump, peace-loving bird for that queer old game.

Those Darn Muggles: Kennilworthy's Chapter 5

Chapter 5 is Kennilworthy Whisp's shortest, which is understandable since it deals with Muggle matters. This is somewhat like the humor behind Harry and his friends finding out how little it takes to pursue a career in Muggle Relations (*OP* 656-57)—*one* O.W.L. (and that's *in* Muggle Studies), along with "*enthusiasm, patience, and a good sense of fun.*" To magic folk, we're just not that interesting (dare I say, not that bright?), and Rowling's narrators often make quick work of us on the pages of her books.

One of Zacharias Mumps's bits of advice to avoid being seen playing Quidditch by Muggles is to "play at night" (15). Now *that* reminds me a bit of a certain night-time secret vampire baseball game; does that ring a *bell* with any of you? Mumps's concerns about Muggles seeing Quidditch being played were surely well founded since eventually the game could not be played within a hundred miles of a Muggle town (16). All these efforts at secrecy culminate in the late seventeenth century in the often-mentioned International Statute of Wizarding Secrecy (16). As has been noted by many Rowling readers, the date of this statute is in variance; for example, it's cited as 1692 here and in *Fantastic Beasts* (xv), but backdated to 1689 in *Deathly Hallows* (318). The later date would link the time period of magic folk's going "invisible" to the notorious Salem witch trials here in America, which works for me; but, frankly, the older I get, remembering *anything* within three years' accuracy is problematic and all bets are off that I will (sorry, Ludo).

Let the Games Begin to Change: Kennilworthy's Chapter 6

Following Kennilworthy Whisp's shortest chapter, dealing with Muggle matters, comes his longest chapter, dealing with the emergence of modern-day Quidditch. Zacharias Mumps, our fourteenth-century historian with the surname of a disease, describes the huge pitch, which is the length of one and two-thirds football fields, and the transition from baskets to goalposts. The old basket scoring method is reminiscent for American basketball fans of Dr. James Naismith's peach baskets in the gymnasium in Springfield, Massachusetts—the beginning of the sport of basketball, a uniquely one-man-invented sport. Harry, you may recall, is reminded of basketball as Oliver Wood first explains the rules of Quidditch to him in *Sorcerer's Stone* (167-68).

In the *Daily Prophet* article "Bring Back Our Baskets!" it seems that the Quidditch players at Barnton were the ultimate "homers"—talk about home-pitch advantage with those contrasting basket sizes. Given all the trouble goblins seemed to have caused in Newt's account of the being/beast classifications, it's interesting here that the contentious goblins get the blame for Quidditch riots (20). That there were "goblin agitators" over a change in Quidditch seems as unlikely as Griphook and Gornuk in the stands at Hogwarts cheering Harry on to catch the Snitch. Those stalwart fans referenced in the *Daily Prophet* article who thought they had seen "the end of the game as we know it" might have Muggle parallels in those who bemoaned the outlawing of spitballs or the flying wedge or an unlimited time to shoot in what we know as baseball, football, and basketball respectively. All of those Muggle games and more have, like Quidditch, evolved but not ended.

Here are a number of other parallels between the most popular sport in the wizarding world and certain Muggle sports:

- § Whisp's account of how Chasers, aided by Gripping Charms, are able to catch, hold, and throw Quaffles with one hand reminds me of basketball players palming the ball.
- § The red color of Quaffles to improve visibility is similar to yellow tennis balls replacing the white balls several years ago. The old white ones, when they'd been used in many a match, often became dimmed and soiled and hard-to-see.
- § The bewitching of Quaffles so they wouldn't fall and bounce so far away after a missed catch reminds me of kids shooting baskets

on the driveway who've let some air out of the ball so their missed shots don't bounce all the way into their neighbor's hydrangeas.

§ Still another parallel to Muggle sports comes when Quidditch added scoring areas in which Keepers were expected, but not required, to stay—making Keepers' roles much like those of hockey and soccer goalies.

§ When Whisp mentions that Beaters, because of "a good deal of physical strength" needed to play this position (25), have generally been wizards rather than witches, I thought of the burliness of an NFL lineman of maybe 320 pounds as contrasted with, say, a wiry cornerback of 180 pounds. Such linemen are not only large but have that "good deal of physical strength"; some can bench press great weights (or maybe could bench press the cornerback, or two or three place kickers).

§ The 1884 rule that "only the Chaser carrying the Quaffle could enter the scoring area" (25) parallels violations in soccer and hockey related to offside (or offsides). Who is attacking to score with (or without) the Quaffle or ball or puck varies with each sport, but there are rules, and there will be penalties if the scoring attempt isn't according to them.

§ To bring in yet another Muggle sport, "stooging" (25) seems at least a first cousin to holding or pass interference in American football. Rowling probably intends some wordplay here since stooging involved "Chasers beating the Keeper up" (26)—as *goons* and *stooges* in gangster lingo often beat people up. As far as I can tell all this has nothing to do with Moe, Larry, and Curly, but as Chasers I suspect they would give any opposing Keeper more than his money's worth. Notice the "freckled-faced six-year-old" kid quoted in the *Daily Prophet* article (26) who is keenly disappointed in the banning of stooging. He says, "Me and me dad like watching them Keepers flattened. I don't want to go to Quidditch no more." Maybe it's all just as well for this kid; now he can stay home and work on his nominative and demonstrative case pronouns and his double negatives.

§ Seekers are, Kennilworthy tells us, of "immense importance" on Quidditch teams (26). They are "most likely to be fouled"; and even though "there is considerable glamour" in being a Seeker, "they are usually the players who receive the worst injuries" (27).

Not only does this describe Harry's experiences as a Seeker quite accurately, it is also quite descriptive of a football quarterback, a baseball pitcher, and, to a lesser degree, a basketball point guard. To elaborate Brutus Scrimgeour's injunction: "Take out the Seeker or quarterback or pitcher or point guard," and you will win the game. Brutus's point may be brutal, but it's often been quite true. In fact, *The Blind Side*, a 2006 book by Michael Lewis and a 2009 film directed by John Lee Hancock, focuses on the importance of the left tackle in American football *to keep someone* from taking out the quarterback and winning the game (not to mention telling a heartwarming story along the way).

§ Notice in Kennilworthy's "Rules," that at no time may a Quidditch player's feet touch the ground during a match—much like a water polo player cannot touch the bottom of the pool at any time.

§ In long matches, Quidditch time outs— or, for you purists, times out—may be as long as two hours. That is one long time out. Can you imagine the great Kareem Abdul-Jabbar in the twilight of his career coming back on the court after a two-hour delay? Frankly, though, we may be only a Super Bowl or two away from a two-hour half-time show.

§ Quidditch penalty shots are similar to those in soccer or ice hockey (27-28), and injured players are *not* substituted for. Thus one team may be short-handed, as in water polo or as in hockey with the old penalty box. Man up or power play, anyone?

§ In a "stop the presses moment," Kennilworthy tells us that a Quidditch game ends with *either* the catching of the Golden Snitch *or* "by mutual consent of the two team Captains" (28). Sure. Right. I can see the Slytherins up by a hundred and ninety and Flint says to Wood, "Let's just end this here; what do you say, Oliver?"

§ The "Fouls" of Quidditch (28-30)—the ten that are described out of the seven hundred that have been committed, that is—are at times much like those in American football. Blagging—grabbing the tail of an opponent's broom "to slow or hinder" (29)—seems like holding. Blurting—"[l]ocking broom handles"—is reminiscent of a face mask penalty. Cobbing—vigorously elbowing an opponent—would be paralleled in perhaps an unnecessary roughness penalty. Cobbing could elicit a ref's whistle in basketball as well and would probably be some kind of foul in many Muggle sports, depending on one's interpretation of "excessive" or even "elbow." Referees tend to frown on elbow action. Snitchnip—a player other than the Seeker "touching or catching the Snitch"—seems comparable to an ineligible receiver penalty in American football.

§ For good measure, other Muggle sports penalties come to mind as well. Wouldn't Flacking be like basketball goal tending? Moreover, before the dunk was legal, today's basketball slam or flush would have been just a Muggle version of Haversacking.

§ Here's one more parallel: those Muggle baseball pitchers who try to do funny things to the ball (whether with saliva or a fingernail file) so the ball will do funny things on the way to home plate would be guilty, in Quidditch terms, of Quaffle-pocking, a foul which involves altering the Quaffle so that it "falls more quickly or zigzags" (30).

I'm impressed by Rowling's intuitive knowledge of how sports rules evolve. As any sports enthusiast or even observer knows, every sport undergoes a slow evolution over time shaped primarily by concerns for and concessions to safety and fairness. I served for several years at Pepperdine University as the Faculty Representative to the NCAA, and I am a life-long sports fan; so I'm not speaking purely theoretically when I say that rules are problematic. Rules are forever bent to the point of breaking, and fouls, if we were to see the whole list, must be in the hundreds. Athletes, whether magic or Muggle, whether in the air, on the court or field or the ice or in the water *compete*. And, somehow apparently non-athlete J.K. Rowling knows or intuits this and, through a purely imaginary sport, convinces us that competition is complicated and must be controlled.

This is why, I suppose, there have almost always been referees. In Rowling's sports world the referees were once "only the bravest witches and wizards" (30). If Quidditch referees can die during a "friendly match," if their own brooms can Portkey them to the Sahara Desert, if they must "watch the antics of fourteen players at once" (31), undergo flying tests and written tests, be fair and impartial and "not jinx or curse offensive players even under pressure," all this would take an extraordinary witch or wizard indeed. By the way, Quidditch referees, like their Muggle counterparts, may find it hardest of all to "prove, through a series of intensive trials" (31) that they will not curse those who so often curse them. Even today, these worthy "zebras" get comments like, "Hey ref, are you *blind*?" And, needless to say, they are not, nor are they deaf.

Before we leave Kennilworthy's longest chapter, let's revisit five little matters. First, we're reminded again that Bludgers were once called "Blooders" (21). Either the old or the new name fits, and both are good puns. The Blooders surely caused many an ancient Quidditch player to become bloody, just as modern players are bludgeoned by the renamed balls. Then or now, you don't want to find yourself blooded, bludgeoned, or bloodied. Secondly, the post-rock Bludgers were made of lead, then iron (22); so I wouldn't be at all surprised if American witches and wizards at some point a few decades ago played Quidditch with stainless steel Bludgers (especially near Pittsburgh). Third, I like the absurdity that the Golden Snitch that was never caught in the 1884 match on the moor might be (23) "still living wild on the moor." A non-living thing *still living* there on the moor? Here's *still* one *more* (sorry) matter: Zacharias Mumps mentions that "a fast Keeper" may leave his own defended goal, go to the other end of the pitch and score a goal, and return to defend his own end (24). With all due respect to Zacharias, he maybe should have described such a Keeper as *really*, *really*, *really* fast; after all, the pitch is five hundred feet long.

Fifth and finally, reread Kennilworthy's comments that argue that it's probably best for all magic folk that the Department of Magical Games and Sports has never made the full list of seven hundred Quidditch fouls "available to the wizarding public" (28). Might this be somewhat parallel in the history of Christianity to the Reformation era when the Church was opposed to the laity having access to scripture? Think of (or research) the roles of Luther, Tyndale, or Wycliffe in making the scriptures available to the masses, and see if you think Rowling is subtly drawing a parallel here. Following the Reformation, everyone was able to read the bible; and the empowered establishment opposed that, not unlike Kennilworthy's reservations that magic folk, knowing about *all* the many fouls of Quidditch "might get ideas" (28). And, as one who *has* read the documents in question, the privileged Kennilworthy concludes that "no public good can come of their publication" (29). Isn't one of the relatively few "lessons of history" that more information is better than less? I wouldn't relish the idea of reading about the other six hundred and ninety Quidditch fouls, but that's what lawyers are for. And yet, I didn't read the entire Old and New Testament of the bible for myself until I was in my early fifties. And what a summer *that* was—to see for myself what all was there *and not*. So, sorry, Kennilworthy, but I'd say if it's been a published, the public should be able to decide for itself the nature of the publication for good or ill. Sure, they might get ideas, but that's happened before, and it's not always a bad thing.

The Alliteration League: Kennilworthy's Chapter 7

Like Rowling's wacky numbers involved in magical monetary denominations, she uses some unlikely numbers in regard to Quidditch as well. We learn that the first World Cup was played in 1473 (39), an odd year unlike the years when the Soccer World Cup or Summer or Winter Olympics are held. Similarly, the number of teams in Britain and Ireland is thirteen, another odd choice of an odd number (and often traditionally unlucky in Rowling's works as well) since six Quidditch matches would be in progress on a given day while one team is idle. We know by now too that Rowling seems to like her alliteration better than the average writer. Strangely, of the thirteen British and Irish teams, only the Puddlemere Uniteds are non-alliterative. Whether this is relevant or not, Puddlemere is the only non-existent location where these Quidditch teams are from; all the rest are real places (with a couple of minor spelling variations). Technically, the Appleby Arrows are a team with assonance in the title, but, overall, this is a veritable Alliteration League. Muggle professional football, baseball, and basketball teams have only a small percentage of alliterations involving city and nickname, in a few cases because the franchise has changed (as with the once alliterative Boston Braves). The Seattle Seahawks, Jacksonville Jaguars, and Tennessee Titans; the Pittsburgh Pirates and Philadelphia Phillies; and the Cleveland Cavaliers, New York Knicks, and the L.A. Lakers could play in Rowling's Quidditch world—as could a few from other areas of Muggle sports, such as the Boston Bruins and Pittsburgh Penguins.

I like to suggest that you consider these matters regarding the thirteen British and Irish Quidditch teams:

- § I thought maybe the Bats of Ballycastle were Bludger-beating-type bats until I read about Barney, the fruit bat who's batty over Butterbeer (32-33). The Muggle counterpart might be Tony the Tiger touting the grrrreatness of Frosted Flakes.
- § In honor of the most famous Caerphilly Catapult in history, the Dangerous Dai Commemorative Medal is given to the League player "who has taken the most exciting and foolhardy risks during a game" (33). I wonder if the word "commemorative" refers to Dai or to the (posthumous?) winner of that year's award. How many times might *that* award have been accepted by the surviving spouse?

§ Alas, every sport has its Chudley Cannons (33-34), holders of "longest-period-since-last-a-champion" position. Chicago Cubs fans can appreciate the Cannons' revised motto—from "We shall conquer" to ". . . hope for the best"— and might caution the Cannons not to allow Steve Bartman anywhere near the pitch during a crucial Quidditch match (Google time?). Reading about the orange-clad Cannons reminds me of Ron's orange décor in his room (*CS* 40) and of Dumbledore's graveyard humor about these perennial Quidditch cellar dwellers—that he will die just as surely as the Cannons will finish last in the league (*DH* 683).

§ Those famous Falmouth Falcon beaters, Kevin and Karl Broadmoor, may or may not be twins, but they surely remind me of Fred and George. We Americans pronounce this bird nickname differently than the British do. Atlanta NFL fans especially need to remember that the first syllable of Falmouth's Quidditch team nickname rimes with *pall*, not *pal*.

§ Unique in Quidditch is the always all-female Holyhead Harpies team. The legendary match Whisp describes here (34-35) took place between the Harpies and the Heidelberg Harriers. I've spent a good deal of time in Heidelberg, and I think I can say with some certainty that this Quidditch team is not aptly named. Heidelberg is one of the least harried haunts in all of Europe; it would be like an American team named the Pleasantville Harriers. Also, I like the assumption on Harrier Rudolf Brand's part that such a worthy opponent as Gwendolyn Morgan would be worthy (and would want) to be his wife. The harpies of old often taloned those who harried them; *this* Quidditch-playing Harpy concussed a Harrier who would have married her. Considering the Harpies that Kennilworthy names—Glynnis Griffiths and Gwendolyn Morgan—along with future Harpy Gwenog Jones, I wonder if a witch has to have a first name beginning with *G* in order to *be* a Harpy.

§ The Kenmare Kestrels are Seamus Finnigan's favorite team for obvious Irish reasons. By the way, the great Irish poet Gerard Manley Hopkins's poem "The Windhover" describes the beauty of a kestrel's flight.

§ The Montrose Magpies are the Dominant Ones—once again, here there are parallels with Muggle sports. The Magpies are the

New York Yankees of Quidditch, or, from earlier times and other sports, the Boston Celtics or Dallas Cowboys. I like the fact that Whisp notes that the Magpies "have fans across the globe" (35), thus illustrating the bandwagon or fair-weather-fan effect. This is what Ron practically accuses Cho of with regard to her support of the Tutshill Tornados, you may recall (*OP* 230). Magpie Eunice Murray illustrates the confidence (or arrogance) of the perennial winner. Eunice's declaring Snitch-catching to be "too easy" (35) is reminiscent of Babe Ruth's alleged pointing to the fence before homering over it or of Joe Namath's famous guarantee of a Super Bowl win. Magpie Hamish MacFarlan's career after Quidditch, becoming Head of the Department of Magical Games and Sports (35-36), parallels that of a Ludo we know. Coincidentally, these Yankees of Quidditch wear, as Magpies should, black and white (sans, I assume, pin stripes).

§ The Pride of Portree and Puddlemere United teams are a couple of those kind of weirdly nicknamed teams like the Miami Heat, Orlando Magic, or Tampa Bay Lightning. When a fan can't say *a* or *an* in front of his or her favorite team, then the nickname doesn't seem to work as well. Compare, "The ball is stolen by a Laker" to "The ball is stolen by a Heat." Quidditch fans of these two teams can't yell to a streaking Seeker, "Go, you Pride" or lament that the foul was called "on a United" as naturally as they can cheer for a racing Arrow Chaser or boo a cobbing Falcon. This is a rhetorical disadvantage of major proportions.

§ I find it of interest that Kennilworthy mentions the connection between former Pride captain Catriona McCormack and The Weird Sisters (36), taking us back to the Yule Ball of *Goblet of Fire*. Similarly, in the Puddlemere passage, Whisp refers to Celestina Warbeck (Molly's favorite singer and Fleur's *not*), whom we'll hear much more from (too much for Fleur) in *Half-Blood Prince* (330-33). Puddlemere is the "oldest team in the League" (36), so maybe *that* explains their unique non-alliterative nickname; they didn't know alliterative names would be the norm. (Like the first professional baseball team, the Cincinnati Red Stockings, perhaps didn't realize that naming yourselves after hosiery would only spread to Boston and Chicago.) If you're thinking that maybe alliteration hadn't been invented in 1163, forget that; they're all over the place in *Beowulf*. In fact, maybe the *Beowulf* poet used them all up for a while. Back to the attire of a United (note the awkwardness of that phrase), I'm not at all sure why the robe is adorned with "two crossed golden bulrushes" (36). Golden bulrushes?—that makes me wonder if there's a drawing of baby Moses hidden behind them. One minor mention of this Quidditch team is upcoming in Rowling's Book 7 of the Potter series. In *Deathly Hallows* Molly asks Harry if a stray sock with those golden bulrushes on it belongs to him (87-88). Harry reminds Molly that he is not a Puddlemere fan, though someone at the Burrow might be a United fan—and a one-socked one at that.

§ Tutshill Tornados Seeker Roderick Plumpton once caught a Snitch with tornadic speed (37); he might agree with Eunice "too easy" Murray that Snitch catching should be harder. More about Plumpton's "catch" later. Rowling lived for a time in Tutshill as a child, incidentally. The Wigtown Wanderers wear blood-covered robes with a meat cleaver emblem; and the Wimbourne Wasps once bent the rules a bit. These last two *W* team descriptions are especially rich in humor. The Parkin siblings, the original fifteenth-century Wanderers, were aided by their sideline supporter father, butcher Walter Parkin, who caused "intimidation" in opponents simply by holding "a wand in one hand and a meat cleaver in the other" (37). Now, *that's* intimidation; if Walter had known about *Sectumsempra* he could have been out for the opponent's blood (literally) with either hand. Finally, don't you wonder if the Wimbourne Wasps wrought a little havoc and bent a few rules when they introduced their Arrow opponents to the wasps' stings? I like especially the fact that the team "adopted the wasp as their lucky emblem" (38) after this incident. *Lucky*? It wasn't as if fans held jars of buzzing wasps on the sidelines for luck; a Beater batted stinging wasps at his opponent and put the poor stung Seeker *on* the sidelines. That's some example of the old cliché "Make your own luck," isn't it? The most famous former Wasp in Rowling's books is Ludo Bagman. Now retired, he's still a fan of the Wasps—"also known as 'Stingers'" (38), and he likes to wear his old, now too-tight Quidditch attire.

The Wide World of Quidditch: Kennilworthy's Chapter 8

In his account of how Quidditch spread from Britain to the continent and beyond, Whisp gives us a Norwegian poet's early fifteenth-century reference to the game in a bit of doggerel (39). The poet's name is Ingolfr the Iambic, which is doubly problematic because it would seem doubtful that he was much of a golfer in his day (and in his climate), and the Iambic poet writes his quatrain primarily in anapestic, not iambic, poetic feet. In non-academic terms, that is to say his verse is not ta-DUM, ta-DUM, ta-DUM; instead it's ta-ta-DUM, ta-ta-DUM, ta-ta-DUM, two unaccented syllables before the accented one. Maybe "Nongolfr the Anapestic" would be a more accurate name for the poet, though considerably less humorous.

The other Quidditch allusion in literature which Whisp cites is found in the work of one of Ingolfr's contemporaries, a French playwright named Malecrit (39). This is *recherché* humor indeed. One whose name, from Latin roots, suggests *bad critic* wrote a play called, in English, "Alas, I've Transfigured My Feet," in which a character has to play Keeper and stop Quaffles and thus cannot help carry a cow or, perhaps, given the title of Malecrit's play, help transfigure feet. By the way, do you think Rowling wants us to make a connection between the title of Malecrit's play and Ingolfr's iambics transfigured into anapestic feet? Or is that a stretch of *way* too many feet?

The first Quidditch World Cup was the proverbial doozey, wasn't it? There were wicked transfigurations, an attempted decapitation, and, predictably, Transylvanian tricks with vampires (bats, that is). Whisp tells us that the European Cup began in 1652 (40) and is played every three years, which means that most European champions will *not* advance to compete in that year's world cup. Have you considered how infrequently the Quidditch European and World tournaments would coincide with one having begun in an even year and happening at three-year intervals and the other having begun in an odd year and occurring every four years? It's like being back in Algebra I and facing those word problems: "If two planes left Kansas City, one at 3:30 and the other at 5:00, the second plane traveling at 1.5 X the speed of the other . . . ." Remember those? Here's one thing that may be a problem with Rowling's numbers: since the World Cup of 1994 (*Goblet of Fire* time) is 521 years after the first one of 1473 and the Cup "has since been held every four years" (40), wouldn't there have to have been one span of three or of five years in there somewhere, since 521 is not evenly divisible by four? Maybe one of those flights out of Kansas City got fogged in and the Cup was canceled that year.

There's a nice comic touch with regard to each of the remaining European teams. The Vratsa Vultures, "pioneers of the long goal" and shooting from great distances (40), are comparable to U.S. football teams known for their passing game, especially the long bombs, or basketball teams that live and die by the three pointer. The French team is "famed for their flamboyant play" and their "shocking-pink robes" (40). I would say that "flamboyant," "play," and "shocking" grow out of stereotypes of things that go on small-time in Quiberon, and big-time in Paris. As I said in my last section, it seems ironic that pastoral Heidelbergers are "fiercer than a dragon and twice as clever" and even more ironic that the team from peaceful Luxembourg is known as the Bombers, "celebrated for their offensive strategies and always among the top goal-scorers" (41). I suspect Rowling has encoded some kind of joke in the wee bit she says about the Quidditch team from Portugal since she once lived there, but I have no idea what it might be. Braga is the oldest city in Portugal, which is something for Bragans to brag about, but doesn't seem relevant to the Broomfleet seven. This is another of those problematic nicknames too: "The Quaffle's been intercepted by a Broomfleet" or "Penalty to the Broomfleets." Finally among the European teams, the brief comments about the Grodzisk Goblins take us back to the Wronski Feint as executed to perfection by Viktor Krum in *Goblet of Fire* and forward to the discussion of the maneuver at the conclusion of *Quidditch Through the Ages*.

Rowling's humor is rich as she has Kennilworthy take us around the rest of the world Quidditch-wise. The European herbologists who introduced the game to New Zealand "on an expedition there to research magical plants and fungi" (41) is perhaps a veiled reference to Captain Cook's landing at Australia's Botany Bay and introducing much more than just a game to the aborigines. I appreciate the macaw-like colors of the New Zealand Macaws team, as well as their phoenix mascot "Sparky"—a little less formal and pluckier (sorry) a name for a phoenix than Fawkes. The only question, and meaning no disrespect to Sparky, is if you're the Macaws, why do you have a phoenix mascot? Similarly, an old friend of mine went to a high school in West Virginia whose nickname was the Blue Devils, but whose colors were purple and gold. Go figure.

It's good to know that alliteration is international, in Rowling's world anyway. Throughout Europe, Australia, and Africa, the teams, like those in Britain and Ireland, share the initial consonant sounds. The Vratsa Vultures, Quiberon Quafflepunchers, Heidelberg Harriers, Bigonville

Bombers, Braga Broomfleet, Grodzisk Goblins, Moutohora Macaws, Thundelarra Thunderers, Woollongong Warriors, Patonga Proudsticks, Tchamba (silent *T*) Charmers, Gimbi Giant-Slayers, and Sumbawanga Sunrays collectively illustrate alliteration without borders. As with the British and Irish locations of teams, all of the above, with the exception of Thundelarra, are real place names in the various countries (with one variation of spelling—Patong*o*, Uganda). Thundelarra is the name of an exploration company in Perth, but I'm glad Rowling included it. In this word I can hear *thunder*, *Thumbelina*, *Cinderella*, and *Toora, Loora, Loora*. On a more serious note (and almost all notes are more serious than my last one), I wonder if Rowling wasn't up to something with her cryptic and succinct comments about some of the African teams. The fact that Quidditch is "becoming increasingly popular throughout the African continent" (42) sounds somewhat like saying the African nations are becoming increasingly like industrialized nations, more Europeanized. "Uganda in particular" is an "emerging" nation which held its own in a match with a British team "to the astonishment of most of the Quidditch-playing world" (42-43). Why are the players from Togo "masters of the reverse pass"; and why does the team from Tanzania delight fans "across the world" with "formation looping" (43)? I have no answers to these questions, which are themselves questionable even to ask. But after reading 4100 pages of innocent or seemingly irrelevant comments Rowling makes in the Potter books, she just makes me wonder about the smallest things sometimes.

Now, at long last, Kennilworthy Whisp comes to the Quidditch teams of North America. I suspect an American historian specializing in the pre-national period could find some significance in Rowling's first paragraph of the "North America" section. After all, more than Quidditch "reached the North American continent in the early seventeenth century"; and many "wizard settlers," as well as many Muggles I'm sure, "hoped to find less prejudice in the New World" (43). The Canadian teams—the Moose Jaw Meteorites, Haileybury Hammers, and Stonewall Stormers—are all three alliterative, of course, and all three are from real towns in Saskatchewan, Ontario, and Manitoba respectively. Kennilworthy next concentrates matters in the U.S., especially on Quodpot, an explosive and more flamboyant version of Quidditch. Rowling's subtle satire here may be directed at the U.S.'s tendency to make things bigger, longer, more exciting, and more explosive—even at the expense of it all exploding in our faces. Think of Rugby with its scrums transformed into American football with its West Coast spread offenses; think of a quiet cricket match compared to the baseball World Series. More is better in the U.S. (or, in Abraham Peasegood's case even before it *was* the U.S.), so the simple Quaffle-turned-Quod explodes, the seven-member team becomes eleven (as in American football), and, overall, it's *quid pro quod*. Two more things: Quodpot involves getting the quod in the pot. This is how Americans tend to name sports; consider the names of our major sports and what's involved with playing them—baseball, football, and basketball. Not complicated, is it? Secondly, there's an Arnold Peasegood mentioned (barely) in *Goblet of Fire* (86). Maybe his ancestors played Quodpot, which is better than your ancestors being crackpots I guess.

Back to the main *Q* game now: Kennilworthy tells us that Quidditch "is gaining popularity in the United States" (45)—which, sorry U.S. soccer fans, sounds like some observations we've heard about *that* imported sport for about fifty years now. The Texas team could have been nicely and neatly alliterative if Rowling had named them the Sweetwater Stars. But in the Lone Star State everyone is a star, hence "All-Stars," but I would still count the Sweetwater All-Stars, maybe, as a delayed alliteration. As for Sweetwater, it is the "Wind Turbine Capital of Texas" (that could be good for a future bar bet), it has a population of just under 12,000, and the town has an annual rattlesnake round-up (the second weekend of March). If you speak Parseltongue, you might bring home the blue ribbon at that sweet Sweetwater event. How does Rowling come up with the Quidditch cities? The only other U.S. team Kennilworthy mentions plays in Fitchburg, Massachusetts. Fitchburg is more than three times the size of Sweetwater, Texas, approaching 40,000 residents, and the Fitchburg Finches Quidditch team plays there. The town was actually first settled by a man named John Fitch, not by a bird called a finch, but there's no stopping Rowling and her creation of alliterations (*you* try alliterating with *Fitch* and see how little fits). The Finches' captain is interestingly named Maximus Brankovitch III, a name with Latin, Anglo, and Russian echoes, but overall a capitalistic sounding name since *max* and *bank* are embedded there.

Two other parts of the world end Kennilworthy's chapter: South America and Asia. Since Quidditch came to South America as European wizards went there on business involving the Peruvian Vipertooth dragon, we have a linkage between *Quidditch Through the Ages* and *Fantastic Beasts and Where to Find Them*. Finally, notice how the opening paragraph of the "Asia" section (46) almost echoes Rudyard Kipling's famous line, "East is East, and West is West, and never the twain shall meet." Rowling's version might be, "Carpets are carpets, and brooms are brooms, and Quidditch is played on a broom." The exception to relative indifference to Quidditch in Asia is Japan, which parallels that country's extraordinary embracing of baseball. Rowling indulges in a bit of edgy humor with the "setting fire to their brooms in case of defeat" line (46) being an all-too-close reminder of kamikaze or hara-kiri. I don't know about you, but I'm travel weary, so it's back to Britain for the research and development and marketing and sales of the all-important racing brooms without which a Quidditch team couldn't even get off the ground.

Recent Sticky Business:
Kennilworthy's Chapter 9:

The old brooms were crude, uncomfortable, and not too imaginatively named. The Oakshaft 79 (a shaft of oak, I presume) was created in 1879 by Elias Grimstone (47). I'll bet that inventor Elias, like inventor Eli Whitney, grimly kept his nose to the grindstone when he was about the business of developing the better broom. You need only compare figure A in *Quidditch Through the Ages* (3) with Figure F (48) to appreciate the cushioning work wrought by Smethwyck, not to mention a number of unnamed or unknown wizards or witches who seemed to "get it" with regard to streamlining and aerodynamics. Parallels between the history of the broom industry and the Muggle automobile industry permeate Kennilworthy's chapter. The cushioning accomplished by Smethwyck made brooms "more comfortable than ever before" (47)—as did the development of shock absorbers, power steering, and power brakes in automobiles. Even the vocabularies are similar, as Rowling writes of the Cleansweep's "cornering" or the Comet's "braking" (49). The witch who first crossed the Atlantic on a broom in 1935, Jocunda Sykes, did so on an Oakshaft. I'll bet she was jocund after she pulled off that long flight. In the Muggle world, Charles Lindberg's transatlantic flight came in 1927. I wonder if magic folk sang "Lucky Jocunda" or danced to the Jocunda Hop eight years later.

More Muggle parallels and good humor are in the next parts of Kennilworthy's chapter. Rowling the wordsmith is still at it with the Moontrimmer, a broom that can achieve great altitudes—trimming the moon as it were. And then there's the super-fast Silver Arrow which, like a you-know-what shot into the air, causes Madam Hooch to remember it fondly when she encounters Harry's state-of-the-art Firebolt in *Prisoner of Azkaban* (254). The details of the Cleansweep's early days seem similar to Henry Ford's assembly lines and mass production of Model T's and Model A's. The Cleansweep was "produced in numbers never seen before," and all the Quidditch players had one "within a year" (49). Next came the Comets beginning with the Comet 140, the number of the first tested success, which reminds me of why Salvarsan 606 was numbered 606 (Google at your own risk). The "Cleansweep-Comet competition" (50) calls to mind the Ford-General Motors competition during the glory days of American automobile industry preeminence. Do you think there's any significance in Rowling's one-paragraph dismissal of the Tenderblast and the Swiftstick, manufactured by Ellerby and Spudmore, a "Black Forest company"? These manufacturers with British names began their business in 1940 in Germany. Are there any political implications there? I'm not sure, but one of those brooms made in the Black Forest "never achieved" the speeds of Comets and Cleansweeps, and the other was "never used" in Quidditch. Next, Rowling has Kennilworthy recall the old Shooting Star brooms (50). They were both cheap and (increasingly with age) slow. So by the time Ron is riding his (at least) fourteen-year-old, third-class-carriage of a broom in *Chamber of Secrets*, no wonder butterflies pass him by (46). The Universal Brooms Ltd. firm only lasted twenty-three years and "went out of business in 1978" (50). Are there any old Edsel owners out there who feel the pain of the Shooting Star folk; and, come to think of it, wouldn't Arthur Weasley, if born a Muggle American, have owned an Edsel? I can hear him now: "No, Molly, I know it's not a Plymouth or a Chevy or even a Nash, but there you are."

Finally, the wizarding world enters into the world of the Nimbus. With unprecedented turning ability, un-thought of speeds, unparalleled handling and unquestioned reliability, the Nimbus was the gold standard. Should we say the Rolls Royce of brooms? And, anticlimactically, Kennilworthy reminds readers that the pseudo-Nimbus, the pale imitation of a classic, was a Twigger, made by the aptly named Flyte and Barker, who like a circus *barker*, surely claimed more than was delivered by the faulty *flights* of this broom supposedly superior to the then nonpareil Nimbus. Those less-than-savvy witches and wizards who bought the Twigger 90, who had "more Galleons than sense," (51), were probably wowed by the bangs and whistles, in this case the Warning Whistle and the Self-Straightening Brush. Obviously, as Kennilworthy wrote, he didn't know of brooms to come, of developments and inventions after 1990. He is lavish in his praise of the Nimbus, the then state-of-the-art racing broom. The advent of the Nimbus brooms "galvanised" the broom world (50), and nothing like a Nimbus "had ever been seen before" (51). I can imagine Whisp wondering what could possibly exceed the qualities of a Nimbus. The answer will come like a *firebolt* from heaven in a few years; and "the broom world," like so many other worlds within our world, will be "galvanised" again and again as we all continue to see one more wonder than we've ever seen before. And, as the late Kurt Vonnegut was fond of saying, "So it goes."

Putting the Moves On: Kennilworthy's Chapter 10:

What Kennilworthy Whisp says about the feeling of being "short-changed" at a Quidditch match that ends too soon with a quick Quidditch Golden Snitch snatch (52) brings to mind the uniqueness of how Rowling ends her imaginary sport. Whether there are clocks counting down (as in American football) or up (as in the rest of the world's football), whether there are innings or quarters or halves or periods, virtually all Muggle sports will last a good while. Sure, if it's 42-0 at the end of the first quarter of a football game, or 63-19 at the half of a college basketball game, we all kind of know how things will end up, and it's all basically over. Or, if a baseball team is down three games to none in a championship series, we *know* they'll never come back, right Boston Red Sox fans? But, seriously, think of a game that could end in three-and-one-half *seconds*. Surely the witches and wizards who paid their Galleons for those prized nose-bleed seats in the sky that day Roderick Plumpton got the Snitch would have felt robbed indeed. And just to add to the craziness that Rowling created with Quidditch, this potentially seconds-long game can also last for days, weeks, or months—or, theoretically, forever (remember that Snitch still living on Bodmin Moor since 1884?).

Now, here are some observations on Whisp's accounts of some famous Quidditch moves and maneuvers:

§ The Bludger Backbeat is, like a tennis player's powerful backhand, a powerful weapon indeed.

§ The Dopplebeater Defence is an example of two hands (not heads) are better than one. Moreover, Dopplebeater reminds me of *doppelganger*—the German word meaning a *double goer* and applied in English usages as a twin, a look-alike, or an alter ego. In this Quidditch case, the doppel gangs up on the opponent and sends the Bludger flying at twin speed. Speaking of twins, wouldn't you figure that Fred and George tried this move at least a time or two?

§ The Double Eight Loop reminds me, by way of contrast, of some of Keeper Ron's early worst efforts when he's hanging around the side of the far goal, which would mean, maybe, Ron is doing one-half of one-half of a *single* eight loop. Sorry, Ron, but you *were* pretty bad at times, mate.

§ The Hawkshead Attacking Formation sounds like the old long-since-outlawed flying wedge formation on kick-off returns in the early days of American football, first used by Harvard against Yale, those two perennial football powers of long ago. It was banned after only a couple of seasons when officials figured that every time it might be employed, there will be blood. Hawkshead Chasers using the Attacking Formation would have to make sure the Chaser with the Quaffle is at the point of the arrowhead; that would be the proper Hawkshead *staging* to avoid *stooging*.

§ Parkin's Pincer doesn't sound that dangerous, but bear in mind that the inventors of this move had the meat-cleaver-bearing father as back up and wingman down on the ground. And, since Parkin's Pincer is still another alliteration, notice that out of Rowling's thirteen Quidditch moves described in this final chapter, seven are alliterative, including all the *P* ones. She just can't seem to stop herself.

§ So, was the all-time-record-breaking-three-and-one-half-second Snitch catch the world's first and only successful execution of the Plumpton Pass? Or, was it an accident? To add to the familiar old line, I can imagine Plumpton saying, "Nothing up my sleeve—whoops, there *is* something up my sleeve, the Snitch, the game winner." If this accident-over-hero theory is too much for you to swallow, recall Harry's first Snitch capture: an accident *he* swallowed. Here's another way to consider the fastest Snitching in Quidditch history: in claiming this as an international Quidditch move, did Plumpton have something up his sleeve literally or figuratively?

§ The Porskoff Ploy seems comparable in U.S. football to a pitch out or to any option play. Pinpoint timing and deftness would be, as Kennilworthy says, "of the essence." The Irish team successfully uses the maneuver at the World Cup in *Goblet of Fire* (106-07). I am assuming Petrova Porskoff is a woman, since Petrova is almost always a woman's first name. If so, this would be the only one of the thirteen Quidditch moves invented by a witch.

§ The Reverse Pass, obviously the Quidditch version of the "no-look pass," is what it is—whether executed in the air, on the court, on the field, on the ice, or in the pool; and "[a]ccuracy is difficult" indeed (53). Just ask anyone who has tried this move and has been intercepted or has fumbled, anyone who has thrown the ball over the right shoulder when his or her teammate was behind the left.

§ Though the Sloth Grip Roll and the Starfish and Stick maneuvers may be insulting to and exploitative of stereotypical images of two- (or three-) towed sloths and of regenerative members of the Asteroidea order, I doubt that any members of those species of, as Newt would say, fantastic beasts would have a problem with Kennilworthy Whisp. Yet, you never know how many creatures have their Muggle human champions out there somewhere or, maybe I should say, somewhere out there. Kennilworthy had better hope that some sloth-rights group or a starfish lobby isn't after his hide. You might recall that during Angelina Johnson's very frustrating year as Gryffindor's Quidditch captain, she plans to practice "a new move called the Sloth Grip Roll" (*OP* 351). It is indeed a new Quidditch move since Rowling had just invented it for *Quidditch Through the Ages*. That the Starfish Without Stick "should never be attempted" is obvious even without Figure G (54). The Starfish *Without* Stick indeed; Rowling is doing her *shtick* about starfish and sticks.

§ I'd be really careful about being actually hit by the fake punch known as the Transylvanian Tackle since it might draw blood and *then* where would I be among the vampire bats faithful? Victim of a (I hope not) sucker punch?

§ Does Rowling intend a boomerang reference in the Woollongong Shimmy—given the sound-alike link between *boomerang* and *Woollongong*? I guess not since the move seems more about zigzagging than boomeranging. So it looks like that idea will return to me and whack me in the back of the head.

§ The last of Rowling's Quidditch maneuvers is the Wronski Feint. As I say in *Repotting Harry Potter*, there may be a pun intended in Wronski and *wrong sky* feint, but suffice it to say here, in ending our return to *Qudditch Through the Ages*, no wonder Rowling so loves feints and fakes and misdirections in Quidditch. For 4100 pages of Harry's story, she has been "pretending to have seen the Snitch far below," ([55]) only to have it soaring, all along, high above our heads.

The last page of Kennilworthy Whisp's book is, I believe, both straightforward and parody—both a tribute and a mock-tribute to the game, or subject, at hand (56). Toast-like, Rowling has a wistful Whisp wish that the game of Quidditch may long continue, evolve, and be enjoyed by all. Much like Newt Scamander affirms that magizoology matters, and much like we all wish our hobbies, our avocations, and our passions will endure and prevail and be beloved by all, Kennilworthy, quite understandably, wishes we could all thrill to the "poetry and power of Quidditch." And that makes me wish that you will continue to thrill to your favorite "sport." It may not be Quidditch or basketball, football, baseball, soccer, hockey, water polo, hurling, or curling or billiards or chess. In fact, it may not be a sport at all. But, whatever it is that moves us most deeply, *that's* what takes us away from the ground and lifts us into the sky. And whatever it is that elevates our pulses, gives us goose bumps, and stands our hair on ends, *that*, as Kennilworthy says, is the "most glorious of sports!" That's *our* own "poetry and power"; and isn't it almost magic when we find *that* game to play? Rowling's little book seems to ask between the lines, "What's your Quidditch?" That is to say, based on the Latin for *quid*, what's your *this*—your *this*-itch? What is your passion, your poetry, your power? Although the *quid*, the *this*, has been, in one sense, the same through the ages, it's also unique to every person, magic and Muggle alike. Quidditch anyone?

Chapter 4: A Return to Beedle the Bard

Worlds Collide: Rowling Readies Us for the Tales

In J. K. Rowling's *The Tales of Beedle the Bard*, magic and Muggle matters come together as we have Hermione the translator, Dumbledore the commentator, and Rowling the annotator and illustrator all contributing to the volume. Speaking of the latter, I really appreciate Rowling's drawing (prior to the table of contents) which nicely previews all five tales to come—much more impressively so than Mary GrandPré's cover illustration does in my view. Moreover, each time Rowling footnotes one of Dumbledore's points, or when she writes on McGonagall's behest that the professor has never abused her Animagus powers (81, footnote 2), she is a veritable intermediary between magic and Muggle worlds.

Rowling's introduction gives us Beedle's background and an overview of magical and Muggle fairy tales. As I have suggested in *Repotting Harry Potter* (293), "Beedle the Bard" may suggest the Beatles, those twentieth-century bards of song, as well as the You-Know-Who of Avon. Recall too that a *beadle* is a town official (as in the bad beadle in *Sweeney Todd*); this homonym for Beedle is a later spelling of a Middle English word, *bedel*, which meant *messenger*, which fits nicely for the teller of Rowling's tales. In addition, though there's no connection with our bard, Rowling does a good deal with beetles (the bugs) in the Potter books—think of an annoying reporter's Animagus form and of a gentle giant's eye color. Rowling tells us that little is known about Beedle, that he lived in the 1400s, was a native of Yorkshire, and that, based on the likeness in "the only surviving woodcut" of him, he had a "luxuriant" beard" (ix). All of the above, incidentally, is a bit reminiscent of a Muggle bard, Geoffrey Chaucer, who lived and wrote his tales in the fourteenth century. There are many gaps in his biography and few likenesses of him, but in all portraits Chaucer is bearded though, beardless as I am, I'm not quite sure how to judge the "luxuriant" nature of facial hair.

Although Rowling goes into little detail in her introduction regarding the role that fairy tales play in the lives of magic folk and Muggles, you may find it of interest that Bruno Bettleheim pursues this subject extensively in his 1976 classic study *The Uses of Enchantment: The Meaning and Importance of Fairy Tales*. Rowling does mention that "virtue is usually rewarded, and wickedness punished" in such tales (vii). The "obvious difference" between magic and Muggle fairy tales, according to Rowling, is that in the latter "magic tends to lie at the root of the hero's or heroine's troubles" (vii-viii). An obvious exception would be the story of a young woman whose name Ron thinks sounds like a disease, Cinderella. I appreciate especially Rowling's point too that even though characters in magical fairy tales can themselves perform magic, they still encounter problems, that "magic causes as much trouble as it cures" (viii). This generalization is descriptive of much of what happens in the Potter books—most fundamentally in the magic of Lord Voldemort and of Harry respectively. One further contrast Rowling notes is that witches in Beedle's tales often are proactive and take matters into their own hands, as opposed to young women in Muggle tales "taking a prolonged nap or waiting for someone to return a lost shoe" (ix). (Offense intended for Aurora and Cinderella.) With regard to an overview of the tales to come, Rowling writes that those who triumph in these stories "are not those with the most powerful magic, but rather those who demonstrate the most kindness, common sense, and ingenuity" (x). This, of course, could be said of all of Rowling's heroes and heroines in the Potter books, her own epic fairy tale.

Rowling once again blends magic and Muggle matters in referencing the cooperation of Headmaster McGonagall in the printing of Dumbledore's commentaries, in her reference to Hermione Granger's new translation, and in her comments that she is sure Dumbledore would be a "delighted" supporter of the Children's High Level Group (xi-xii). Speaking of Dumbledore, Rowling tells us that the headmaster wrote his Beedle commentaries about eighteen months before his death (xii-xiii). This would be late 1995 or early 1996 (since Dumbledore died in June, 1997) or during the dark days of the events of *Order of the Phoenix*. Knowing Dumbledore as we Potter readers do, it seems not at all surprising that he would be thinking about the meaning of fairy tales during those dark days. Rowling mentions the incompleteness of Dumbledore's remarks on the final Beedle story, "The Tale of the Three Brothers," and speculates that what the headmaster told his "favorite and most famous pupil" about truth may explain the "omission" of the explicit meaning of the tale. That truth is, in Dumby's words, "a beautiful and terrible thing, and should therefore be treated with great caution" (*SS* 298) is quoted here and perhaps suggests that innuendo and symbolism communicate truths more effectively and deeply than explicitness and didacticism. Thus Dumbledore and Harry and Muggle readers of both *Deathly Hallows* and *The Tales of Beedle the Bard* must resist the temptations of the Hallows and pursue our own Horcruxes, lest we pay "so terrible a price" (xiv) as the wise headmaster who foolishly placed a ring on his finger.

I would like to end this discussion of the introduction to Beedle's tales with a brief note of my own on Rowling's "A Note on the Footnotes" (xiv). How's that for absurdity—a note on a note about footnotes? One last time before we begin the first tale, Rowling the Muggle editor reminds us that she will explain Dumbledore the wizard commentator's terms in annotations that follow by way of "clarification for Muggle readers"—so worlds once again come together. I think Rowling has nicely prepared our *heads* for these *tales* (sorry); so are you ready to Beedle?

Rowling's Physician in Spite of Himself: Afterthoughts on "The Wizard and the Hopping Pot"

How do fairy tales traditionally begin? "Once upon a time . . . ," right? Not surprisingly, Beedle, like the Brothers Grimm and countless others, begins this tale, as well as "The Warlock's Hairy Heart" and "The Tale of the Three Brothers," with a reasonable facsimile of the famous opening phrase (1, 43, 87): "There was once . . ." (1). The "kindly old wizard" of Beedle's first tale was a helpful friend to "his neighbors" (1). From the problems these neighbors encounter, along with their inability to solve them, most readers surely will conclude that those in need are Muggles. In fact, Dumbledore tells us so in his commentary, referring to them as the wizard's "non-magical neighbors" (11). Thus the old wizard's actions, like Arthur Weasley's interests and actions and like Kingsley Shacklebolt's remarks on the Potterwatch radio broadcast in *Deathly Hallows*, indicate clearly that he is, to use the problematic term, a Muggle lover. His son clearly is not; he is "of a very different disposition to his gentle father" (2). And how universal is *that* line? A Muggle-friendly father has a Muggle-hating son, or at least a trouble-hating son. Because troubled folks seek his help—from the "brat's warts" (I like the sound of that; it reminds me of *bratwurst*) to the lost donkey, to the ill child. To the son, like Lucius Malfoy and countless others, a non-magical person is "worthless" (2).

So comes refusal-to-help incident number one, the sprouting of the brass foot, and the *clang, clang, clang* not of the trolley, but of the cooking pot (5). By the way, doesn't the foot in Mary GrandPré's cover art look pretty flesh-and-blood, rather than brassy? And where are the warts? In Beedle's tale only three villagers make their needs known to the wizard, but what happens to the pot indicates others' needs as well—it is "spewing out bad cheese and sour milk and a plague of hungry slugs" (7). Remember Ron's wand woes, slug fans? Needless to say, the wizard could not eat or sleep, and who could? If there's one thing I hate it's a hopping, warty, one-brass-footed, banging, braying, groaning, slopping, choking, retching, crying, whining, spewing cauldron. But "the pot refused to leave" (7)—much like dilemmas and problems don't just go away, and much like the poor, which we have with us always. Rowling's drawing of the pursuing pot is noteworthy, since her rendering of the foot also looks more flexible than immovable brass; but the real question is, "What's that beetle (?) doing coming out of the cauldron?" (8).

Next in the tale comes the transition, transformation, or conversion—whichever shoe fits—as the wizard says, "Bring me all your problems, all your troubles, and your woes!" (8). This line echoes Jesus' words "Come to me, all you who are weary and burdened, and I will give you rest" or "Let the little children come to me" (Matthew 11:28, Matthew 19:14—*New International Version*). After a night of helping and healing, the wizard son sees the sun rise, sees the light, and he slippers the now muffled brass foot. I like the fact that Beedle doesn't tell us the foot disappeared; it's *there*, as real as was the son's initial hard-heartedness, but it's "muffled at last" (10)—just as our consciences are silenced, our angers abated, and our darker sides enlightened, even though sometimes only after we can neither sleep nor eat and repentance was slow to come.

Before we leave the tale itself and look at Dumbledore's commentary, consider with me another parallel between this son's story and Jesus' ministry. The Great Physician, to use one of the many common epithets referring to Jesus, lived many years before his public ministry began, before he "went about his father's business" to alter Jesus' own words. On occasion once Jesus began to heal people, he was apparently beleaguered, so much so that Mark writes, "Jesus could no longer enter a town openly but stayed outside in lonely places. Yet the people still came to him from everywhere." (Mark 1:45). Our wizard son in the tale is reluctant at first, even hostile, to do for the ever-increasing number of people in need what his father had done. Yet he does eventually take away the warts, restore the lost donkey, and heal the ill child—the first three of the many needs he initially ignores and later meets. Taking away warts might be suggestive of *taking away sins*; the donkey restored is reminiscent of *seeking and finding the lost*; and the child's full recovery is, of course, a literal manifestation of *healing the sick*. All of the italicized words above suggest the business of Jesus the son—at least echoed in Beedle's tale. I'm not suggesting "The Wizard and the Hopping Pot" is Christian allegory, but I thought these parallels worth mentioning, just as an afterthought.

Dumbledore in his commentary points out initially the "amazing" survival of such an early pro-Muggle tale as this one (11). In placing Beedle's tale in historical context, the headmaster mentions confrontations between Muggles and magic folk, like the one whereby Nick the Hogwarts ghost (nearly) lost his head (12, footnote 1). In this same footnote, and on a more serious note, think of Dumbledore's own sister's life when you read about those young wizarding family members "whose inability to control their own magic made them noticeable, and vulnerable, to Muggle witch-hunters." In later times, in a climate of separation of matters magical and Muggle, therefore, the "revised story" of the Hopping Pot demonizes the Muggles and generally is a tale with implications and applications about one-hundred-and-eighty degrees from the original. Dumby tells us that some children presently are told this revised version by parents who are "generally anti-Muggle" (14). I assume Narcissa told young Draco this version. Speaking of Malfoys, I love the fact that great great great something Brutus Malfoy, using his position as editor of *Warlock at War*, advances that seventeenth-century theory that a Muggle-loving wizard is a weak-magic wizard—a theory refuted by Albus himself (16-17, footnote 3). Brutus, aside from associations with Roman history, is a name that sounds like *brutish*—which may be what Dumbledore would think of Brutus's views. Recall too that we find a reference to Brutus Scrimgeour in *Quidditch Through the Ages* ([iv]); I can't say whether or not that Brutus was brutish, but he did write *The Beaters' Bible*.

One last humorous touch in Dumby's commentary affords another parallel to the Muggle world of fairy tales. Mrs. Beatrix Bloxam has sanitized several of Beedle's tales into syrupy, bowdlerized versions that are safer for the kiddies in her view, but unacceptable to young readers in Dumbledore's view (17-19). Such changes as Beatrix makes in the wizard son's tale (Beatrix names him Wee Willykins) are comparable to changes in Muggle tales, like "The Three Little Pigs" ending with the wolf being cooked for dinner in a boiling kettle of water (Joseph Jacobs's 1890 version) or just running away (Walt Disney's cartoon adaptation of 1933). Beatrix Bloxam's objections to the tales and her fears for the "little angels" who read them (17-18) serve as a good satire on certain "Harry haters" of a few years ago—the concerned parents who feared their little angels would embrace sorcery from reading the Potter books (which most of *those* Beatrix types hadn't read). Here are two final matters regarding our hygienic tale teller's name:

§ *Beatrix* Potter is the author of the Peter Rabbit tales of the early 1900s (her last name might ring a bell). Moreover, perhaps *Bloxam* suggests *buxom* which, apart from the well-known anatomical meaning, can, according to *Webster's Collegiate*, mean "obedient, tractable . . . offering little resistance," which may be what Mrs. Bloxam wants little angel readers to be and do.

§ Beatrix Bloxam's "infamous" saccharine adaptations of the stories are collected under the title *Toadstool Tales* (17). Though she would lose the alliteration, Mrs. Bloxam should possibly have chosen *Mushroom Tales* to protect her kiddies further from harm.

There's Nothing in the Water: Afterthoughts on "The Fountain of Fair Fortune"

It's not surprising that Rowling chooses for one of Beedle's tales to have a fully alliterative title. What *is* surprising is that only one does (though parts of "The Warlock's Harry Heart" and "The Tale of the Three Brothers" contain alliteration). She indulges herself in still more *f* sounds early in this tale; in her second paragraph, she employs "fight," "Fountain," "Fair," "Fortune," and "forevermore" (20). In "The Fountain of Fair Fortune" Beedle tells us that those who travel to the Fountain include magic and Muggle folk alike (21), and that the blessings are received on what I assume to be the summer solstice during the daylight hours of this "longest day," June 20 or 21. We're used to three witches in literature and lore from John Updike's in Eastwick to Shakespeare's in *Macbeth.* The three witches in this tale bear interesting names:

- § Asha is the name of an organization dedicated to providing education for underprivileged children in India, as well as being an acronym for a number of other organizations. Most significantly, it is the Hindi word for *wish* or *hope.*
- § Altheda is a name with Greek origins meaning "like a blossom"; she will gather some herbs (I know, they're not exactly blossoms) at a very important point later in the tale. It could also be linked to *althos*, Greek for *healing.*
- § Amata is linked to a form of the Latin word for *love*, *amo.* Beedle's witch's name is also the name of a Roman mythological queen whose daughter's union with Aeneas causes Amata's suicide. Though only loosely related, love and despair over a lover are both associated with this name, historically and in Beedle's tale.

Asha has suffered lost health, Altheda lost means, and Amata lost love. Soon after the three witches set out, the *creepy* part of the tale gets them involved with the "dismal-looking knight, who was seated on a bone-thin horse" (23). Do you recall Don Quixote's steed Rocinante? It appears this knight's mount and Quixote's could be stable mates (in a stable without much oats). In a bit of a link to the Potter books, Rowling somewhat echoes here the incident in *Deathly Hallows* wherein a fourth, unwanted character, the Death Eater Yaxley, Disapparates from the Ministry along with Harry, Ron, and Hermione (*DH* 267-70). Similarly, the creepers result in Sir Luckless joining the witches as this threesome becomes a foursome—to the anger of Asha and Altheda. It is Amata who gets caught up in the armor of the knight, which is rather ironic since Amata will get caught up in the amour of the knight as well. We learn that this Muggle knight has no knightly skills (24), and we Potter readers are reminded of Sir Cadogan—with one noticeable difference: Sir Luckless *knows* he's inept. What's more, Sir Luckless lacks confidence and is certain he has no chance of beating the witches to the fountain.

The three witches solve the three trials with their tears, their sweat, and their memories while Sir Luckless, unluckily, tries all the wrong solutions to their problems. His materialistic, actually metallic, attempts to help the group move forward all fail. Neither sword nor coin nor shield can conquer the Worm or the words on the ground or on the stone. The very human elements are what work the wonders. Drinking the tears of Asha, the Worm turns away: sorrows surcease and tears provide the transition, just as the mother's tears fill the Hopping Pot (and just as the tears are most significant to bring change in William P. Young's unusual but compelling novel *The Shack*). I can't help but wonder if there's any significance in the Worm in the tale being "white . . . bloated and blind" (26), a rather curious detail. Altheda's drops of sweat are proof of the labor expended even when no progress seemed to be made. The sweat drops evidence effort, which is *then* rewarded with progress. And Amata's removal of her memories of the lost love (removed by wand much like Potter characters remove memories for the Pensieve) causes the flooded stream waters to recede and enables the foursome to proceed to the end.

What's better than a happy, fairy-tale ending wherein someone lives "happily ever after"? How about four someones living happily ever after. We're left with a healed Asha who, so we're told at the start of the tale, suffered from "a malady no Healer could cure" (21). Altheda the herb healer extraordinaire will earn a fortune bringing others' health back to them. And, maybe best of all, Amata is well rid of the memory of one who had deserted her and is now loved by and in love with a man worthy of "her hand and her heart" (33). Here are four more afterthoughts about "The Fountain of Fair Fortune":

§ Bathing in the fountain seems to have given Sir Luckless the confidence, the luck, he needed even if the waters weren't really magic at all. This is comparable to Ron's excellent performance in Quidditch after drinking the *non*-Felix-spiked pumpkin juice. There too it's the *mind* that's magic, not the liquid the character drinks or bathes in.

- § An undeniably inept Muggle is the one who bathes in the Fountain on that June day. A major underdog named Luckless is the winner, against all odds. Anything can happen, especially if love is involved.
- § Sir Luckless is full of love for aptly named Amata; his triumph is that he loves "the kindest and most beautiful woman he had ever beheld" (33), and that is a most fair fortune indeed, with or without a fountain being involved.
- § In this tale, as in "The Wizard and the Hopping Pot," I sense an echo of Christian tradition and ritual as Sir Luckless, baptismal like, "emerged from the waters with the glory of his triumph upon him" (33). Like the Christian concept of casting off the old self, becoming a new person, and wearing a new name, our knight in Beedle's tale may cast aside that "rusted armor" and never be known as "Luckless" again. As if born again, I suspect Luckless was called by his beloved Amata something other than his former name. Sir Luckless's "baptism" changes his luck because his heart is changed, not because the waters themselves were the transforming agent; there's nothing in the water. In fact, Beedle's last words tell us that those waters "carried no enchantment at all" (34). As I did with regard to the Christian elements in "The Wizard and the Hopping Pot," I offer all these observations as underlying parallels, and I am not suggesting in any way the necessity of reading this tale a certain way or the suggestion that the tale is Christian allegory.

Dumbledore's commentary is not so much analysis of the tale as it is an anecdote about a dramatic performance gone wrong, gone horribly wrong. In one of the richest humorous passages in *The Tales of Beedle the Bard*, Dumby tells us of the efforts of former Hogwarts Herbology professor Beery (the surname of a prominent family of American actors) to perform a Christmas pantomime of this Beedle tale. To put it mildly, as Dumby does, things turned out rather badly—so badly in fact that Beery forever after thought performing this tale about luck to be unlucky (35, footnote 2). Rowling gives us a couple of fun facts about Professor Kettleburn in Dumby's commentary. The professor's first name is Silvanus (36), which is appropriate for one who surely spent a lot of time in the Forbidden Forest (*silvanus* is Latin for *forest*). Further, we learn exactly how many of Kettleburn's remaining limbs remain for him to spend his years of retirement with: one and a half (39, footnote 4). Hagrid's predecessor should have thought long and hard about introducing an Ashwinder—and an enlarged one at that—on a wooden stage. The Ashwinder's eggs, Newt Scamander tells us in *Fantastic Beasts and Where to Find Them*, are in essence incendiary bombs (2). In addition to problematic matters involving flammable beasties, Professor Beery had to deal with major actor issues since there is no love left between "Sir Luckless" and "Amata," the woman named after love. To make matters worse, there is outright warfare between the students playing Asha and Amata (37). I was also surprised to notice that apparently Headmaster Dippet had even more trouble with his Care of Magical Creatures professor than Dumbledore had with Hagrid (39, footnote 4); now *that's* saying something.

There's even more "good stuff" in Dumby's slapstick-like essay following this Beedle tale. Brutus's objections to Beedle centuries ago are paralleled to Lucius Malfoy's demand for banning a story wherein a Muggle seems to be about the business of "*interbreeding*" with a witch (40). Dumbledore, in his response to Mr. Pureblood, reminds Lucius that hardly any one witch or wizard *is* pureblood, all of which "marked the beginning" of *bad* blood between Lucius and Albus. What this Dumbledore commentary reminds me of, though, causes me to smile: the dramatic fiasco that most of us have probably witnessed or even been a part of on the stage. I'm not talking about the play that transports us to other worlds, but the play that falls apart before our very eyes. Check out the Christmas pageant in John Irving's *A Prayer for Owen Meany* or Michael Frayn's farce *Noises Off*. Such fiascos at the hands of rank amateurs or well-meaning young student performers might understandably have led to Headmaster Dippet's "blanket ban" on future performances, thus establishing "a proud non-theatrical tradition that Hogwarts continues to this day" (39). With apologies to Shakespeare, might we say that the play's *not* the thing that will catch the conscience of the kids.

Before we leave the "Fountain of Fair Fortune" tale, look again at Rowling's drawing of the fountain itself (34). I wonder why the symbol linked to "The Tale of the Three Brothers" adorns the bottom basin, why the all-seeing eye the next, why an omega is on the basin second-from-the-top, and why the *whatever* appears on the top basin. The serpent with bat wings forms the staff of the fountain, and a lot of barely legible, or downright illegible, letters line the rims of all the basins. So, as to the specifics and symbols of what all these fountain matters might mean, no ideas are spouting forth to me.

Who Needs a Heart When a Heart Can be Broken: Afterthoughts on "The Warlock's Hairy Heart"

Beedle chose a weird title for this tale—a story which, as Dumbledore says, is "grisly" (55). The part of the title that is alliterative is a strange phrase, though not so much to those of us who know the music of Bruce Springsteen. We know about a *hungry heart*, but a hairy one is quite a different matter. Having come away from Rowling's drawing of the fountains with few answers and explanations, ironically, I feel confident in pointing out a few details in Rowling's illustration that begins Beedle's next tale (43). Rowling has drawn a book and a lute (sources of love poetry and song, referenced later), and note the spilled red wine, symbolic of failed love and/or bloodshed, as well as the dagger, the instrument of our warlock's demise. The key in the drawing, though not in the tale, suggests the manner in which our warlock has locked his heart away.

The warlock's initial decision to secure his heart is a result of how foolish and weak people in love seem to him to be; when they lose their hearts, they lose their dignity (43). So he takes steps to "ensure his immunity" and to make certain that "none succeeded in touching his heart" (43-44). As if all this is not ominous enough, the warlock guards his heart by Dark Arts. Does this sound familiar, Potter readers? Recall someone who does not love, has no friends, operates alone, and is the very Lord of the Dark Arts? Our warlock here, like Voldemort centuries later, "transferred his greatest treasure to the deepest dungeon" (45). I'll say more later about the similarity of hiding away the heart and of securing the soul as Horcruxes.

Twice in Beedle's tale he refers to the warlock's heart as a treasure, in fact as "his greatest treasure"—once in the passage quoted in the previous paragraph and later when the warlock leads the maiden down to the dungeon "where he kept his greatest treasure" (49). The bible verse quoted on the Dumbledores' gravesite in Godric's Hollow, you may recall, is from Matthew 6:21: "Where your treasure is, there will your heart be also" (*DH* 325). It doesn't bode well for this warlock that his treasure/heart is locked in a dungeon. This tale takes a new direction when the warlock relents to peer pressure from non-peers, his servants, and decides to take a wife, motivated essentially by spite and scorn to do so. Reread the description of his ideal mate (46-47) and notice that she would be aristocrat, heiress, and trophy wife all in one (no pre-nup necessary). It is quite telling too that the would-be wooer of this ideal wife, this "prize" as she is called (47), pays suit by having other singers sing his love songs and by speaking the "stolen" words of love poems to the maiden (49).

Sensing the warlock's heartlessness, she is taken to the dungeon and beholds the warlock's protected, casketed heart (50), and *that's* not a pretty sight. This heart had "never fallen prey to beauty, or to a musical voice, to the feel of silken skin" (50). I might add too that this heart had never been broken or felt pain or grown stronger because of these things. Instead, it had "grown strange during its long exile" (51). I'm reminded of Hawthorne's story "Ethan Brand" about a character, isolated from humankind, whose heart turns to stone, or of the lines from Yeats's "Easter 1916": "Too long a sacrifice/ Can make a stone of the heart." The bloody conclusion to this Beedle tale involves the warlock's desperate attempt to cut out the beating heart of the maiden in order to feel the emotions of a normal heart. The tale suggests as a moral: once you've lost love and life in your own heart, you can't find it in the heart of another.

Dumbledore seems quite right in saying "The Warlock's Hairy Heart" is "by far the most gruesome of Beedle's offerings" (54). I would say that two hacked-out hearts in hand(s) and fallen warlock prostrate over previously fallen maiden lying in a pool of blood qualifies adequately as "gruesome." Much about this tale is Poe-esque, an example of what Edgar called "the grotesque," a tale of powerful and singular effect in the end. Poor Beatrix Bloxam, as an innocent child (yeah, right), heard the tale "by accident," "inadvertently," and apparently repeatedly as she "developed the habit of sleepwalking back to the same keyhole every night" (55, footnote 1) to hear the tale again and again. In addition to the subtle satire directed at the eavesdropping, loving-to-be-shocked Beatrix, Dumbledore's commentary is rich and eloquent.

Noting that the tale "speaks to the dark depths in all of us" (55), the headmaster points out that it addresses a great temptation of magic: "the quest for invulnerability" (56). In particular, this tale deals with the desire to be invulnerable to heartbreak and to the vicissitudes of loving—the wooing, the winning, and sometimes the losing of the hearts of others. In a Hemingway story called "In Another Country," one of the characters whose wife has died suddenly and unexpectedly advises a younger man never to marry, never to put himself in a position to lose; in essence, he is telling his friend to lock away his heart and never give it to another. T. S. Eliot's J. Alfred Prufrock decides not to ask an "overwhelming question," not to proclaim his love, not to sing his love song. In the ironically titled poem "The Love Song of J. Alfred Prufrock," Prufrock seems to resolve that he will lead a careful, controlled, and, obviously, lonely life. Prufrock is too careful, too cautious to give his heart away; he is the patron saint of the cautious who fear to love. These literary characters stand in contrast to millions of us "fools who love," as Dumbledore says; and, saddest of all, they, like Beedle's warlock, are heartless yet still not invulnerable to pain. As the wisest of wizards says here in his commentary: "To hurt is as human as to breathe" (56). And as Søren Kierkegaard says in *Fear and Trembling*, to be human is both a terrible and a wonderful experience. Another of Dumbledore's observations about the warlock is telling: "in seeking to become superhuman this foolhardy young man renders himself inhuman" (59)—an understandable observation from one who witnessed Tom Riddle becoming Lord Voldemort.

In addition to being invulnerable, Dumbledore points out, the warlock in the tale "wants to remain forever uninfected by what he regards as a kind of sickness" (58). Love *is* a "sickness" of sorts; to be in love, to be lovesick, is to be thoroughly vulnerable and completely infected by feelings for the heart of another. In such a state, the pure-hearted, the ones truly in love, don't need to have the music played or the love songs sung or the stolen poetry of another recited. *They* compose and sing and write the notes of love themselves, figuratively if not literally. The maiden in the tale knows this and knows instinctively that she is being wooed by one who has no heart. Harry's ability to love and Voldemort's inability even to conceive of love is a leitmotif running all through the Potter books, subtly providing readers with the all-important differences between having a hairy heart and having a Harry heart.

It is quite understandable that Dumbledore mentions the parallels between the casketed heart and the parts of the soul secured as Horcruxes. The foolish safeguarding of the heart to avoid love is similar to the unholy severing of the soul to avoid death, and even though Adalbert Waffling may waffle on some matters, he is firm in this observation: "*the source of life* [the heart?], *the essence of self* [the soul?]" are the "deepest mysteries" that no wizard should tamper with (59). Speaking of tampering with the heart, Dumbledore notes that the quest to create a "true love potion" is ongoing, but, citing Hector Dagworth-Granger, Dumby agrees that no potion yet devised can create love (57, footnote 3). And, come to think of it, if it were possible to create such a potion, wouldn't the teenaged, brokenhearted Severus have lifted it somehow to Lily's lips?

Let's consider four minor matters before we leave the heartless warlock. First, Rowling's footnote on the use of the word "warlock" as opposed to "wizard" is informative and explains the rarity of the former word in the Potter books (56, footnote 2). The older usages of "warlock" almost involved a pun, since those wizards were skilled *war*riors. In modern times, the martial associations are not necessary; a wizard of great "skill or achievement" becomes known as a warlock. Thus we certainly understand why "warlock" can be used properly to describe Dumbledore, but not, say, Mundungus. I recall from my limited exposure to magical terms, pre-Rowling, that "witches" were female magic people, and "warlocks" were male magicals. This I took as a matter of course from watching old films like René Clair's 1942 *I Married a Witch*, Richard Quine's 1958 film *Bell, Book, and Candle*, and the 1960s CBS television series *Bewitched*. Secondly, the name Rowling gives to the founder of the Most Extraordinary Society of Potioneers, Hector Dagworth-Granger, is interesting indeed. Two of the names have military associations. Hector is a Trojan warrior immortalized by Homer in the *Iliad*, and Sir Thomas Dagworth was a fourteenth-century English soldier in the Hundred Years' War (if magical, both Hector and Dagworth would have been warlocks, I suppose). Despite Hermione's response when Slughorn asks her if she might be kin to Dagworth-Granger (*HP* 185), Hermione's Muggle dentist father may have had magical ancestry if, as I have mentioned before, we assume a Muggle-born magic person's parents must both have a "recessive gene" for magic.

Thirdly, I really appreciate the humor of Rowling's explanation of the "everyday" expression "to have a hairy heart" (59-60). This supposedly describes a "cold or unfeeling witch or wizard" and is comparable perhaps to a non-committal Muggle who gets "cold feet" or who is a "cold fish"—everyday expressions in our world. Albus's "maiden aunt Honoria" (60) did the *honor*able thing in calling off that engagement to her hairy-hearted wizard fiancé—or did she? After all, he was rumored to be a Horklump fondler, which Honoria found "deeply shocking" (are the Horklumps shocking, or is it the fondling of them, or both?). The two footnotes that grow out of the Aunt Honoria incident, by the way, are nice links between *The Tales of Beedle the Bard* and *Fantastic Beasts and Where to Find Them* (60, footnotes 4 and 5). Whether you read Newt's description of Horklumps in *Fantastic Beasts* or Dumbledore's here, don't you love Dumby's line that it's "very difficult to see why anyone would want to fondle them"? And, considering that, worst-case-scenario-wise, Honoria might have married a hairy-hearted Horklump-fondler—that was a narrow escape indeed. Yet all this was only "rumored," and maiden Aunt Honoria is left alone with her honor. Fourthly, Rowling ends Dumbledore's commentary with a bit of subtle satire in that "self-help book" which "has topped best seller lists"—and don't they always? If Dr. Phil were a wizard, I can easily imagine him authoring *The Hairy Heart: A Guide to Wizards Who Won't Commit*. Or would Dr. Phil be a warlock?

She Who Cackles Last: Afterthoughts on "Babbitty Rabbitty and Her Cackling Stump"

The sound of "Babbitty Rabbitty" reminds me of what rabbits do: they go hippitty hoppitty. Also, in Beedle's title, it's not difficult to see which word is a witch word: witches, the old crone variety anyway, *cackle*, so some cackling is surely going to be linked to such a one in the tale. It's apparent as the story unfolds that the setting is indeed a "long time ago" (61) since it takes place before the 1689 (or 1692) International Statute of Wizarding Secrecy, as there is a mutual awareness of the "others" among both magic and Muggle folk in the tale.

This next-to-last of Beedle's tales is the longest as well. Rowling's artwork is outstanding (61). Notice the axe that will cut down Babbitty's tree, the fake wand broken *from* a tree, the king's crown, the dead dog's collar (I guess—alas, poor Sabre), and rabbit tracks. If you're in doubt initially about the nature of the "foolish King" the story centers around, Dumbledore makes it clear that he's a "foolish Muggle" king (82). In fact, he's a foolish Muggle king who thinks he's going to master and monopolize magic—yeah, right. To eliminate real magic in his kingdom, he forms the Brigade of Witch Hunters, armed with their "pack of ferocious black hounds" (61). Real-life parallels abound: from the literal witch hunters in late seventeenth-century Salem, Massachusetts, to the metaphorical hunts of Stalin and his purges, of Hitler and his Party, and even of McCarthy and his affidavits. Moreover, the black hounds of this king's witch hunts are reminiscent of Black Shirts, Brown Shirts, SS, Gestapo, KGB, and other ferocious aids to the witch hunting process.

How ironic it is that the foolish king wants to employ an "Instructor in Magic." As the wise headmaster says in his commentary, the king "both covets and fears magic" and "believes that he can become a wizard simply by learning incantations and waving a wand" (82-83). Dumbledore documents the findings of the wise wizards of the past: "wizards and witches are born, not created" (83, footnote 4). So magic is not a skill Muggles—even Muggle kings—can acquire and demonstrate to others (despite the dazzling effects achieved by David Copperfield, Doug Henning, or other Muggle "magicians"). Yet once this "cunning charlatan" (62)—a dangerous combination—enters the tale the masses *are* swayed, and their Muggle king begins to look like he's magic after all. I find it interesting that among the charlatan's tricks and devices, he attains "a silver chalice or two" (62-63). This is reminiscent of Thomas B. Costain's

1952 popular novel *The Silver Chalice*, which is about an evil character, a charlatan named Simon Magus (Simon the Magician), who lived during the time of Jesus' "magic" and who swayed the masses with his pseudo-magic.

Much like the warlock who hid his heart is affected by the words of his servants in the previous tale (46), the king is susceptible to wounded pride as he hears Babbitty the old washerwoman laughing at his wandwork, actually his twig twirling, and his hopping. Her "cackling" cuts to the heart, and the king had better, as the old cliché goes, put up or shut up. Once the charlatan discovers true magic in Babbitty, to his evil credit he comes up with a plan that should have worked. After all, the Lady's hat disappears, the horse flies (did Babbitty say *Leviequinus*?), but the third magic challenge is another matter. Sabre the dog can't be brought back from the dead; "for no magic can raise the dead" (72). Actually, and somewhat sadly, Dumbledore tells us that it was "through this story that many of us first discovered that magic could not bring back the dead" (78). Dumby goes on to recall that magical children believed "that our parents would be able to awaken our dead rats and cats with one wave of their wands" (78-79). This reminds me of a poem I recommend to you. It's by John Crowe Ransom and is called "Janet Waking"; it tells of a young girl weeping and begging her father to make her dead pet hen awaken and rise and walk upon the grass again.

On a lighter note, Dumbledore quotes an observation of "the eminent Wizarding philosopher" Bertrand de Pensées-Profondes (79-80). "Bertrand" might be so named as to remind us of the eminent Muggle philosopher Bertrand Russell, and the hyphenated surname for one, like Rowling, knowing more than a little Latin and French, would suggest *Profound-Thoughts*. Bertrand reminds us succinctly, albeit not gently, that as for bringing the dead back to life, "*Give it up. It's never going to happen*." Understandably, since the return to the living of those lost is so often and so profoundly in the thoughts of Harry, notice the Rowling footnote referencing all the near-attempts of magic folk to accomplish the impossible and bring back the departed (79, footnote 1). She mentions photographs and portraits that move and talk to the living, the Mirror of Erised, ghosts like Harry's friend Nick; and, though *not* mentioned, we the living think too of the essences of Harry's parents and friends in the graveyard scene in *Goblet of Fire* and in the forest in *Deathly Hallows*.

Meanwhile, back to the king, the charlatan, and the cackling witch: after the dead dog stays that way (to quote Bertrand, "*It's never going to happen*"), I love the way the shrewd but doomed charlatan turns on his accomplice. His spin is that the witch is negating the king's magic with counter-spells (72). Babbitty then Apparates or transfigures herself or becomes her rabbit(ty) Animagus other self and fools and foils them all. She cackles last. I agree with Dumby (86 and footnote 6) that she seems to threaten the Cruciatus Curse before it even has a name or is forbidden, telling the Muggle king he will "feel like an axe stroke in your own side, until you will wish you could die of it!" (75). So, in the end, much to the dismay, I suspect, of every Malfoy from Lucius back to Brutus, here in Beedle's tale is another positive step in magic-Muggle relations and coexistence. The Muggle king relents in his witch (and wizard) hunting; he issues a protective proclamation for all magic folk "allowing them to practice their magic in peace" (75); and he erects a commemorative statue to Babbitty, who, in rare rabbit form, has hopped off "far away" from this place where a statue of pure gold stands in tribute to her (76).

Now, finally, back to the matter of Babbitty's transforming into a rabbit. Dumbledore classifies the old washerwoman as an Animagus (80). Rowling writes an elaborate apologia for Minerva McGonagall's status as an Animagus (81, footnote 2), and Dumby mentions that those who change into their animal forms often do so when there is "a great need of disguise or concealment" (81)—think of the hunted criminal Sirius living long as a dog and eating rats during his time of concealment. Though Dumbledore admits Beedle his fair share of poetic license, he questions Babbitty-the-rabbit-Animagus's ability to speak or, if she's transfigured instead of Amimagused, her human cognitive powers in general (84-85). So Beedle does indeed seem to be exercising his poetic license and giving Babbitty the best of all worlds—the ability to take the form of a rabbit, retaining the power of speech in rabbit form, and all along having the knowledge of a human so as to foil evil Muggles and hop away to—what?—wash royal linens on another day for another king.

We're left with one more thing to ponder: *was* Babbitty modeled on the "famous French sorceress Lisette de Lapin" (81)? And was Lisette an Animagus who turned into a rabbit to escape her execution (82)? Here are three brief observations on the subject: (1)Madam de Lapin would be, like Sirius the dog/man or Lupin the wolf/man, aptly named if she's a rabbit/woman since *lapin* is French for *rabbit*; (2)if she did transform herself into a "large white rabbit," she wasn't too large to hippitty hoppitty through the bars of her prison cell; and (3)there's something inherently comedic and whimsical about large white rabbits. Lewis Carroll introduced us to the White Rabbit, Mary Chase gave us Harvey, James Thurber drew numerous rabbit cartoons, and Hugh Hefner gave us, well, you know.

So did *this* rabbit in Beedle's tale, Lisette de Lapin, contribute to the madness of King Henry VI (82 and footnote 3)? Or, when you think about it, Crazy Hal didn't really need any person's (or rabbit's) help to achieve pure lunacy, did he? This is quite predictable, but Rowling shows that she knows her European history well with regard to her fictitious folk in this tale of Beedle's. The year that the rabbit/woman escapes from France to England, 1422, is the very year Henry VI assumed the throne of (then) both England and France—at the age of nine months. So, who knows, maybe as the years went by, Lisette de Lapin was the rabbit behind the throne, cackling at her Muggle king's antics much like Babbitty had at hers.

One Out of Three Is Not Bad: Afterthoughts on "The Tale of the Three Brothers"

The fifth and final Beedle tale is the shortest, being less than half the length of two of the others. Dumbledore's commentary, however, is his longest, being twice the length of two of his others. Since I've read *Deathly Hallows* a few more times than I've read *The Tales of Beedle the Bard*, I almost expect to hear Ron's and Harry's interruptions of Hermione's reading of the tale as I read it here. You may recall that Molly Weasley told her children about the "Three Brothers" with a midnight setting (*DH* 406) rather than the setting being at Beedle's twilight time (87). By the way, in Rowling's drawing of the brothers approaching the bridge, that sun seems awfully high in the sky for twilight (90); then again, maybe it's the moon. The initial drawing to accompany the tale neatly gives us wand, stone, and cloak with death as the skull in their midst (87).

The adjectives to describe each brother are interesting: the oldest is "combative," the middle brother is "arrogant," and the youngest is "the humblest and also the wisest" of the three (88-89). Beedle nicely uses their respective natures to explain the brothers' motivations and choices here and their actions and fates later. It's significant that Death breaks off the elder branch for the wand, picks up the stone for the Resurrection Stone, but gives "his own Cloak of Invisibility" to the youngest brother (88-89). The latter action makes me wonder if Death, in order to remain invisible to those he's about to surprise, has another Invisibility Cloak back in his Death closet. (By the way, Death as an unforgettable invisible narrator is one of many elements that make Markus Zusak's *The Book Thief* an extraordinary novel; check it out.)

It's no surprise that there are *three* brothers since so much literature and lore and so many fairy tales (by Beedle and by Muggle writers alike) have three pigs or mice or wishes or billy goats gruff. In Rowling's number of brothers (and gifts from Death) and in the second brother's having to turn the stone three times in his hand, the author ends her employment of numerous *three*'s which permeate the Potter books from beginning to end, many of which I've discussed before. From the number of days Harry is unconscious in *Sorcerer's Stone*, to the period of his confinement to his Privet Drive room in *Chamber of Secrets*, to the number of times the wall must be addressed before the Room of Requirement appears, to the countdown for using a Portkey or starting a Quidditch game, to the number of Hallows in Book 7—Rowling, it seems safe to say, *loves* things in threes, including our three favorite Hogwarts students.

While I'm on the subject, I might add that literary trinities are often intended as archetypal symbolism. It's tempting here in this tale of the Hallows trinity to associate the wand with God (both involve power and might, even omnipotence), the stone with Jesus (both are associated with life, death, and resurrection), and the cloak with the Holy Spirit (both are in a sense non-material and can't be seen). The eventual dispensation of all three Hallows in Book 7 seems consistent with these associations since (1)Harry will see the wand again later, as the dead will see God *after* this life; (2)Harry chooses to let the stone remain lost, as he will be reunited with his loved ones who've preceded him in death *after* this life; and (3)Harry has the cloak now in *this* life, just as Christians believe that the Holy Spirit dwells in the living. These are merely parallels and echoes of matters associated with the Holy Trinity. As I have said before in this book, I don't offer this as *the* way to interpret the symbolism of the Hallows or mean to suggest that they are elements in a Christian allegory. It's just that as a literary analyst given things "hallowed" and in threes, how could I resist suggesting these parallels?

Notice that when the Elder Wand passes from the elder brother to whom it was given, the thief takes it from his sleeping victim rather then winning it in a duel. In his commentary, Dumbledore points out that the Elder Wand passes to another when the former possessor is overcome "usually by killing him" (104)—but, as the plot of *Deathly Hallows* illustrates, not necessarily overcoming by death. With regard to the second brother, the very unsatisfactory nature of his reunion with the girl he had loved and lost to death contains a phrase reminiscent of the Ministry scene in *Order of the Phoenix*. The girl was separated from the middle brother "as by a veil" (92). Dumbledore's comment is that this brother was "meddling in the shadowy art of necromancy" (95), which editor Rowling reminds us "has never worked" (95, footnote 1). William Faulkner's character Emily Grierson, however, in a story called "A Rose for Emily," achieves a unique way of being with a deceased lover (check out *that* story, though not too late at night).

The hero of Beedle's story, the humble and wise brother, lived a long life since Death could not find him beneath the Invisibility Cloak. I assume this implies that he was "invisible" to Death because he was among the living and not preoccupied with, or in a sense looking for, Death. It is on *his* terms and in *his* time—after he has lived the proverbial "rich, full life"—that the youngest brother is ready to take off the Cloak, be seen then by Death, and accompany his "old friend" and depart life. As the tale ends we have Rowling's drawing of his tombstone (93). Despite the flaws and faded places on the stone, you can read "IGNOTUS PEVERELL," see the sign of the Deathly Hallows, and make out what I take to be TEMPUS FUGIT down near the ground. The skull, skeletal fingers, and drawings of the casket and the crossed bones all remind us that this is a place of death. What do you think is written on the lowest part of the tombstone, ending in ANE?

After Dumbledore admits "The Tale of the Three Brothers" was his favorite boyhood tale—in contrast to his brother Aberforth's favorite "Grumble the Grubby Goat"—he relates the moral of "The Three Brothers" quite explicitly: "Human efforts to evade or overcome death are always doomed to disappointment" (94). The various attempts to "evade or overcome death" would apply to those like Xenophilius Lovegood, who believe in the Deathly Hallows; those like young Albus and Gellert, who pursued the Deathly Hallows; those like Nicolas Flamel, who possessed or pursued the Sorcerer's Stone; and those like Lord Voldemort, who split their very souls in an effort to thwart death. All of these and indeed all who would win a victory over death in their lifetimes "are always doomed to disappointment." Death, Dumbledore goes on to say, is "a wily enemy who cannot lose" (95). The wisest brother, like the wise headmaster himself during the events of *Half-Blood Prince*, "having narrowly escaped Death once," understands that "the best he can hope for is to postpone their next meeting for as long as possible" (94-95). Dumbledore then gently debunks the legend that those who believe possession of all three Hallows can bring the possessor immortality (96). He quotes Alexander Pope's aphorism about hope, from the *Essay on Man*, and begins his discussion of the cloak, the stone, and, at some length, the Elder Wand. In Rowling's footnote on Invisibility Cloaks and Disillusionment Charms, she both reminds us that Dumby doesn't need a cloak to be invisible (something we've known since *Sorcerer's Stone*) and allows us to see how unusual Harry's cloak is since most cloaks are far from "infallible" (97, footnote 3), which we come to appreciate fully in *Deathly Hallows.*

Dumbledore next gives us still more reminders that no stone (or any other object) is going to bring back the dead in any satisfactory way or form (97-99). Consider the irony of the skeptical commentator doubting the existence of two of the Hallows, the perfect cloak and the stone, and explaining away the "power" of the "unbeatable" wand, which itself has "been beaten hundreds of times" (106). These comments, if you'll recall, Dumbledore is writing about a year and a half before his death. Even the wisest of wizards has a lot to learn late in life, doesn't he? Remember, editor Rowling addresses the headmaster's commentary on this tale, saying that he "reveals a little less than he knows—or suspects" about the story of the three brothers (xiii).

In the final part of Dumbledore's commentary, he gives us a good bit of wandlore—some of which we've gotten as far back as *Sorcerer's Stone* (when Ollivander tells Harry that the wands choose the wizards) and some of which we get in *Deathly Hallows* (such as the stories of Emeric, Egbert, Godelot, and the others who once wielded the wand). Especially ironic are Dumbledore's comments that a wand is usually buried with its owner; that, as we've mentioned before, the Elder Wand is "usually" won by killing the former possessor; and that a wizard who uses a "second-hand wand" (or in Harry's case in *Deathly Hallows* a third- or fourth-hand wand) might find the results unsatisfactory (104). Dumbledore also mentions that in the long history of the Elder Wand, it seems never to have been in the possession of a woman. I can't improve on Dumby's observation about this matter; I can only quote it: "No witch has ever claimed to own the Elder Wand. Make of that what you will" (106, footnote 9). Similarly, there is no feminine counterpart for the word *warlock*. Make of *that* what you will.

Predictably, and with the hindsight and insight we have from reading *Deathly Hallows* before *The Tales of Beedle the Bard* was translated and made available to us, we find much irony in the last part of the commentary regarding choices—those made by the brothers in the tale, by Dumbledore, and, implicitly, by Harry and by us all. Dumbledore concludes that "humans have a knack of choosing precisely those things that are worst for them" (107). And if that line from Dumbledore's commentary on the tale of the brothers sounds familiar, it is almost verbatim what the headmaster tells Harry in *Sorcerer's Stone* (297). There, the line comes just after he has explained to Harry that the Flamels will now die, and that the Sorcerer's Stone was "really not such a wonderful thing" since it brought all the "money and life" you could want, which would clearly be the choice of almost all of us, but which, obviously from the passage in Book 1 and here in *The Tales*, is *not* the best choice. If money (or the power to get it with the Elder Wand) and life (or the power to bring loved ones back to life with the Resurrection Stone) are what's *worst* for people, notice what, then, must be *best*. Living out a natural life span during which the mind has become "well-organized" so that death is "but the next great adventure" (*SS* 297). As Dumbledore tells the then eleven-year-old Harry, it's like going to bed at the end of the day—or, in the case of the Flamels, the end of a "very, *very* long day."

Admitting that even he would have found it difficult to choose the Invisibility Cloak, Dumbledore ends his self-portrait in words, assuring us that despite his cleverness, "I remain just as big a fool as anyone else" (107). Near the end of *Deathly Hallows* Harry is faced with choices not unlike those offered to the three brothers, and he chooses wisely and well, keeping the cloak and dispensing with the wand and the stone. Like Ignotus Peverell, Harry, when his natural time has come, will take off the cloak and leave it to his children, who will leave it to theirs. This is his heritage and his legacy. It involves forswearing the temptations of power and of bringing back the dead, and it means greeting his old friend Death when his time comes. We would expect no less of the Harry we've come to know, would we? Most who have read Harry's story and those who will in years to come will not have an opportunity, figuratively speaking, to wield the wand or turn the stone, but all will wear the cloak until it's time to take it off and give it over to their children. Isn't it a pleasant thought that we too, like the wise brother, might not fear Death as a mortal enemy, but great him "as an old friend." But I hope—since it springs eternal—that day is far in the future for us all—as it was for the youngest brother in the tale.

Meanwhile, since *tempus fugit*, let us *carpe diem*, enjoy each other's good company, and escape every now and then by reading—or, just as good and sometimes even better, by *re*reading a good book. Remember, I am the *Re-* guy, and I certainly found the Potter books, *Fantastic Beasts and Where to Find Them*, *Quidditch Through the Ages*, and *The Tales of Beedle the Bard* joys to reread as I was writing this book. I do feel a minor disappointment about *Beedle the Bard*, however: it contains only five tales—definitely a case of more would be better. One tale which is referenced in *The Tales of Beedle the Bard* is a title without a tale. Twice Dumbledore mentions "Grumble the Grubby Goat" (94, 106), just whetting our appetites and leaving us wondering about Albus's brother's favorite story. We know that Grumble "attracted flies" (106), and we can safely assume that he was grubby. And yet even the title leads to serious questions to ponder: was it *because* this goat was grubby that he grumbled, or was he grubby because he grumbled? And what role did those flies play in all this? These are questions for the ages—or at least for Aberforth.

Endnote

As much as Rowling gives us, she leaves us wanting more. Even after the 4100 pages of Harry's saga and the additional 249 pages (counting introductions) of the ancillary books, wouldn't we all love just a bit (all right, *quite* a bit) more? In April 2010 I was signing copies of *Repotting Harry Potter* at a book festival at UCLA. At one point, a nine- or ten-year-old child stopped at my booth, picked up a copy of my book, flipped through it, put it down, then picked it up and flipped through it again. Finally, she asked, "Is this book new?" I told her that it was fairly new, that it had come out a little over a year ago. Her eyes lit up, and she asked, "So this is the story of what happens to Harry after *Deathly Hallows*?" I told her no, that my book is not a new Harry Potter adventure, that it is one of many books *about* the Harry Potter books. She seemed on the brink of tears, and I felt as if I had said, "No, Virginia, there's *not* a Santa Claus." Think of this: if you're ten years old and you have loved Rowling's Potter books already as a young child, then of course you think with your heart, and wishful thinking leads you to believe that a grey-haired professor on an April afternoon at UCLA can sell you the next Harry Potter adventure. I'll always remember that child and that moment; I love what it says about falling in love with books and always wanting more.

But the good part, the happy ending, the fairy tale ending if you will, is that there *is* more—more and more books forevermore. And even if there'll never be an eighth Harry Potter book, there are eight times eighty great ones that you and I haven't even opened yet. That child need not be disappointed for long. I'm sure she'll find her next great adventure written by someone other than Rowling about someone other than Harry, again and again and again. I know because *I've* done just that since *I* was ten. And another happy ending is that the child can go back to *Harry* again and again, and his story reads quite differently when you're ten than when you're a bit, or a lot, older. I'd like to see her face when she next finds her favorite story, but I kind of know that look when I see it. I've taught great books at great universities for well over thirty years now, and I've seen that look that comes from reading a book you love, one you regret to finish, one that leaves you wanting more. It's a wonderful thing to *feel* for yourself, and, believe me, it's always a beautiful sight to see in others.

So keep reading, my friends, keep picking up a new (or an old, but new to you) book, keep looking for your next great reading adventure. It's either being written right now, or it was written centuries ago—or anywhere in between. Yet if it's a really great book that you read, you won't be able to tell the difference. The place and time from which it comes will, like magic, become *your* here and *your* now with every page you turn.

Acknowledgements

I am grateful foremost for the continued support of Dr. Maire Mullins, my division chair at Pepperdine University, and for the inspiration of Dr. Helen Deese, who initially encouraged me to read the Potter books. For their suggestions and ideas I thank my fellow Potter Pundits, John Granger and Travis Prinzi. For his expertise and professionalism, I thank Robert Trexler of Zossima Press. In addition, I want to thank these friends, family members, and colleagues for their ideas and their encouragement toward what would become *Rowling Revisited*: Bob and Dena Beaudine, Jane Thomas Burke, Cyndia Clegg, Doug and Mary Cooper, Michael Ditmore, David Dowdey, Allison Ensor, Avery and Pat Falkner, Michael Gose, Evelyn Greer, David Holmes, Stacey Hood, Bill and Nancy Ingram, Arlene and Mark Mallinger, Genny Moore, Carolyn Nicks, Ken and Libby Perrin, Rosalind Seabrook, Cliff and Wanda Sinkler, Alexi Thomas, Jennifer and Nathan Thomas, Katherine Netterville Welch Thomas, Blair and Matt Weisbecker, and Alonzo and Katherine Welch.

Appendixes

For virtually my whole life I have enjoyed, among other things, animals, sports, and books. So focusing on Rowling's ancillary books about beasts and about the wizarding world's favorite sport and best-known tales has been a pleasure. I thought you might benefit from the following appendixes which list where in the Potter books Rowling refers to or focuses on various beasts and to the game of Quidditch, in addition to references to the many books written by and for wizards and witches. Each appendix is selective (I don't reference someone just using the word "dragon" or "Quidditch"), but does (I hope) contain all significant passages dealing with the subject at hand. References to the beasts and to the books remain essentially the same throughout the Potter books, but the Quidditch references decline, of course, as Harry leaves the sport behind him at least for a while. Moreover, with regard to references to books, about forty percent involve Hermione—reading, reporting on what she's read, or showing her frustration that she may be the only person to have read *Hogwarts: A History*. Finally, notice in Appendix C that there are no book references in almost the entire last half of *Deathly Hallows*, though, as we all know, there's plenty of action there.

Appendix A: Fantastic Beasts and the Pages Where You'll Find Them

Harry Potter and the Sorcerer's Stone

Reference	Page
Dragons guard Gringotts; Hagrid has always wanted one	64-65
The first glimpse of Fluffy, the three-headed dog	160-61
Harry, Ron, and Hermione encounter the mountain troll	174-77
Norbert hatched in Hagrid's cabin; taken away by Charlie's friends	231-41
A Forbidden Forest encounter with centaurs Ronan and Bane	252-54
The discovery of the dead unicorn	255-56
Firenze meets Harry	256-59
The trio gets past Fluffy with a little flute playing	275-76

Harry Potter and the Chamber of Secrets

Reference	Page
The boys de-gnome the Weasleys' garden	35-37
Ron tells Harry about the ghoul in the attic	41
Lockhart's pixie lesson	101-02
Hagrid has been advised about kelpies by Lockhart	114-15
Fred and George experiment with a salamander	130
Harry meets Fawkes the phoenix	206-07
Harry and Ron encounter Aragog and the Acromantula	275-79
The basilisk description from a library book	290-91
Fawkes in the Chamber	315-22
The basilisk in the Chamber	317-20

Harry Potter and the Prisoner of Azkaban

Hagrid's lesson on Buckbeak and the other hippogriffs	113-18
Lupin's lesson on Red Caps and kappas	141
Hagrid's lesson on flobberworms	142
Lupin tells Harry about grindylows	153-54
Snape's lesson on werewolves	171-73
Snape says kappas are common in Mongolia	172
Lupin's lesson on the hinkypunk (a beast not in *Fantastic Beasts*)	186
Flitwick's classroom is decorated with fairies	189
Hagrid's flobberworms die from eating too much lettuce	220
Hagrid builds a bonfire full of salamanders	235
Security trolls guard the corridor	269-70
Hagrid's exam involves keeping a flobberworm alive	317
Lupin's exam involves a grindylow, Red Caps, and a hinkypunk	318
Buckbeak is "executed"	331
Lupin transforms into a wolf	380-81
Harry and Hermione rescue Buckbeak	400-15

Harry Potter and the Goblet of Fire

Crookshanks chases a gnome at the Burrow	60
Leprechauns at the World Cup	104-12
The howling ghoul in the Weasleys' attic	154
Hagrid's lesson on Blast-Ended Skrewts	196-98

Giant palomino winged horses bring in the Beauxbatons students	243, 245
The Blast-Ended Skrewts are almost three feet long	264
The Blast-Ended Skrewts are over three feet long	295
Harry sees the dragons for the Triwizards' first task	325-29
Cedric and the Swedish Short-Snout	351
Fleur and the Common Welsh Green	352
Viktor and the Chinese Fireball	352-53
Harry and the Hungarian Horntail	353-56
Hagrid's class deals with nearly six-feet-long Blast-Ended Skrewts	368-71
Fairies are used for Yule Ball decorations	413
Grubbly-Plank's unicorn lesson	436, 440
Rita Skeeter reveals that Hagrid bred manticores and fire-crabs	438
Harry's struggle with grindylows	495-96
Merpeople during the second task	497-505
Merpeople have a pet grindylow	498
Buckbeak in the cave with Sirius, Harry, Ron, and Hermione	521, 523, 532
Hagrid's lesson on nifflers	542-45
The Blast-Ended Skrewt in the maze during the third task	625-26
The sphinx in the maze during the third task	628-30
The giant spider in the maze during the third task	631-32
Fawkes the phoenix heals Harry's leg	698

Harry Potter and the Order of the Phoenix

Dead puffskeins under the sofa at Grimmauld Place	101
The de-doxying of the curtains at Grimmauld Place	102-05
Dung has sold knarl quills to Fred and George	171
Harry sees thestrals for the first time	196-201
Grubbly-Plank's lesson on bowtruckles	259-61
Grubbly-Plank covers porlocks, kneazles, crups, & knarls for O.W.L.s	323
Harry soaks his hand in essence of murtlap	324
Grubbly-Plank makes first reference to thestrals by name	358
Hagrid's lesson on thestrals	444-49
Hagrid's lesson on crups	552
Firenze begins his teaching career	597-605
Margorian confronts Hagrid	697-99
Harry's O.W.L. involves a knarl, a bowtruckle, and a fire-crab	717
Nifflers in Umbridge's office	723-24
Harry, Hermione, and Umbridge encounter the forest centaurs	753-57
The forest centaurs vs. Grawp	757-59
Harry angers a bowtruckle	759-60
The ride to the Ministry on thestrals	762-68

Harry Potter and the Half-Blood Prince

Buckbeak is renamed "Witherwings"	53
Slughorn splashes dragon blood	65

Ginny's pet is a miniature puffskein named Arnold	121, 132
Cormac and his uncle hunted nogtails	144
Harry, Ron, and Hermione greet Buckbeak at Hagrid's cabin	227-28
A garden gnome is atop the Weasleys' Christmas tree	329-30
Harry watches a gnome struggle with a worm	344-47
Luna says Gurdyroots ward off Gulping Plimpies	425
The death and burial of Aragog, the great Acromantula	480-85
The lament of the phoenix	614-15
Merpeople sing at Dumbledore's funeral	642-43
Centaurs pay their respects to Dumbledore	644

Harry Potter and the Deathly Hallows

Elphias Doge barely escaped chimaeras during round-the-world trip	18
Thestrals are used in the seven Harrys venture	53
Ron shows Harry the ghoul in the attic	97-98
Hagrid gives Harry the mokeskin pouch for his seventeenth birthday	120
Luna is bitten by a gnome	140-41
Hermione warns the others about the Erumpent horn	401
Xeno says Luna is fishing for Freshwater Plimpies	402, 404, 418
Xeno points out billywig propeller on the bust of Rowena Ravenclaw	404
Xeno mentions invisibility cloaks made from Demiguise hair	410-11
The Erumpent horn explodes	419-20
Luna refers to her father's use of billywig wings on the statue	513

Harry, Ron, and Hermione encounter the Gringotts dragon	535-36
Harry, Ron, and Hermione escape Gringotts on the dragon	541-46
Firenze fights and is wounded in the Battle of Hogwarts	608, 661, 745
Ron and Hermione use basilisk fangs to destroy a Horcrux	623
Giant spiders join in the Battle of Hogwarts	639, 646-47
Hagrid chides centaurs for not fighting	728
Centaurs, Buckbeak, and thestrals join in the Battle of Hogwarts	733-34
Harry tells his son Albus not to worry about thestrals	757

Appendix B: Quidditch Through the Pages

Harry Potter and the Sorcerer's Stone

Reference	Page
Draco's first mention of the game to Harry	77
Harry asks Hagrid about Quidditch	79
Upcoming flying lessons and talk of Quidditch	143-44
Harry flies for the first time	148-50
McGonagall finds a Seeker	150-53
McGonagall sends Harry the Nimbus Two Thousand	164-65
Oliver Wood explains the rules of the game to Harry	166-70
Harry's first match, Gryffindor vs. Slytherin; Gryffindor wins	184-91
Harry discovers that Snape will referee the next match	216-17
Gryffindor vs. Hufflepuff; Gryffindor wins	220-24

Harry Potter and the Chamber of Secrets

Harry explains Quidditch to Colin	106-07
First practice of the year thwarted by Slytherins	107-12
Gryffindor vs. Slytherin; Harry hit by rogue Bludger; Gryffindor wins	166-72
Quidditch match cancelled because of attack on two students	254-56

Harry Potter and the Prisoner of Azkaban

Rules of the game and Wood's pep talk to the Gryffindors	142-44
First match to be against Hufflepuffs because of Draco's "injury"	168-69
Gryffindors vs. Hufflepuffs; dementors appear; Hufflepuff wins	175-82
Harry flies on the Firebolt for the first time	253-56
Gryffindor vs. Ravenclaw; Harry flies against Cho; Gryffindor wins	257-62
Gryffindor vs. Slytherin for the Quidditch Cup; Gryffindor wins	304-13
Ron tells Harry about the upcoming World Cup	431, 434

Harry Potter and the Goblet of Fire

The World Cup invitation; Vernon's reaction; Harry's excitement	30-38
The World Cup final match	105-16
Dumbledore announces there will be no Quidditch this year at Hogwarts	183-84

Harry Potter and the Order of the Phoenix

Seamus puts up his Kenmare Kestrels poster	217
Cho and Ron discuss her being a Tornados fan	230-31
References to Wood playing for Puddlemere United	264, 557
Ron and Harry practice before Ron tries out; Gryffindor practices	289-94
Angelina plans to practice the Sloth Grip Roll	351
Angelina will have to get Umbridge's permission to reform the team	355
Gryffindor's team is permitted to reform	376

Practice in wind and rain; Harry uses the Sloth Grip Roll	378-80
Ron's confidence wanes during practices and before his first match	400-404
Gryffindor vs. Slytherin; crowd sings mocking song	406-11
Harry gets the Snitch; Harry and George fight Slytherins	411-12
Umbridge bans Harry, Fred, and George from Quidditch	416-17
Arthur is in Quidditch great Dai Llewellyn Ward at St. Mungo's	487
Gryffindor vs. Ravenclaw; Gryffindor wins match and Quidditch Cup	701-02

Harry Potter and the Half-Blood Prince

Name-dropper Slughorn mentions Gwenog Jones of the Harpies	71, 147
Harry, Hermione, Ron, and Ginny play two-a-side Quidditch	105
Harry is named Gryffindor Quidditch captain	106
McGonagall and Katie Bell talk to Captain Harry	175-76
Captain Harry's Gryffindor try-outs	223-26
Hermione has met Gwenog Jones of the Harpies	280
Gryffindor vs. Slytherin; Ron thinks he has drunk *Felix Felicis*	294-95
Zacharias Smith commentates; Gryffindor wins	295-98
Gryffindor vs. Hufflepuff; Luna commentates	411-17
Harry is injured by McLaggen and will not play Quidditch again 415-17	

Harry Potter and the Deathly Hallows

Molly asks Harry about a Puddlemere United sock	87-88

Ginny has a picture of Gwenog Jones on her bedroom wall	115
Dumbledore wills Harry the Snitch he caught in his first Hogwarts match	126-28
Harry discovers that Regulus Black was a Quidditch Seeker	187-88
A History of Magic mentions Bowman Wright, inventor of the Snitch	319
Dumbledore says his death is as certain as the Cannons finishing last	683
The Snitch opens in the forest, and the Resurrection Stone is inside	698

Appendix C: The Books in the Potter Books

Harry Potter and the Sorcerer's Stone

Reference	Page
Harry's textbooks, including *Fantastic Beasts and Where to Find Them*	66-67
Hermione's "extra books" to read on the train to Hogwarts	106
Hogwarts, A History mentioned for the first time	117
One Thousand Magical Herbs and Fungi referenced in Snape's class	138
Hermione has checked *Quidditch Through the Ages* out of the library	144
Harry reads *Quidditch Through the Ages*, has it confiscated by Snape	181-82
Books where Hermione looks in vain for Flamel's name	197-98
Harry looks up "Dittany" in *One Thousand Magical Herbs and Fungi*	229
Hagrid consults dragon books in the Hogwarts library	230
Hagrid has checked out *Dragon Breeding for Pleasure and Profit*	233

Harry Potter and the Chamber of Secrets

Molly's books in the Burrow	34
Lockhart's book consulted on how to de-gnome	35-36
Ron's Muggle comic book	40
Hogwarts second-year school books	43-44
Lockhart's *Magical Me* book signing	58-61
Lucius Malfoy takes Ginny's *A Beginner's Guide to Transfiguration*	62-63
Hermione reads *Voyages with Vampires*	86-88, 96-97

Lockhart picks up Neville's copy of *Travels with Trolls*	99
All copies of *Hogwarts: A History* are checked out of the library	147
Hermione compliments *Gadding with Ghouls*	162-63
Hermione checks out *Moste Potente Potions* for Polyjuice instructions	164
Ron gives Harry *Flying with the Cannons* for Christmas	212
Ron tells Harry about *Sonnets of a Sorcerer* to show dangers of books	230-31
Hermione reads *Ancient Runes Made Easy*	254

Harry Potter and the Prisoner of Azkaban

Harry is reading *A History of Magic* under his covers	5
Hermione gives Harry *Handbook of Do-It-Yourself Broomcare*	12
Hagrid sends Harry *The Monster Book of Monsters*	13
Bookstore manager relieved that Harry already has monster book	52-53
Harry gets his third-year Hogwarts books	53-54
Bookstore manager cautions Harry about *Death Omens* book	54
Hermione reads about the Shrieking Shack in *Sites of Historical Sorcery*	77
Trelawney's class reads tea cups based on *Unfogging the Future*	104-06
Hagrid explains how to open *The Monster Book of Monsters*	112-13
Hermione knows about Apparating from reading *Hogwarts: A History*	164
Hermione stuffs *Unfogging the Future* into her bag and leaves the class	298
Ron reads books on hippogriffs to help with Buckbeak's defense	300

Harry Potter and the Goblet of Fire

Harry reads *Flying with the Cannons* while at the Dursleys'	18
Hermione has read *An Appraisal of Magical Education in Europe*	123
Hermione has read *The Rise and Fall of the Dark Arts*	141
Hermione has learned from *Magical Education in Europe*	165-66
Hermione knows Hogwarts is hidden from reading *Hogwarts: A History*	166
"Moody" lends Neville *Magical Water Plants of the Mediterranean*	220
Ron and Harry make up predictions using *Unfogging the Future*	221-23
Hermione points out that *Hogwarts: A History* omits house-elves	238
Harry searches library books to prepare for the first task	338-39
Cedric drops his copy of *A Guide to Advanced Transfiguration*	340
Hermione gives Harry a copy of *Quidditch Teams of Britain and Ireland*	410
Harry searches library books to prepare for the second task	485-89
Hermione knows about surveillance from reading *Hogwarts: A History*	548

Harry Potter and the Order of the Phoenix

Harry packs *Quidditch Teams of Britain and Ireland* in his trunk	52
Molly consults *Gilderoy Lockhart's Guide to Household Pests*	103
Harry's new D.A.D.A. textbook is *Defensive Magical Theory*	160
Harry and Ron use *The Dream Oracle* to interpret their dreams	237-38
Umbridge has the class read Chapter 1 in *Defensive Magical Theory*	240-41
Harry and Ron use *Dream Oracle* as Umbridge observes Trelawney	312-13
Hermione tells Umbridge she has read all of *Defensive Magical Theory*	316

Hermione knows boy-girl policies from reading *Hogwarts: A History*	353
On probation, Trelawney slams *The Dream Oracle* down	365
Umbridge has the class read Chapter 3 of *Defensive Magical Theory*	367
Necessary books appear in Room of Requirement for D.A.	390
Hermione knows about Apparating from reading *Hogwarts: A History*	500
Lupin and Sirius give Harry *Practical Defensive Magic* for Christmas	501
Harry claims he has left his copy of *Fantastic Beasts* to visit Hagrid	605
Hermione is reading *Intermediate Transfiguration*	705
Hermione is not very charming in her use of *Achievement in Charming*	709

Harry Potter and the Half-Blood Prince

Hermione is reading *Advanced Rune Translation*	129
Slughorn gives old copies of *Advanced Potion Making* to Ron and Harry	183-84
Harry first follows the Prince's directions in his Potions book	188-93
Harry disguises the old Potions book as a new one	220
Harry tries *Levicorpus* from the Potions book	237-39
Madam Pince thinks Harry's Potions book is a marked library book	307-08
Slughorn introduces Harry to the author of *Blood Brothers*	315
Harry uses Potions book to submit a bezoar and is praised in class	376-78
Hermione seeks information on Horcruxes in *Magick Moste Evile*	381
Snape demands Harry's Potions book after he uses *Sectumsempra*	524
Harry hides his Potions book in the Room of Requirement	526-27

Harry Potter and the Deathly Hallows

Harry reads about the upcoming *The Life and Lies of Albus Dumbledore*	22-28
Hermione decides which books to take on the journey to find Horcruxes	93-100
Hermione takes *Spellman's Syllabary* in case she needs to translate runes	94-95
Hermione takes *Hogwarts: A History*	96
Hermione has read about Horcruxes in *Secrets of the Darkest Art*	102
Ron gives Harry *Twelve Fail-Safe Ways to Charm Witches*	113
Dumbledore wills his copy of *The Tales of Beedle the Bard* to Hermione	125-26
Hermione examines and studies the tales in *Beedle the Bard*	133, 202
Ron tells Harry and Hermione about the stories in *Beedle the Bard*	134-35
Harry looks through Rita Skeeter's biography in Umbridge's office	252-53
Hermione uses *Spellman's Syllabary* to study *Beedle the Bard*	316
Hermione discovers the inked in-symbol in *Beedle the Bard*	316
Hermione reads from Bathilda Bagshot's *A History of Magic*	318-19
Harry and Hermione read from *The Life and Lies of Albus Dumbledore*	352-59
Hermione compares the *A* in Albus with the symbol in *Beedle the Bard*	394
Hermione refers to the Erumpent description in *Fantastic Beasts*	401
At Xeno's house, Hermione reads "The Tale of the Three Brothers"	406-09
Hermione has looked up "Peverell" in *Nature's Nobility*	427

Bibliography

NOTE: In my teaching, research, and writing, the following books and articles have been of interest and of use to me. I hope you may find them to be as well.

Anelli, Melissa. *Harry, A History: The True Story of a Boy Wizard, His Fans, and Life Inside the Harry Potter Phenomenon.* New York: Pocket Books, 2008.

Anatol, Giselle Liza, ed. *Reading Harry Potter.* London: Praeger, 2003.

Baggett, David and Shaun E. Klein, eds. *Harry Potter and Philosophy: If Aristotle Ran Hogwarts.* Chicago: Open Court, 2004.

Birmingham, Carrie. "Harry Potter and the Baptism of the Imagination." *The Stone-Campbell Journal,* 8 (2005), 199-214.

Bloom, Harold. "Can 35 Million Book Buyers Be Wrong? Yes." *The Wall Street Journal.* July 11, 2000.

Byatt, A. S. "Harry Potter and the Childish Adult." *The New York Times.* July 11, 2003.

Colbert, David. *The Magical Worlds of Harry Potter.* New York: Berkley, 2004.

Gibbs, Nancy. "Person of the Year Runner Up: J. K. Rowling." *Time*, 31 December 2007 and 7 January 2008: 100-104.

Granger, John. *Harry Potter's Bookshelf: The Great Books Behind the Hogwarts Adventures.* New York: Berkley, 2008.

_____. *How Harry Cast His Spell: The Meaning Behind the Mania for J. K. Rowling's Bestselling Books.* Carol Stream, IL: Tyndale, 2008.

_____. *Looking for God in Harry Potter.* Carol Stream, IL: Tyndale, 2004.

_____. *The Deathly Hallows Lectures.* Allentown, PA: Zossima Press, 2008.

Heilman, Elizabeth, ed. *Harry Potter's World: Multidisciplinary Critical Perspectives.* New York: Routledge Falmer, 2003.

Killinger, John. *God, the Devil, and Harry Potter: A Christian Minister's*

Defense of the Beloved Novels. New York: Thomas Dunne, 2002.

_____. *The Life, Death, and Resurrection of Harry Potter.* Macon, GA: Mercer University Press, 2009.

Mulholland, Neil, ed. *The Psychology of Harry Potter.* Dallas: Benbella Books, 2006.

Morris, Tom. *If Harry Potter Ran General Electric.* New York: Doubleday, 2006.

Neal, Connie. *The Gospel According to Harry Potter.* Louisville and London: Westminster John Knox Press, 2008.

_____. *What's a Christian to Do With Harry Potter?* Colorado Springs: Water Books, 2001.

Nel, Philip. *J. K. Rowling's Harry Potter Novels.* New York: Continuum, 2001.

Prinzi, Travis. *Harry Potter and Imagination: The Way Between Two Worlds.* Allentown, PA: Zossima Press, 2008.

_____, ed. *Hog's Head Conversations: Essays on Harry Potter.* Allentown, PA: Zossima Press, 2009.

Roper, Denise. *The Lord of the Hallows.* Denver: Outskirts Press, 2009.

Spartz, Emerson and Ben Schoen. *Harry Potter Should Have Died: Controversial Views from the Fan Site.* Berkeley, CA: Ulysses Press, 2009.

Vander Ark, Steve. *The Lexicon: An Unauthorized Guide to Harry Potter Fiction and Related Materials.* Muskegon, MI: RDR Books, 2009.

Whited, Lana, ed. *The Ivory Tower and Harry Potter: Perspectives on a Literary Phenomenon.* Columbia: Univ. of Missouri Press, 2003.

Here are some of the best-known Potter-related web sites for you to visit if you're not already familiar with them:

www.HogwartsProfessor.com
www.hp-lexicon.org
www.jkrowling.com
www.mugglenet.com
www.thehogshead.org
www.the-leaky-cauldron.org

INDEX

This index will lead you both to a number of classical literary works and to numerous contemporary and pop culture sources that I cite in *Rowling Revisited.* It lists athletic, biblical, cinematic, historical, literary, and other parallels to Rowling's works.

About the Author

Dr. James W. Thomas is Professor of English at Pepperdine University, where he has taught since 1981. He has published several articles and reviews and has presented numerous scholarly papers over the years. His previous books are *Lyle Saxon: A Critical Biography* and *Repotting Harry Potter: A Professor's Book-by-Book Guide for the Serious Re-Reader.* Since 2006, Professor Thomas has taught classes at Pepperdine on the Potter books, both as first-year seminars and as upper-division courses. He has lectured and served on panels at five Harry Potter conferences and has been interviewed about Rowling's books by *Time* magazine, several newspapers, and NPR. Along with John Granger, Travis Prinzi, and others, Professor Thomas is a "Potter Pundit," participating in a number of podcasts on Rowling-related matters. He and his wife Kanet live in Westlake Village, California. They have three children and five grandchildren.

Other Titles of Interest

Harry Potter

The Order of Harry Potter:
The Literary Skill of the Hogwarts Epic
Colin Manlove

Colin Manlove, a popular conference speaker and author of over a dozen books, has earned an international reputation as an expert on fantasy and children's literature. His book, *From Alice to Harry Potter*, is a survey of 400 English fantasy books. In *The Order of Harry Potter*, he compares and contrasts *Harry Potter* with works by "Inklings" writers J.R.R. Tolkien, C.S. Lewis and Charles Williams; he also examines Rowling's treatment of the topic of imagination; her skill in organization and the use of language; and the book's underlying motifs and themes. He intentionally moves away from what the *Harry Potter* books may signify (their moral, religious or philosophical meanings) to focus on what they are – a brilliant construction of style, imagery and invention.

Harry Potter & Imagination: The Way Between Two Worlds
Travis Prinzi

Imaginative literature places a reader between two worlds: the story world and the world of daily life, and challenges the reader to imagine and to act for a better world. Starting with discussion of Harry Potter's more important themes, *Harry Potter & Imagination* takes readers on a journey through the transformative power of those themes for both the individual and for culture by placing Rowling's series in its literary, historical, and cultural contexts.

Deathly Hallows Lectures:
The Hogwarts Professor Explains Harry's Final Adventure
John Granger

In *The Deathly Hallows Lectures,* John Granger reveals the finale's brilliant details, themes, and meanings. Even the most ardent of *Harry Potter* fans will be surprised by and delighted with Granger's explanations of the three dimensions of meaning in *Deathly Hallows.* Ms. Rowling has said that alchemy sets the "parameters of magic" in the series; after reading the chapter-length explanation of *Deathly Hallows* as the final stage of the alchemical Great Work, the serious reader will understand how important literary alchemy is in understanding Rowling's artistry and accomplishment.

Hog's Head Conversations: Essays on Harry Potter
Travis Prinzi, Editor

Ten fascinating essays on Harry Potter by popular Potter writers and speakers including John Granger, James W. Thomas, Colin Manlove, and Travis Prinzi.

C. S. Lewis

C. S. Lewis: Views From Wake Forest - Essays on C. S. Lewis
Michael Travers, editor

Contains sixteen scholarly presentations from the international C. S. Lewis convention in Wake Forest, NC. Walter Hooper shares his important essay "Editing C. S. Lewis," a chronicle of publishing decisions after Lewis' death in 1963.

"Scholars from a variety of disciplines address a wide range of issues. The happy result is a fresh and expansive view of an author who well deserves this kind of thoughtful attention."
Diana Pavlac Glyer, author of *The Company They Keep*

The Hidden Story of Narnia:
A Book-By-Book Guide to Lewis' Spiritual Themes
Will Vaus

A book of insightful commentary equally suited for teens or adults – Will Vaus points out connections between the *Narnia* books and spiritual/biblical themes, as well as between ideas in the *Narnia* books and C. S. Lewis' other books. Learn what Lewis himself said about the overarching and unifying thematic structure of the Narnia books. That is what this book explores; what C. S. Lewis called "the hidden story" of Narnia. Each chapter includes questions for individual use or small group discussion.

Why I Believe in Narnia:
33 Reviews and Essays on the Life and Work of C.S. Lewis
James Como

Chapters range from reviews of critical books , documentaries and movies to evaluations of Lewis' books to biographical analysis.
"*A valuable , wide-ranging collection of essays by one of the best informed and most accute commentators on Lewis' work and ideas.*"
Peter Schakel, author of *Imagination & the Arts in C.S. Lewis*

C. S. Lewis: His Literary Achievement
Colin Manlove

"This is a positively brilliant book, written with splendor, elegance, profundity and evidencing an enormous amount of learning. This is probably not a book to give a first-time reader of Lewis. But for those who are more broadly read in the Lewis corpus this book is an absolute gold mine of information. The author gives us a magnificent overview of Lewis' many writings, tracing for us thoughts and ideas which recur throughout, and at the same time telling us how each book differs from the others. I think it is not extravagant to call *C. S. Lewis: His Literary Achievement* a *tour de force*."

Robert Merchant, *St. Austin Review*, Book Review Editor

C. S. Lewis & Philosophy as a Way of Life: His Philosophical Thoughts
Adam Barkman

C. S. Lewis is rarely thought of as a "philosopher" per se despite having both studied and taught philosophy for several years at Oxford. Lewis's long journey to Christianity was essentially philosophical – passing through seven different stages. This 624 page book is an invaluable reference for C. S. Lewis scholars and fans alike.

Speaking of Jack: A C. S. Lewis Discussion Guide (pub 2011)
Will Vaus

C. S. Lewis Societies have been forming around the world since the first one started in New York City in 1969. Will Vaus has started and led three groups himself. *Speaking of Jack* is the result of Vaus' experience in leading those Lewis Societies. Included here are introductions to most of Lewis' books as well as questions designed to stimulate discussion about Lewis' life and work. These materials have been "road-tested" with real groups made up of young and old, some very familiar with Lewis and some newcomers. *Speaking of Jack* may be used in an existing book discussion group, Sunday school class or small group, to start a C. S. Lewis Society, or as a guide to your own exploration of Lewis' books.

Mythopoeic Narnia: Memory, Metaphore, and Metamorphosis in C. S. Lewis's The Chronicles of Narnia (pub 2011)
Salwa Khoddam

Dr. Khoddam, the founder of the C. S. Lewis and Inklings Society (2004), has been teaching university courses using Lewis' books for over 25 years. Her book offers a fresh approach to the *Narnia* books based on an inquiry into Lewis' readings and use of classical and Christian symbols. She explores the literary and intellectual contexts of these stories, the traditional myths and motifs, and places them in the company of the greatest Christian mythopoeic works of Western Literature. In Lewis' imagination, memory and metaphor interact to advance his purpose – a Christian metamorphosis. *Mythopoeic Narnia* helps to open the door for readers into the magical world of the Western imagination.

C. S. Lewis Goes to Heaven: A Reader's Guide to The Great Divorce (pub 2011)
David G. Clark

This is the first book devoted solely to this often neglected book and the first to reveal several important secrets Lewis concealed within the story. Lewis felt his imaginary trip to Hell and Heaven was far better than his book *The Screwtape Letters*, which has become a classic. Clark is an ordained minister who has taught courses on Lewis for more than 30 years and is a New Testament and Greek scholar with a Doctor of Philosophy degree in Biblical Studies from the University of Notre Dame. Readers will discover the many literary and biblical influences Lewis utilized in writing his brilliant novel.

George MacDonald

Diary of an Old Soul & The White Page Poems
George MacDonald and Betty Aberlin

The first edition of George MacDonald's book of daily poems included a blank page opposite each page of poems. Readers were invited to write their own reflections on the "white page." MacDonald wrote: "Let your white page be ground, my print be seed, growing to golden ears, that faith and hope may feed." Betty Aberlin responded to MacDonald's invitation with daily poems of her own.

Betty Aberlin's close readings of George MacDonald's verses and her thoughtful responses to them speak clearly of her poetic gifts and spiritual intelligence. Luci Shaw, poet

George MacDonald: Literary Heritage and Heirs
Roderick McGillis, editor

This latest collection of 14 essays sets a new standard that will influence MacDonald studies for many more years. George MacDonald experts are increasingly evaluating his entire corpus within the nineteenth century context.

This comprehensive collection represents the best of contemporary scholarship on George MacDonald. Rolland Hein, author of *George MacDonald: Victorian Mythmaker.*

In the Near Loss of Everything: George MacDonald's Son in America
Dale Wayne Slusser

In the summer of 1887, George MacDonald's son Ronald, newly engaged to artist Louise Blandy, sailed from England to America to teach school. The next summer he returned to England to marry Louise and bring her back to America. On August 27, 1890, Louise died leaving him with an infant daughter. Ronald once described losing a beloved spouse as "the near loss of everything". Dale Wayne Slusser unfolds this poignant story with unpublished letters and photos that give readers a glimpse into the close-knit MacDonald family. Also included is Ronald's essay about his father, *George MacDonald: A Personal Note*, plus a selection from Ronald's 1922 fable, *The Laughing Elf*, about the necessity of both sorrow and joy in life.

A Novel Pulpit: Sermons From George MacDonald's Fiction
David L. Neuhouser

"In MacDonald's novels, the Christian teaching emerges out of the characters and story line, the narrator's comments, and inclusion of sermons given by the fictional preachers. The sermons in the novels are shorter than the ones in collections of MacDonald's sermons and so are perhaps more accessible for some. In any case, they are both stimulating and thought-provoking. This collection of sermons from ten novels serve to bring out the 'freshness and brilliance' of MacDonald's message."

from the author's introduction

Behind the Back of the North Wind:
Critical Essays on George MacDonald's Classic Children's Book (pub 2011)
Editors, John Pennington and Roderick McGillis

This collection of 16 essays by various scholars is the first compendium on a particular MacDonald book – *At the Back of the North Wind.* This novel makes a good representative study because it bridges the world of the "realistic" and the fanciful, including a fairy tale and some nonsense poetry. Plus it deals with a central MacDonald theme - death. Essays run the gamut from exploring MacDonald's Christian worldview, to examining the tension between fantasy and reality, to grappling with *North Wind* as children's literature. In every case, the essays illuminate a complex book. This book is also an excellent companion to the critical and scholarly edition of *At The Back of the North Wind* by Pennington and McGillis published by Broadview Press.

Other Titles

To Love Another Person:
A Spiritual Journey Through Les Miserables
John Morrison

The powerful story of Jean Valjean's redemption is beloved by readers and theater goers everywhere. In this companion and guide to Victor Hugo's masterpiece, author John Morrison unfolds the spiritual depth and breadth of this classic novel and broadway musical.

Through Common Things:
Philosophical Reflections on Popular Culture
Adam Barkman

"Barkman presents us with an amazingly wide-ranging collection of philosophical reflections grounded in the everyday things of popular culture – past and present, eastern and western, factual and fictional. Throughout his encounters with often surprising subject-matter (the value of darkness?), he writes clearly and concisely, moving seamlessly between Aristotle and anime, Lord Buddha and Lord Voldemort. . . . This is an informative and entertaining book to read!"

Doug Blomberg, Professor of Philosophy, Institute for Christian Studies

The Eye of the Beholder:
How to See the World Like a Romantic Poet
Louis Markos

This accessible guide to Romantic poetry focuses almost exclusively on short lyrical poems (the exceptions are Coleridge's *Rime of the Ancient Mariner*, Blake's *Marriage of Heaven and Hell*, and Wordsworth's "Preface to Lyrical Ballads"). A detailed bibliographic essay on each poet is provided that cites critical studies of their work.

Virtuous Worlds:
The Video Gamer's Guide to Spiritual Truth (pub 2011)
John Stanifer

According to a recent report, there were 34.2 million units sold of video game hardware or "consoles" in 2009. This does not include much larger sales numbers for the actual games. Popular titles like *Halo 3* and *The Legend of Zelda: Twilight Princess* fly off shelves at a mind-blowing rate. John Stanifer, an avid gamer, goes beyond a general overview and shows readers specific parallels between Christian faith and the content of their favorite games. Written with wry humor (including a heckler who frequently pokes fun at the author) this book will appeal to gamers and non-gamers alike. Those unfamiliar with video games may be pleasantly surprised to find that many elements in those "virtual worlds" also qualify them as "virtuous worlds."

Spotlight:
A Close-up Look at the Artistry and Meaning of Stephenie Myer's Twilight Novels
John Granger

Stephenie Meyer's *Twilight* saga has taken the world by storm. The four novels that tell the paranormal romance of Bella Swan and Edward Cullen are international bestsellers that readers everywhere are discussing and re-reading again and again. But why are the books so popular? Critics have dismissed them as "Harlequin trash" and "literary junk food." But is there more to *Twilight* than a love story for teen girls crossed with a cheesy vampire-werewolf drama? *Spotlight* reveals the literary backdrop, themes, artistry, and meaning of the four Bella Swan adventures. *Spotlight* is the only book that explains *Twilight*-mania and is the perfect gift for serious *Twilight* readers wanting to learn why the books have become as popular as they are.

The Iona Conspiracy (from The Remnant Chronicles book series)
Gary Gregg

Readers find themselves on a modern adventure through ancient Celtic myth and legend as thirteen year old Jacob uncovers his destiny within "the remnant" of the Sporrai Order. As the Iona Academy comes under the control of educational reformers and ideological scientists, Jacob finds himself on a dangerous mission to the sacred Scottish island of Iona and discovers how his life is wrapped up with the fate of the long lost cover of *The Book of Kells*. From its connections to Arthurian legend to references to real-life people, places, and historical mysteries, *Iona* is an adventure that speaks to eternal truths as well as the challenges of the modern world. A young adult novel, *Iona* can be enjoyed by the entire family.

CPSIA information can be obtained at www.ICGtesting.com
Printed in the USA
LVOW09s1551141014

408703LV00003B/616/P